DOWN
to the
WIRE

Jeff Miller

Foreword by Dick Williams

Taylor Publishing Company
Dallas, Texas

Published by Taylor Publishing Company
        1550 West Mockingbird Lane
        Dallas, Texas 75235

Designed by David Timmons Graphic Design

Library of Congress Cataloging-in-Publication Data

Miller, Jeff, 1955–
    Down to the wire / by Jeff Miller : foreword by Dick Williams.
        p.   cm.
    Includes index.
    ISBN 0-87833-783-0 : $18.95
    1. American League of Professional Baseball Clubs—History.
    I. Title.
    GV875.A1M55   1992
    796.357'64'0973—dc20   91-43039
                                                              CIP

Printed in the United States of America

10 9 8 7 6 5 4 3 2 1

To David and John,
men who lead by example

ACKNOWLEDGMENTS

I give sincere thank yous to the people who aided me in research: Stew Thornley, Cappy Gagnon, Tracy Ringolsby, Bob Pulley, Manny Lim, Joe "747" Adams, Roy J. True, Chip Atkison, Tim Wheatley, Bob Mayes, Dick Johnson, Dona Sieden, Steve Garabedian and the Sports Museum of New England, and Steve Gietscher of *The Sporting News*.

Thanks, of course, to those who were directly involved in the great race of '67—and American League baseball in the '60s in general—who were so willing to share their time and their memories: Bob Allison, Mike Andrews, Luke Appling, Ken Berry, Ken Brett, Gates Brown, George Cantor, Dean Chance, Galen Cisco, Mike Epstein, Whitey Ford, Jim Fregosi, Russ Gibson, Fred Gladding, Jim Gosger, Calvin Griffith, Ken Harrelson, Ernie Harwell, Mike Hershberger, Joe Horlen, Willie Horton, Jim Kaat, Al Kaline, Harmon Killebrew, Bobby Knoop, Lew Krausse, Mickey Lolich, Mickey Mantle, Dick McAuliffe, Denny McLain, Tom McCraw, Sam Mele, Don Mincher, Rick Monday, Jim Northrup, Tony Oliva, Rico Petrocelli, Jim Price, Rich Reese, Rick Reichardt, Bill Rigney, Bill Robinson, Frank Robinson, "Buck" Rodgers, Bill Rohr, "Moose" Skowron, George Scott, and Dick Williams.

To Jim Donovan, my editor, a special thanks for taking a chance on a first-time author, and for all of his hard work and patience. To copy editor DeAnna Lunden, know that yours wasn't a thankless job.

And the biggest thanks of all to my family—my wife, Frances, and children, Kim, Jason, Kevin, and Joe—who over the past two years gave up a lot of nights out and afternoons at the park, and were force-fed more than they ever wanted to know about the 1967 season.

CONTENTS

Sixteen pages of photographs follow page 116

FOREWORD

It was September 1966, and the Boston Red Sox had just fired their manager, Billy Herman. I was managing the Red Sox farm team at Toronto, the first managing job I ever had. Dick O'Connell, the Red Sox general manager, came out to see me in Columbus, Ohio.

I didn't think this was a courtesy visit. I knew I had a shot at the Red Sox job. I had ended by playing career with Boston and knew the country club ways of the team. Dick O'Connell gave me that chance.

And I knew the Red Sox had a chance—to win more games than we lost, at least. What followed was a great four-team pennant race that went down to the final inning of the season.

Baseball was a lot different then. No playoffs. No Astroturf. Hey, no pinetar. It was much more disciplined. I don't know if you'd call it fear, but the players totally respected what the manager and the coaching staff had to say. And if the manager wasn't around and the coach was telling you something, he was the manager.

The players were easier to deal with back then because you didn't have to deal with the agents. The demise of the reserve clause a few years later was a blessing for the players, and more power to them so they could get their money. But now it's swinging the other way so it's completely out of hand. Now in most cases, the player just answers to one person—that's his agent. That's the guy who's going to get him his big, lucrative contract. A manager's hands are more or less tied on the field now.

There wasn't any big money then. It was a business then. But it's a big, big business now. Not only baseball but the other sports, too. I could go back to when I played for the Brooklyn Dodgers in the fifties, when they had all the good players—Snider, Robinson, Campanella, Hodges, Reese, etc. I think the highest-paid player on that ballclub was making $50,000. When I had the Oakland club in the early '70s, I think Reggie

Jackson was the highest-paid player, and that was $80,000. Now, it's millions.

The fans didn't get involved with the contracts and the money. Nor did the media. We had an outstanding media in New England, probably the best in the country back then. We didn't always see eye-to-eye. They covered us like a silk glove. If you survived them, that was quite a job. But there's a lot more internal coverage now. The media gets into the private lives of the big stars. It's tougher for the player now, because of all the TV, all the magazines.

I think the playoffs are the hardest thing now. Once you win those playoffs, then you're in the World Series and the rest is gravy—even the loser's side. This is the going thing—they've used it in other sports—and it's a much bigger moneymaker. Look at the strike-shortened year, 1981, when the two "half" champions met in a pre-playoff. The best club was Cincinnati, and they didn't get in the playoffs at all.

We lived in an apartment complex in Peabody. We had a three-bedroom apartment. Sometimes my youngest son would sleep with us in the master bedroom. Bobby Doerr, one of my coaches and a Red Sox great, lived out that way. So did Mike Andrews. And Rico Petrocelli. Jim Landis lived across the hall. I was a disciplinarian and tried to keep a distance from my players, but there was a closer-knit atmosphere. There's no doubt about it.

And they had something to play for. That ring doesn't mean as much to a lot of people. Nor that World Series check. Back then, it could double a player's salary in a lot of cases.

It was a tremendous year, 1967, not just for us with the Red Sox but for all of baseball.

And there will never be another year like it.

DICK WILLIAMS
October 1991

INTRODUCTION

Maybe the folks at Honeywell Program Systems were just plain bored in the spring of 1967. Whatever the reason, someone at Honeywell used the company computer to determine that the chances of a four-way tie in one of the major leagues' pennant races was 30,315,229 to 1. The odds decreased greatly for a three-way tie—212,552 to 1—and were relatively skimpy for a two-way deadlock—1,467 to 1.

Why the fellas at Honeywell went to this trouble remains a mystery. Going into the 1967 baseball season, there had been only five ties in major league history and never one involving more than two teams. Only a handful of races went into the closing weeks with more than two teams having a legitimate chance of winning the pennant.

Two of the best multiteam races occurred in 1908. In the National League, the Chicago Cubs won by only a game each over the New York Giants and the Pittsburgh Pirates. Over in the American League, Ty Cobb and the Detroit Tigers nipped the Cleveland Indians by one-half game, with the Chicago White Sox placing third, 1½ games out.

Then there was the wild National League finish of 1964. Going into the final day, the St. Louis Cardinals were tied for the lead with the Cincinnati Reds. The Philadelphia Phillies, who had blown a 5½-game lead with eleven games to play, were a game out in third place, hoping to gain a tie and force a three-way playoff by beating the Reds. Philadelphia did beat Cincinnati, but St. Louis rallied to beat the last-place New York Mets and win the pennant by a game over the Reds and the Phils. A look at the final standings shows San Francisco finished only three games out in fourth place, but the Giants never really put themselves in position to be serious contenders during the final week of the season.

But of all the great races, never had four teams remained tethered together for most of the season—and for virtually all of the final four weeks. Never had there been a race that challenged Honeywell's odds of 30,315,229 to 1.

Until September 1967.

Of all of America's professional sports, major league baseball remains the most unchanged. For over one hundred years, the four bases have been separated by ninety feet. A pitcher still needs three strikes to retire a batter; a team still needs three outs to retire its opponent in an inning.

Other sports have felt compelled to change their games every few years, treating them like cars that must be given gaudy new fenders so they will continue to sell. *Let's allow football players to play offense or defense, but not make them play both. . . . Since seven-footers are dominating basketball, let's help the little guy by making shots taken twenty-five feet from the basket worth three points instead of two. If letting eight teams play for the league championship creates interest, then letting sixteen teams in the playoffs would be twice as good, right?*

Consider that one of baseball's biggest furors occurred with adoption of the designated hitter in 1973, the simple modification of *one* one-platoon player. What baseball fan would argue that a batting order featuring a pitcher would be superior to one featuring a designated hitter? Yet fans remain divided over whether the DH is good for the game. To some (myself included), baseball just isn't baseball with the DH. Baseball was meant to be played with the nine-man unit that must perform its best at the bat and in the field (to use the terms "offensively" and "defensively" would sound too much like football).

Baseball, the way it was meant to be played. How often do you hear fans of football, basketball, or hockey speak in those terms? Is there a football purist, as there is a baseball purist?

Because baseball is played on a different plane in regard to its past, the World Series is a superior specimen when compared to the Super Bowl, the NBA Finals, and the Stanley Cup playoffs. Because of baseball's format of two separate leagues that never meet during the regular season, the World Series is a fresh battle between two teams that haven't played each other all season. In some cases, the teams have never met at all during their histories, apart from spring training games. The other sports leagues have actually drifted closer to this with the bloating of their memberships, limiting interconference games to a trickle. But the fact remains that the Los Angeles Lakers and the Chicago Bulls do meet during the regular season before playing for the NBA title, as do the Minnesota North Stars and the Pittsburgh Penguins in the NHL. And despite the limited contact between NFC and AFC teams during the regular season, there have been Super Bowl games that were rematches of regular-season games.

Baseball's purity remains one of its greatest strengths. But even that was slightly sullied when the majors begrudgingly split into divisions beginning with the 1969 season. Before then, baseball always was assured of matching the best team in the National League against the best team in the American League in the Series. You played to win, to finish first, to make the World Series. You didn't play to stay close, to assure yourself of a playoff berth, then keep your fingers crossed that somehow you'd be a better team in short series—like making C's in a course all year long, only to have the outlandish hope that you can waltz out of the final exam with an A. And, indeed, some sports teams have been able to ace their finals and walk away with championships. That nearly happened in the 1991 Stanley Cup Finals. The North Stars, the worst of the sixteen playoff qualifiers, upset three opponents to reach the finals. With a two games to none lead over Pittsburgh, they were two wins away from becoming a Stanley Cup champ that had finished the regular season with a losing record.

Baseball hasn't stooped to this price slashing yet. But the expansion of each league from ten to twelve teams in 1969 did lead to baseball doubling its allotment of first-place teams with the creation of East and West divisions, the belief being that twelve-team units would be unmanageable from a marketing standpoint. No longer is the World Series assured of matching the best teams from each league. In fact, with the balance of power in each league shifting, the World Series now can be a forum for the third- or fourth-best team in a league. Witness the 1973 New York Mets; with less than two months left in the season, they were mired in last place in the NL East with the *New York Post* polling its readers on which Met executives they believed should be fired. Thanks to an epidemic of mediocrity that plagued the division throughout the season, the Mets were crowned NL East champs with an 82–79 record. That was 16½ games poorer than the NL West champions, the Cincinnati Reds, and ranked fourth among all NL teams. Yet a short series, best-of-five NL playoff, with the league rotation awarding New York the final game at home, allowed the Mets to upset the Reds and go to the World Series, where they came close to knocking off the Oakland A's.

Even playoffs won by the superior teams have altered the World Series. In preplayoff days, the Series opponents were assured of having the same number of off days between the end of the season and the start of the Series. Even if one team had to battle to the final Sunday and the other clinched the pennant two weeks earlier, each team had equally sufficient time to prepare for the Series. This included setting up a pitching rotation in which a manager could start his ace in Game One if he chose. While the playoffs have brought an excitement all their own, staggered finishes can force one team to reach the Series with its pitching rotation out of kilter. Sure, an Orel Hershiser can step right out of Game Seven of a playoff and help an inferior Los Angeles Dodgers team beat Oakland in five, but give me a Series in which both teams enter on even terms.

That why I hold preplayoff baseball—or at least its postseason play—in higher esteem than its current counterpart. That's why it was sad to see the passing of the classic pennant race, in which all involved knew that the winner went straight to the World Series, not to this further Series qualification test that baseball formally calls the League Championship Series. And there was none better than the 1967 American League pennant race, in which four teams virtually shared first place with 3 1/2 weeks to play. All four were within a game and a half of each other with three days left in the season, and three *still* were in contention on the final day.

The personalities of these teams further enhanced the quality of the hunt. The Chicago White Sox were akin to a one-legged man nearing the tape in the mile run, winning with magnificent pitching and negligible hitting; the Detroit Tigers hadn't been to the World Series since 1945, and twenty-year veteran Al Kaline, one of the game's greats, was wondering if he would ever play in the Series; the Minnesota Twins had survived a mutinous journey that saw a managerial change early in the year and fingerpointing up until the final game; and the Boston Red Sox went into spring training with a rookie manager and 75–1 odds of going from ninth place to first place. As the race continued, none of the teams was strong enough to dominate. Some baseball followers say that detracts from the status of the 1967 race in baseball history. To me, that only enhances it. It was Everyman's race.

Come for a memorable ride through one of the most unpredictable pennant races in history and, arguably, the best ever.

Jeff Miller
August 1991

1

THE SHUFFLE

Judging by the crowd figures, the American League games played on September 6, 1967, weren't anything special. All of 9,098 took time out on an Indian-summer Wednesday afternoon in Minnesota to watch Cleveland left-hander Luis Tiant pitch and hit his way to a 3–2 victory over the Twins. That night in Chicago, a Comiskey Park crowd announced at 12,203 had to wait four hours and forty-three minutes for a wild pitch by California's Pete Cimino to score pinch-runner Bill Voss and give the White Sox a 3–2 win. In Detroit, the Tigers swept a doubleheader from the Kansas City Athletics before 17,363 onlookers. The highlight of the twin bill was Tigers pitcher Earl Wilson becoming the major leagues' first twenty-game winner in the nightcap. This he accomplished with the help of his fourth home run of the season.

But these otherwise mundane games, when added to the mosaic of the season to date, created a design never before seen. With less than a month remaining in the season, four teams—the White Sox, the Twins, the Tigers, and the idle Boston Red Sox—were virtually tied for first place in the ten-team league:

TEAM	WINS	LOSSES	PCT.	GAMES BEHIND
Chicago	78	61	.561	—
Minnesota	78	61	.561	—
Boston	79	62	.560	—
Detroit	79	62	.560	—

Some experts turned up their noses at the race, noting the relatively weak records of the combatants. At the leaders' pace, the American League winner would finish with only ninety-one victories for the 162-game season, one of the worst championship finishes ever. But there was no denying the anticipation of what appeared to be one of the most thrilling Septembers in baseball history. Tigers owner John Fetzer, a private figure whose quotes were almost never splashed across sports pages like those of a George Steinbrenner or Charlie Finley, was spellbound by the season's events and dubbed this frenetic race "the year of the buzzsaw."

Thrilling races had been the exception in the American League, primarily because of the dominance of the New York Yankees from the late 1920s through the early 1960s. But even with the passing of the Yankees dynasty a few years earlier, few baseball fans before the '67 season expected the American League to produce a dramatic race. According to preseason predictions, this pennant was supposed to belong to the Baltimore Orioles, considering how easily they annexed 1966 as their own personal fiefdom. They had shocked the baseball world by pulling away to win their first AL pennant, then flattened the defending world champion Los Angeles Dodgers in a four-game sweep in the World Series. Baltimore boasted a combination of solid veterans—Frank Robinson led the league in home runs, runs batted in, and batting average to become baseball's first Triple Crown winner since the Yankees' Mickey Mantle in 1956—and a young pitching staff that the rest of baseball envied. With arms like Jim Palmer, Dave McNally, and Wally Bunker, there was no reason to believe the Orioles couldn't repeat in 1967 and replace the aging Yankees as the AL's resident power.

THE TEAMS

The '66 season had been a bitter disappointment for the Minnesota Twins, who had taken the Dodgers to a seventh game in the 1965 World Series before losing. The Twins actually had played decent ball in '66 after getting off to a poor start, but were unable to make up enough ground on Baltimore to make it a race. As owner Calvin Griffith looked ahead to 1967, he believed it was time to shed the Twins' image as a team dependent on home-run power. Minnesota headed into the annual winter meetings in Pittsburgh in December 1966 seeking quality pitching that could make the Twins a more balanced team for manager Sam Mele. Minnesota also faced some serious fence-mending in the wake of a change of pitching coaches that reflected a deeper rift within the organization. As the Twins' chances of catching Baltimore in '66 diminished, a rift had developed between Mele and pitching coach Johnny Sain. Sain was an innovative teacher who was steadfast in his belief that pitchers should be treated differently than the rest of the players, almost a team within the team. Mele's first lieutenant on the team was third-base coach Billy Martin, a fan favorite from his days as a helter-skelter second baseman with the great Yankee teams. Mele was Martin's final manager in the majors. They cried together the day the Twins released Martin, ending his twelve-year major league career. Mele kept Martin on as a scout, then as a coach. Martin greatly influenced Mele's managerial style, convincing him not to rely so heavily on the long ball and instead emphasize the running game. Mele gave Martin free reign over the Twins on the bases. Mele also gave Martin general control of the infielders during the game.

Martin and Sain, while teammates in New York, were not close as Minnesota coaches. Their differences increased one day during the 1966 season when Sain believed Martin trespassed onto his turf. During a game in which an opposing runner on third base made a break for the plate, Martin yelled at the Minnesota pitcher to look the runner back—and also yelled at third baseman Rich Rollins to fake covering the bag. Sain confronted Martin, telling him to leave his pitchers alone. More words were exchanged in the dugout, and later on, Mele told Sain that Martin was right in speaking up. Sain viewed that as lack of support from his manager. Another time, a Minnesota sportswriter came into the room in which Mele and the coaches dressed after a game and criticized the pitching of Dave Boswell. Sain snapped back that if the writer knew as much about pitching as he thought he did, he would be a pitching coach instead of a writer. Conspicuous by its absence in this exchange was any support from Mele. Soon after, Sain moved out of the coaches' quarters and dressed with the players in the regular clubhouse. Things became so frosty that bullpen coach Hal Naragon served as an intermediary between Mele and Sain for the balance of the season. Forced to decide between Martin and Sain, Mele would let go of Sain after the 1966 season.

One pitcher who was particularly enraged by Sain's banishment was Jim Kaat, who had led the American League with twenty-five victories and 305 innings pitched in 1966. Kaat wanted to vent his feelings and went to *Minneapolis Tribune* sports columnist Sid Hartman, who had told Kaat he could call on him for a favor any time. This particular favor, though, Hartman couldn't grant because he wasn't about to go against Martin. While Hartman didn't specifically write what Kaat wanted, the *Tribune* not only printed Kaat's "open letter" critical of the Sain dismissal but actually displayed it on the front page.

At the winter meetings in Pittsburgh, the Twins had all but closed a deal that would bring them the starting pitcher they desired from, of all places, the hapless Mets. Though details had not been completed, the trade would bring Mets right-hander Al Jackson to Minnesota along with former All-Star second baseman Ron Hunt and catcher Chris Cannizzaro for pitcher Jim Perry, utilityman Cesar Tovar, catcher Earl Battey, outfielder Jimmie Hall, and one of two infielders—second baseman Bernie Allen or third baseman Rich Rollins. But the Mets decided instead to trade Hunt to the Los Angeles Dodgers along with outfielder Jim Hickman for outfielder Tommy Davis, a two-time batting champ.

That trade, and another that saw the Dodgers send star shortstop Maury Wills to the Pittsburgh Pirates for third baseman Bob Bailey and shortstop Gene Michael, indirectly worked in the Twins' favor. Those two trades put some peer pressure on the Dodgers' suburban neighbors, the California Angels. With the Dodgers making such bold moves after winning back-to-back pennants, LA fans wondered how the Angels could simply stand pat if they hoped to make up ground on the Orioles. The Angels needed hitting and faced a void at first base when Joe Adcock retired to become manager of the Cleveland Indians. Twins owner Calvin Griffith had approached Angels management early at the meetings, inquiring about right-handed starter Dean Chance, who had won the Cy Young Award as the majors' premier pitcher in 1964 with a record of 20–9 and an earned run average of 1.65. Chance had since gone 15–10 and 12–17, his 1966 totals including a league-high 114 walks. But the Angels weren't satisfied with the Twins' offer of Rollins and slugging first baseman Don Mincher. For one thing, the Angels were set with All-Stars Bobby Knoop at second base and Jim Fregosi at shortstop and planned to use young third baseman Paul Schaal as their leadoff hitter. And while they knew they couldn't replace Chance's quality, they wanted to come away from such a deal with another pitcher, starter, or reliever. The Angels asked the Twins about right-handed starter Camilo Pascual and left-handed starter Jim Merritt, but the Twins refused on each inquiry. Minnesota instead turned to the Washington Senators and packaged Pascual with Bernie Allen to land right-handed reliever Ron Kline.

On the final day of the meetings, the Twins and Angels agreed on a swap that sent Chance and a player to be named later to Minnesota for Mincher, Hall, and reliever Pete Cimino. In Mincher and Hall, the Angels had obtained players who had hit more than 20 home runs in less than full-time service in recent years. This would take much of the burden off young Rick Reichardt, who was fourth in the league in batting when he left the team in early August to have his left kidney removed. Cimino, a right-hander, had compiled a 2–5 record and 2.91 ERA in thirty-five games. "We have given Minnesota our best pitcher," Angels manager Bill Rigney said during the news conference announcing the trade, "but we have gotten two players who will definitely give us additional power." Griffith wasn't pleased about parting with two regulars and a reliever but was happy to land Chance. "With a club that can hit a little more than the Angels, he's got to win twenty games," Griffith said.

Chance's former batterymate, California catcher Bob (Buck) Rodgers, worked for Pacific Van Lines during the off-season. Rodgers offered to move Chance to Minnesota. Chance declined. It wasn't the first time Chance had shaken off one of Rodgers' suggestions.

The Detroit Tigers didn't see the need to make drastic changes for 1967 despite the Orioles' dominance. A midseason trade with Boston in '66 had brought right-handed pitcher Earl Wilson to Detroit. That gave the Tigers a solid starting rotation anchored by Wilson, right-hander Denny McLain, and lefty Mickey Lolich, who was effective despite a natural paunch that made him appear badly out of shape. For hitting, there was right fielder Al Kaline, one of baseball's best pure hitters since he won the AL batting title as a twenty-year-old rookie in 1955. There was home-run punch coming from Kaline, first baseman Norm Cash, left fielder Willie Horton, and catcher Bill Freehan.

What the Tigers did need was a steadying influence for a manager. Detroit had begun the '66 season with sixty-seven-year-old Charlie Dressen at the helm, who had begun managing in the majors in 1934. His days with the Tigers were marked by health problems. During spring training in Lakeland, Florida, in 1965, he asked one day to be driven to the airport in nearby Tampa so that he could fly back to his home in California to check on the health of his wife. Actually, it was Dressen himself who was ailing, in the process of having a heart attack and insistent that he be checked out by his personal physician. Dressen was back in the dugout by May but suffered another heart attack May 16, 1966, after the Tigers got off to a 16–10 start. Coach Bob Swift was appointed interim manager and fancied himself a strict disciplinarian, though some of his players didn't find him capable of carrying out his intended mission. But Swift's stint lasted only fifty-seven games; he left the team July 14 with what was diagnosed as food poisoning. The Tigers then turned to Frank Skaff, another coach, to take over the team.

Dressen's problems were compounded by a liver infection, and he died August 10. Swift, it turned out, was not suffering from food poisoning but from lung cancer. Only a few weeks after the Tigers finished third, Swift died. And the Tigers weren't sold on Skaff, who had produced a 40–39 record. Management even called some of the players to ask their opinions of Skaff. The consensus was that Skaff was a nice guy but overmatched in the job of handling a major league ballclub.

The Tigers approached Bill Rigney, who had managed the California Angels for six years, with an offer of a three-year deal worth $75,000 annually. Rigney declined, sticking with his $45,000 contract with the Angels. The Tigers eventually made a surprising choice on October 3, 1966, by selecting Mayo Smith. Smith, fifty-two, was neither active on the field nor successful in his previous major league managing experience. A four-year term with the Phillies ended midway through the 1958 season with the team in eighth place and never having completed a winning season. He landed in Cincinnati the following spring but lasted only eighty games, being fired with the Reds mired in seventh place. Smith spent the intervening years as a scout with the Yankees and turned down an offer from the Chicago White Sox before the '66 season following the retirement of Al Lopez. Smith was seen as a manager who could subtly guide a veteran team that was more in need of a pat than a spanking. One of his first major moves was to hire the Minnesota castoffs, Sain and Naragon, as his pitching coach and bullpen coach.

If the Tigers were thought to need only a gentle, guiding hand, the Red Sox sought a new manager who could provide a tight grip and ride the team hard. Boston had suffered a club-record fifteenth consecutive losing season in 1966, when it rose to ninth place on the final day. As bad as all the losing was, the Red Sox also were tainted with the label of being a "country club" team—all for one and none for all—content with playing for Tom Yawkey, possibly the most gregarious owner in the majors. Following the firing of manager Billy Herman on September 8, 1966, executive vice president Dick O'Connell recognized the need for a manager who could crack the whip and instill a new attitude. Such a man was managing the Red Sox's top farm club, Toronto, of the Class AAA International League.

Dick Williams had taken the Toronto Maple Leafs to consecutive Governor's Cups, the International League's postseason playoff championship, in '65 and '66. Williams, a journeyman major-leaguer who got his start in the Brooklyn Dodgers' organization, had also helped develop some of the Red Sox's best young talent over the past two years. These were players like outfielder Reggie Smith and second baseman Mike Andrews, players who figured to at least get a shot at making the major league roster in 1967. His players were well versed in fundamentals, as emphasized by the Dodgers during the 1940s under Branch Rickey. For instance, there really was no need to check with the third-base coach with a runner on second base and no one out; the batter knew he was supposed to bunt the runner over to third.

Soon after Herman was fired in early September, O'Connell went to Columbus, Ohio, to meet with Williams while he still was managing Toronto. It was rare at the time that a man earned his first major league managing job without spending time in the majors as a coach. Williams had gone straight from playing to managing in the minors. But he didn't consider O'Connell's trip merely a courtesy visit. He knew the Red Sox had failed miserably in the past when they sought out managers. He knew there were people in his corner in Boston or he never would have been given the chance two years earlier to manager at Class AAA with no previous managing experience. After the International League season ended with a second consecutive playoff championship, Williams drove from Toronto to Boston with Andrews, believing he had a good chance at landing the Boston job.

There were other factors working against Williams besides never managing in the majors. He was only thirty-nine years old and had even played with some of the current Red Sox when he finished his nondescript major league career in Boston in 1964. But these negatives didn't faze O'Connell, who wasted little time in making his decision. The day after the Red Sox finished the season, Williams—sporting the flat-top haircut that exemplified his drill-sergeant mentality—was introduced as the team's new manager. Flanked at his introductory news conference by Yawkey and O'Connell, Williams promised: "We'll win more games than we lose." Reporters raised their eyebrows and their pens, marking down the words and wondering if they would remind Williams of this bold proclamation on the day when the Red Sox clinched a losing record.

Soon after being named manager, Williams returned to his off-season home in Arcadia, California. He was playing gin rummy one night when one of his buddies asked him who he thought would be the contenders in the American League in 1967. "Start with the Red Sox," Williams blurted out, matter-of-factly. His comment was greeted with skepticism and laughter. That Dick, what a kidder. They soon learned Williams wasn't just joking among friends.

Of the four teams that would be virtually tied for the league lead on September 6, 1967, the White Sox went into the season making the fewest major moves. They were a team that historically based its hopes on pitching and defense. Such was the case again in 1967 under second-year manager Eddie Stanky, whose own major league career was typified by scrapping and hustling for whatever he could. Right-handers Gary Peters and Joe Horlen and lefty Tommy John were joined by veteran Jim O'Toole, acquired from Cincinnati, to give the White Sox four quality starters. The bullpen featured the ageless Hoyt Wilhelm. Actually, Wilhelm was quite aged—forty-three to begin the season. But hitters still were having a difficult time figuring out how to hit his fluttering knuckleball. His 1966 ERA of 1.67 in forty-six appearances marked the third consecutive season in which Wilhelm kept his ERA below 2.00. Defense again became a priority because the White Sox had committed a league-high 159 errors in '66. Infielder Don Buford and outfielder Tommie Agee, the AL's Rookie of the Year in '66, gave the team two of the AL's best basestealers. But while Buford and Agee had combined to steal 95 bases and the White Sox led the majors in steals with 153, Stanky was convinced Buford and Agee could steal 60 each.

Agee, with 22 homers, also was the team's main power hitter. And there was hope there would be more hitting throughout the batting order after the White Sox finished last in the AL with a team batting average of .231. First baseman Tom McCraw had batted .559 with eight home runs during the fifteen-game Instructional League schedule in Florida the previous fall. New catcher Duane Josephson was voted the Most Valuable Player in the Pacific Coast League and was called home by White Sox management to rest after leading the Venezuelan League in hitting for much of its winter season. Plus, White Sox general manager Ed Short thought he landed a gem in a trade with St. Louis for outfielder Walt (No Neck) Williams, who had led the Pacific Coast League in hitting at .330. Stanky convinced the American League to experiment in spring training by allowing a pinch hitter to bat twice in a game. The White Sox, of course, featured the best candidate available in pinch hitter extraordinaire Smokey Burgess. Turning forty years old in February 1967, Burgess had led the majors in 1966 by going 21 for 66 in pinch-hit appearances. That gave him a major league record 136 career pinch-hits. And with 11 walks and getting hit once, Burgess reached base 33 times in 79 pinch-hit plate appearances. Add in outfielders Pete Ward and Ken Berry plus veteran shortstop Ron Hansen, and the White Sox believed their nucleus was strong enough to make a run at the Orioles.

SPRING TRAINING

Many of the Red Sox players didn't know what to expect from Dick Williams when they reported to spring training in Winter Haven, Florida. Some who had played for him could tell stories about Williams getting into fights with players and going days without talking to those who had worked their way into his personal doghouse. Some had their doubts when they heard him say at his hiring that the Red Sox would have a winning season. Whom was he kidding? That hadn't happened in Boston since 1958. The team that reported to Winter Haven averaged 24.6 years of age, second youngest in the AL to Kansas City. Fittingly, Williams was the second-youngest manager in the majors to thirty-seven-year-old Dave Bristol, the new manager at Cincinnati.

Williams early hammered home the point that this camp would be no Florida vacation. At an impromptu news conference on the shores of nearby Lake Lulu, Williams set the tone for his first camp: "I am the only chief around here. The rest are Indians." Williams wasn't particularly worried about whose toes he stepped on along the way, even if they belonged to the greatest legend in Red Sox history. Ted Williams had been a fixture at spring training since his retirement following the 1960 season. He routinely would come by and be given his run of the camp, working with the outfielders at his leisure, providing professorial assistance around the batting cage. Dick Williams didn't mind Ted's presence in general; who's to quibble when one of the game's greatest hitters drops in? But Dick wasn't keen on Ted questioning his methods, such as that of having his pitchers play volleyball to promote conditioning. Before Dick knew it, Ted Williams had packed his gear and left camp. No matter. Dick Williams knew he never would forgive himself if he compromised his ideas and failed as a major league manager. He would look back and never know what might have happened had he done everything his way.

The biggest compromise he accepted was agreeing to retain pitching coach Sal Maglie, who had one year left on his contract after the 1966 season. Williams wanted to bring in Darrell Johnson, his pitching coach in Toronto, but was willing to wait a year so that Boston would not have to eat a year of Maglie's contract. Maglie had been nicknamed "The Barber" during his ten-year major league career because his aggressive pitching style often gave batters a relatively close shave. He accepted his lame-duck status and continued to teach his pitchers not to give in to hitters. This came back to hurt the Red Sox at least once—during an intrasquad game, of all places. In March, young slugging right fielder Tony Conigliaro suffered a fractured left shoulder blade when he was hit by a pitch by teammate John Wyatt. Tony C, as he was nicknamed, was not expected to miss the season opener. But this was far from the first time Conigliaro was sidelined by a mishap at the plate. Early in his career he was often hurt, many times paying the price for his propensity to crowd the plate.

Williams was determined to establish a different mind-set, a winning attitude, in camp. During a spring game against the Mets, indications were that this would be a different kind of Red Sox team when Boston scored 10 runs in the ninth inning to win, 23–18. Russ Gibson, a native of the Boston suburb of Fall River and a ten-year minor-leaguer still hoping to make the majors, was enthusiastic enough to concur with Williams's prediction of a winning season. Conigliaro went so far as to pick Boston to finish fourth.

Pitcher Jerry Stephenson didn't share this spring euphoria, probably because he had been demoted to Toronto. "This guy is flaky," Stephenson said of the new manager. "He thinks he's a drill instructor. It's going to be a long season."

One of Williams's more tangible tasks during spring training was to determine whether George Scott would be the regular first baseman or give way to Tony Horton. Scott, the "Boomer," at six feet two and 215 pounds when not enticed by food within arm's reach, had clouted 27 home runs and driven in 90 runs to make the All-Star team as a rookie in '66 while splitting time between first base and third base. He was surprisingly quick for his size and wasn't a defensive liability. What was troublesome was his frequent inability to make contact with the baseball; he struck out a team-record 152 times in 1966. Horton had been signed out of the University of Southern California in 1962 for a bonus reportedly worth $125,000. By the end of the '65 season, he had worked his way up to Boston and hit .294 in sixty games. But he had begun the '66 season in Boston with a horrendous 3-for-22 start and was promptly returned to Toronto. After another solid season at Class AAA, and the Red Sox's committing to playing Joe Foy at third base, Horton was scheduled to battle Scott for first base in 1967.

Pitching appeared to be a problem again for Boston. As the club prepared to break camp, Williams penciled in a five-man starting rotation that had combined for only a 25–33 record in 1966. This included only two pitchers who had spent much of the previous season as starters, righty Jim Lonborg (10–10) and lefty Dennis Bennett (8–8). One of the five was rookie right-hander Bill Rohr, who had not even appeared in a major league game. Williams's bullpen was headed by a couple of right-handers who had come to Boston during the '66 season, Wyatt and Don McMahon.

One pitcher that Williams didn't bring north was Dave Morehead, who had yet to show the kind of stuff that merited the reported $80,000 bonus Boston had paid him in 1961 to sign out of San Diego State. There was a glimmer of stardom in September '65 when he pitched a no-hitter against the Indians. But he also led the majors that year with eighteen losses, then missed most of 1966 with a sore arm. Still only twenty-three years old when he reported to Winter Haven in 1967, his spring numbers were ruined when he allowed 10 runs in $2^{1}/_{3}$ innings in the 23–18 win over the Mets. With his wife, Patty, expecting a child in two months, Morehead had to fight back tears when he learned he would start the season at Toronto.

Meanwhile, Williams's plan of inserting rookies Reggie Smith in center field and Mike Andrews at second base had to be postponed when Andrews was benched with a back injury. He'd initially hurt it during the winter while lifting weights at home in California. He was in and out of the lineup in Florida and finally had to rest his back. Williams decided his best alternative was to temporarily move Smith, who'd begun his pro career as an infielder in the Twins' organization, in from the outfield to fill in for Andrews at second base and bring veteran José Tartabull off the bench as the starting center fielder.

There was no question about who would play left field. That belonged to Carl Yastrzemski, who at age twenty-seven was practically the elder statesman of the ballclub. A veteran of six losing seasons in Boston, Yastrzemski was determined to do all he could to change the Red Sox's fortunes. He had experienced some frustrating times in Boston and weathered trade rumors. Late in the 1966 season, Yaz had told Boston sportswriter Larry Clafin, "I want to play in Boston for the rest of my career. No more politics for me. I want to be the best baseball player I can every inning next season."

Just up the road at Lakeland, the Tigers were fine-tuning what they believed was the best team in the league. The team's lockers were grouped by position, and the clubhouse boy had no idea in which group the new No. 10 uniform belonged. He asked pitcher Mickey Lolich, "Did we make any deals lately?" Lolich, too, was stumped for a while before the answer came to him. "Hey, that's our new manager." Such was the fanfare, or lack of it, that greeted Mayo Smith. That also typified how much front-page news was generated at Tigertown. The most significant change made by Smith was moving All-Star shortstop Dick McAuliffe to second base. Smith gambled that the Tigers would be better defensively with McAuliffe, whose range was limited, at second, and Ray Oyler playing shortstop every day. In two seasons as a part-time player, Oyler had failed to hit .200, but Smith wanted Oyler's glove out there every day and figured the rest of the team would suffice offensively. Oyler never had been a good hitter and usually made matters worse by working himself into a frenzy about it when at the plate. Such was his plight that McAuliffe once took his glove out to the on-deck circle instead of his bat when hitting behind Oyler, certain that Oyler would make the inning's final out. McAuliffe was reluctant to move to second base but agreed to try it when Smith telephoned him at home during the winter. McAuliffe's calling card was his odd, open stance at the plate. A left-handed hitter, he held his hands high, positioned his right foot near the outside of the batter's box, and practically faced the pitcher. He said he patterned the stance after Gil McDougald, a former Yankee infielder, after getting off to a poor start in the minors.

The McAuliffe switch was the main news item at Lakeland. This camp was meant to hone existing skills and attitudes. A typical sight on mornings at Tigertown was Al Kaline, a career .300 hitter, taking early batting practice. "I've been in the majors for fourteen years," Kaline explained, "and I want to know what it's like to play in a World Series." Catcher Bill Freehan was coming off two All-Star seasons but thought he could do more than hit a dozen or so homers, drive in fewer than 50 runs, and hit .234, which he had done in '65 and '66. His goal for the spring was to move closer to the plate and pull the ball more. General manager Jim Campbell provided Freehan, who had to be dragged out of the lineup even when injured, with a capable backup by acquiring Jim Price from Pittsburgh.

Smith announced he would go with a five-man pitching rotation featuring McLain, Lolich, Wilson, Dave Wickersham, and Joe Sparma. That news didn't exactly thrill Sparma, who feared Smith would begin the season using only four starters and would use him only as a spot starter. Under similar conditions in 1966, Sparma, a former Ohio State University quarterback, had pitched only 92 innings with a 2–7 record. He was already, however, benefiting from the presence of Johnny Sain, who spent much of the spring teaching him a slider.

The biggest pitching surprise in Lakeland was twenty-four-year-old Mike Marshall. Signed by Philadelphia as a shortstop in 1961, he had also dabbled in pitching. He was traded to the Tigers' organization in 1966 and had convinced his manager at Montgomery of the Class AA Southern League, Wayne Blackburn, to spend a month each as a shortstop and a pitcher to prove he could make it as a pitcher. He ended up going 11–7 with a 2.33 ERA for the Rebels, proving to the organization that he should try it as a pitcher, and his impressive spring showing against the Tigers earned him a promotion to the bullpen in Toledo of the International League. Another Detroit bullpen project was former Red Sox starter Bill Monboquette. His career got off to a promising start in Boston—a 17-strikeout game in 1961, a no-hitter in '62, a twenty-win season in '63. But two years later, he led the majors in losses with eighteen, was shipped off to Detroit, and failed to maintain a starting job with the Tigers in '66. His goal was to simply stay on the roster.

The Tigers experienced a spring casualty when left fielder Willie Horton injured the Achilles' tendon in his left ankle. Detroit was counting on Horton, who had driven in more than 100 runs in each of his two previous major league seasons, to protect Kaline by hitting behind him in the batting order. But with Horton shelved for at least a month, Mayo Smith was forced to experiment with various lineups and defensive combinations. Still, he headed into the season with plenty of confidence. "I'll take ninety-five wins," he said.

Twins manager Sam Mele was determined to leave spring training in Orlando, Florida, with a team that could do more than simply hit home runs. The entire organization must have been counting on that, too, or else management wouldn't have decided to move back the right-field fence at Metropolitan Stadium in Minnesota by fifteen feet. The company line for the move was that it made it easier for the grounds crew to unroll the tarp. The Twins failed to mention that two of the '66 Twins who made best use of that right-field fence, left-handed hitters Mincher and Hall, were wearing Angels uniforms.

By the time the Twins reported to Florida, talk of the Kaat-Sain-Mele furor had subsided. Mele telephoned Kaat over the winter to clear the air. Kaat admitted that his tone and choice of medium probably were a little brash, but he was unhappy with the move nonetheless. Aside from the arrival of Dean Chance, the talk of camp was the young Panamanian who was making the jump from Class A to starting second baseman. Rod Carew had caught the eye of Twins owner Calvin Griffith during Instructional League play the previous fall. Only twenty-one years old, Carew had strung together three impressive minor league hitting seasons—a .325 average in rookie ball in '64, .303 in the Class A Florida State League in '65, and .292 in the Carolina League in '66. The failure to obtain Ron Hunt from the Mets and the trade of Bernie Allen to the Senators left Minnesota with an opening at second base. Mele was skeptical of promoting Carew all the way to the majors, but Billy Martin helped convince him to give Carew a shot.

There were other question marks in the Twins' infield. With Mincher gone, the team needed a regular first baseman. The logical candidate was slugger Harmon Killebrew. For all of Killebrew's hitting prowess—he had led the American League in home runs four times since 1959—he had bounced around defensively like a pinball, from first base to third base to the outfield. Mele stationed Killebrew at first, which made Rich Rollins the top candidate at third. Cesar Tovar, another player who confounded the Twins because of his ability to play both the infield and the outfield, was put at second pending Carew's progress. But with Martin constantly drilling Carew in the infield—even caroming grounders to him off a concrete wall to improve his reflexes—Carew was ready to be the Twins' regular second baseman for Opening Day.

Rollins had been a familiar face in the Minnesota infield for five seasons, but his batting average had dropped steadily the past three years. Plus, he'd committed more than 20 errors in a season four times, twice leading AL third basemen. Another option was to move in rookie Ron Clark, a slow-talking Texan with a quick bat. In 1966 at Denver of the Pacific Coast League, Clark had hit .294 with 16 home runs and 94 RBIs. He homered and doubled in the first intrasquad game of the spring. But he fizzled at the plate as camp wound down, working his way to the bench. With Carew established at second, Tovar was available to move over to third as well as play center field. Mele finally decided to go with Rollins at third, and flank Tovar in center with power-hitting Bob Allison in left and two-time batting champ Tony Oliva in right. The fourth out-fielder, Ted Uhlaender, would provide left-handed hitting off the bench. To bolster the outfield, the Twins also picked up veteran Walt Bond, a left-handed hitter who had hit .263 with Houston in 1966. Bond made the final roster despite being diagnosed as having leukemia. "Do I look sick?" Bond incredulously asked reporters when questioned about his illness. "Do I look dead?"

At the White Sox's camp in Sarasota, Florida, Eddie Stanky was glad simply to see shortstop Ron Hansen and third baseman Pete Ward report healthy. Each had been on the injured list the previous May—Ward be-cause of a hernia operation and Hansen with a ruptured spinal disk. It was this depleted infield situation that forced the White Sox to obtain veteran infielder Jerry Adair from the Orioles in '66. At catcher, Stanky was pleased to see rookie Duane Josephson step forward and win the job as planned, leaving veteran J.C. Martin as a competent backup.

The White Sox honed their running game, stealing 57 bases in twenty-six spring games. Another reason for optimism was the perform-ance of right-handed starter Bruce Howard. He compiled a spring ERA of 1.54 in 17⅓ innings. The prospect of Howard, who had been only sporad-ically successful in two previous full seasons, pitching as well as Gary Peters and Joe Horlen must have frightened the rest of the American League. With his team set, Stanky could only sit back and hope some hits could find their way to Chicago's South Side. It wasn't a good sign to have your most effective bat belonging to a forty-year-old pinch hitter. By the way, Smokey Burgess went a combined 2 for 7 in four spring games in which he was used as a double pinch hitter. Stanky couldn't help but mock his team's lack of hitting even away from the ballpark. Upon land-ing a measly-looking mackerel on a fishing trip in the gulf, Stanky cracked: "This looks like a White Sox rally."

If Stanky was confident he could produce an exciting winner, Chicagoans weren't quick to pick up on it. An exhibition game at Comiskey Park against the National League's Chicago Cubs attracted a mere 7,727 fans. The previous season, White Sox home attendance had dropped below the one-million mark for the first time since 1958. While the White Sox were still drawing better than the Cubs, rumors persisted that the Allyn family, who owned the team, was considering abandoning the city. There was a viable vacancy not far to the north in Milwaukee, left bare by the Braves after the 1965 season. Such talk picked up momentum when the

White Sox announced they would play an exhibition game in Milwaukee on July 24 against the Twins.

THE OTHERS

In Miami, Orioles general manager Harry Dalton predicted his team's top challengers would be—in no particular order—Cleveland, Chicago, and Minnesota. Frank Robinson was coming into form nicely following minor knee surgery performed the previous autumn, though the knee was slightly swollen. With a set lineup, Baltimore was even blessed with the problem of what to do with the best player in the minor leagues. First baseman Mike Epstein had torn up the International League playing for Rochester, leading the league with 29 home runs and 102 runs batted in and finishing sixth in hitting at .309. A three-year letterman in football and baseball at the University of California—signed to a football scholarship by Bill Walsh and coached by Marv Levy—before signing with the Orioles, Epstein had begun in pro ball in 1965 by being named player of the year in the Class A California League before reaching Rochester.

Those kinds of numbers certainly merited a serious look in a major league spring training camp—unless that team happened to be the world-champion Orioles. Epstein knew he had little chance of unseating veteran Boog Powell, who had hit .287 with 34 homers and 109 RBIs in '66. But he was sure he could fit in somewhere and make a contribution. Yet when Epstein arrived in Miami, Orioles manager Hank Bauer wasted no time in informing him otherwise. "Don't bother," Bauer gruffly warned him. "You're not going to make our ballclub. I'm not going to break this thing up." Nonetheless, Epstein enjoyed an impressive spring that at least assured a spot on the Orioles' roster.

There was concern leaving Miami about pitching. Steve Barber had started an impressive 10–3 in '66 but had only pitched 14 innings after the All-Star break because of arm problems. Despite warnings from pitching coach Harry Brecheen, Barber began throwing hard the first day of spring training. And Wally Bunker, already a three-year mainstay in Baltimore's starting rotation at age twenty-two, complained of a sore elbow.

Soon the gates were locked at places like Joker Marchant Stadium in Lakeland and Chain O'Lakes Park in Winter Haven for another spring. The ten American League teams headed north with the following interleague exhibition records:

Chicago	16–10	Cleveland	13–14
Washington	14–12	California	11–14
Boston	14–12	New York	13–17
Detroit	14–13	Kansas City	11–16
Baltimore	14–13	Minnesota	12–17

2
APRIL

 he Las Vegas oddsmakers pronounced their opinion of who should win the American League pennant in early April:

Baltimore	2–1	California	17–1
Minnesota	3–1	New York	18–1
Detroit	4–1	Boston	75–1
Chicago	6½–1	Kansas City	175–1
Cleveland	10½–1	Washington	175–1

The American League's traditional season opener took place at D.C. Stadium in Washington on Monday, April 10, between the host Senators and the Yankees, the latter coming off their first finish in the AL cellar since 1912. For much of the decade, having the Yankees play in the Washington opener meant getting a sneak preview of baseball's reigning royalty. That no longer was the case. Mickey Mantle, his knees more brittle than ever, had signed his fifth consecutive $100,000 contract and agreed to move from center field to first base, where there would be less wear on his legs. In turn, brash Joe Pepitone was moved from first base to center. Many fans didn't expect veteran pitcher Whitey Ford, a certain Hall of Famer, to return for a sixteenth season. The pain in his left elbow, which he had learned to live with long ago, had become more acute.

There were times the previous season that the circulation problem caused the fingers on Ford's left hand to go numb. He would carry out to the mound a small squirt bottle filled with hot water, occasionally spraying his hand to wake up the nerves. Catcher Elston Howard had returned at age thirty-seven but figured to give way to Jake Gibbs, the former star quarterback at the University of Mississippi who had yet failed to put up big numbers since signing a reported $100,000 bonus in 1961.

But other familiar faces in pinstripes were gone as a new regime headed by general manager Lee MacPhail, who had helped develop the Orioles into champions, decided it was time to tear down and start from scratch. Second baseman Bobby Richardson and outfielder Hector Lopez each retired after twelve seasons. Reliever Pedro Ramos was traded to Philadelphia. Roger Maris, the glory and turmoil of his record-setting 61-home-run season in '61 now a distant memory, was traded to St. Louis for third baseman Charlie Smith. The acquisition of Smith marked something of a dark milestone in Yankee history. Only two years earlier, Smith was a regular with the crosstown Mets, overall the worst team in baseball since their inception in 1962. With Smith manning third base, Clete Boyer, a fixture there for eight seasons, was sent to Atlanta for a promising minor league outfielder named Bill Robinson. Yankees farm director Johnny Johnson eagerly sang the praises of Robinson: "I find it hard to see why he won't make it big." *The Sporting News* asked the following question in a spring headline: BILL ROBINSON—BEST SINCE MANTLE? But the twenty-three-year-old carried the question mark that came with off-season elbow surgery. There was also the matter of Robinson being black. While major league baseball's color line had been crossed twenty years earlier, the Yankees still had not been blessed with many black stars. The pickings had been slim aside from Howard, the team's first black player and the 1963 AL Most Valuable Player.

At least for one crisp April afternoon, with D.C. Stadium adorned in Opening Day bunting, the Yanks looked like the Bronx Bombers of old. A seven-run third inning carried the Yankees to an 8–0 victory over the Senators and manager Gil Hodges. Robinson indeed looked like the next great Yankee, going 2 for 4 with a home run and two RBIs. Mantle had to leave the game in the third inning when he pulled a muscle running the bases after a single. Cruising along with a two-hit shutout was Mel Stottlemyre, whose personal fortunes over the previous two seasons had reflected those of the Yankees—twenty-game winner in '65, twenty-game loser in '66. Because this was the only game of the day in the American League, the Yankees looked down at the rest of the league from first place.

The other eight AL teams were scheduled to display their wares for 1967 the following day. The world-champion Orioles were home against

Minnesota in the marquee matchup of the day, matching lefties Dave McNally and Jim Kaat. New managers were part of the other three games: Dick Williams and the Red Sox at home against Chicago, Joe Adcock and the Indians visiting Kansas City, and Mayo Smith and the Tigers playing that night at California.

It didn't take the Orioles long to satisfy a crowd of 39,812 at Memorial Stadium. They rocked Kaat for four runs in the first inning and went on to win, 6–3. McNally didn't last the fifth inning, but Baltimore reliever Moe Drabowsky, a journeyman who had gained fame for shutting down the Dodgers in the '66 Series, picked up the victory. Cold weather in Boston postponed Williams's debut, but he didn't seem to mind. "We were the first team to call off a game this year, weren't we?" an upbeat Williams asked reporters. "Now, if we can just continue to be first in things. . . ." Adcock and Smith were losers in their openers. The Indians lost to Kansas City, 4–3, while the Tigers couldn't solve Angels starter George Brunet, 5–0 against them in '66. Brunet had a two-hit shutout going to the ninth before Gates Brown, starting in left field for the injured Willie Horton, homered to cut California's winning margin to 4–2. Only 17,839 fans attended the opener at Anaheim Stadium, but they saw Don Mincher begin his Angels career with a 3-for-4 night, including a home run off Denny McLain.

As the season's first month passed, the biggest surprise was that the Orioles proved to be mere mortals—aside from Frank Robinson. The 1966 American League MVP and Triple Crown winner wasted no time getting off to another great start. He homered twice in the second game of the year and closed the month tied for the league lead in homers with Detroit's Al Kaline at five, as the league RBI leader with 14, and with a .351 batting average that trailed only Kaline's .383 among everyday players.

The rest of the Orioles, though, didn't resemble October's heroes. Slugging first baseman Boog Powell hit only .231, All-Star third baseman Brooks Robinson .213, catcher Andy Etchebarren .209, and center fielder Paul Blair .167. Their pitching lagged despite an apparently successful comeback from Steve Barber. Jim Palmer, Wally Bunker, and Dave McNally all struggled through April, as Baltimore finished the month with a 3.21 team earned run average that ranked fifth in the league.

THE TWINS STUMBLE

If Minnesota was expected to provide the Orioles with their toughest competition, the Twins did more than match Baltimore's mediocre start. They were absolutely awful, winning only five of fifteen games and finishing April in the basement. There were a couple of games that amplified the Twins' plight. One was a 4–3 loss at home to the Tigers on April 15 in which first baseman Harmon Killebrew committed a critical error in the seventh inning on a play that should have been an inning-ending DP. Detroit was batting with one out and the score tied, 3–3. A check-swing single to center by Don Wert and a single through the right side of the infield by Gates Brown put the go-ahead run on third base. Those hits gave the Tigers 10 in less than seven full innings against starter Jim Kaat. Twins manager Sam Mele lifted Kaat in favor of right-hander Al Worthington to face the right-handed-hitting Kaline, who had homered off Kaat in the previous inning. Kaline connected with a low slider—he said later he thought he'd actually hit it harder than his sixth-inning home run—but bounced the ball to Zoilo Versalles at shortstop. Versalles bobbled the ball momentarily and tossed to second baseman Rod Carew for the inning's second out, but Carew's relay to first was cuffed by Killebrew as Kaline crossed the bag. First-base umpire Hank Soar called the play safe, allowing Wert to score what proved to be the winning run. Killebrew, a normally mild-mannered player, insisted after the game the call was incorrect.

Little did the Twins realize that true aggravation was really six days down the road in a 12–4 loss at Detroit. In the third inning of that game, Tony Oliva hit a home run, only to have the play officially credited as only a single because Oliva passed runner Cesar Tovar on the bases. The ball was hit to right field, where it appeared Kaline had a chance to make the catch. Tovar was at first base and instead of going halfway between first and second, he retreated toward first base. Oliva and first-base coach Jim Lemon followed the flight of the ball, oblivious to Tovar's position. Oliva rounded first base as the ball landed in the second deck of Tiger Stadium's right-field stands. First-base umpire John Stevens watched as Oliva passed Tovar on the base path. Tovar's run counted while Oliva was ruled out with an RBI that gave Minnesota a 1–0 lead. The Tigers answered with two runs in the bottom of the third, then broke open the game with a seven-run fourth. It got even worse in the sixth, when reliever Jim Ollom failed to cover the plate on a wild pitch that allowed Ray Oyler to score all the way from second base.

Mele followed the embarrassing defeat with a closed-door clubhouse meeting. He noted to reporters afterward that this was the third time in the season's first ten games that Tovar had pulled "a rock" on the bases. It was Tovar's second baserunning blunder against the Orioles alone; he'd been doubled off when Baltimore's Curt Blefary stuck his glove over the fence to rob Rich Rollins of a home run during the first week of the season. In this latest no-brainer, even if Kaline made the catch, there was no way Tovar should have been thinking of tagging up and advancing to second base against Kaline, one of the best-throwing outfielders in baseball.

Down the hall from Mele in the Twins' clubhouse, no one was prepared to accept blame for the base-running blunder. There was Oliva's version: "I hit the ball good. I knew it was out of the park. I was rounding first base when I heard Tovar say to me in Spanish, 'Don't pass me on the bases!' I'm still not sure I went by Cesar. I was running slowly because it was a home run." Tovar's version: "I went halfway to second, then I came back when first-base coach Jim Lemon hollered at me to come back to first and tag up. I hollered at Tony not to pass me."

The only Minnesota player to hit more than one home run in April was Killebrew, with two. He entered the season with 336 career home runs, ranking him eighth among active players and tied with Joe Adcock for twentieth among all players. He had hit more than 40 homers in five different seasons, leading the league four times.

Killebrew had grown up in the small southwest Idaho town of Payette, near the Washington border. Solidly built, he starred in football, basketball, and baseball, graduating from high school in 1954. His favorite sport was baseball, but his ticket to a college education was football. He was scouted by a number of major league teams, but with the death of his father a few years earlier Killebrew was determined to go to college and assure his future financial security. With no baseball scholarships available at the time, Killebrew accepted a football scholarship to the University of Oregon and planned to play football and baseball. The Red Sox were the major league team to show the most interest in Killebrew, and Red Sox scout Earl Johnson made Killebrew promise to call him if he changed his mind regarding pro ball.

What changed Killebrew's mind began, innocently enough, with his sister working in the home office of U.S. senator Herman Walker. When Walker was working on Capitol Hill, he liked to frequent Senators games and got to know team president/owner Clark Griffith. Walker told Griffith he should send someone out to Idaho to check out this Killebrew kid. By coincidence, the greatest star in Senators history—pitcher Walter Johnson—also was from Idaho. Ossie Bluege, a former Senators third baseman turned scout, was dispatched to Idaho.

It rained the day that Bluege planned to watch Killebrew play for the semipro Payette Packers. Some city fathers worked on the field feverishly to try to get it in shape just so the Washington scout could watch Payette's favorite son. They went to the extent of burning gasoline on the infield to make it dry faster. While all of this was going on, Killebrew was waiting out the rain delay, sitting with Bluege in Bluege's car. That's when Bluege asked Killebrew to consider signing as a third baseman with the Senators, though no official offer was extended.

The skies cleared, and Killebrew gave Bluege more than he was looking for. He hit a home run far over the wall in left center in an area that most of the townsfolk said had never been reached before by a home run. Bluege returned to the ballpark the next morning and paced out the home run, estimating the ball traveled 435 feet. He called back to Washington and told Griffith the Senators should do everything they could to sign Killebrew.

The worst thing about becoming a baseball player, Killebrew thought, would be having to trudge through the minor leagues for two or three years before even finding out if he could make it as a major leaguer. But the Senators offered him about $30,000. The size of the bonus dictated that, according to major league rules, Killebrew would have to remain on the major league roster for at least two years. With the money and the time commitment, Killebrew agreed to sign with the Senators. He called Boston's Earl Johnson and told him of Washington's offer. Johnson admitted that the Red Sox were not prepared to spend that kind of money on him and wished Killebrew well.

Killebrew's initial two-year stint with the Senators was a struggle, in part because there was little chance of dislodging regular third baseman Eddie Yost, a Washington fixture since 1947. Joining Washington near midseason, Killebrew played in only nine games in 1954. It helped that the veterans befriended Killebrew rather than treat him like a threat. He didn't make much progress in '55, playing in only thirty-eight games the entire season, hitting .200. Killebrew was hitting .222 when his bonus commitment expired in June 1956, and he was demoted to Charlotte of the Class A South Atlantic League. It was a move that Killebrew actually looked forward to, hoping for a chance to play regularly.

Killebrew rediscovered his home run swing in the minors. He hit 15 home runs in seventy games for Charlotte. At Chattanooga in 1957, he led the Southern League in homers with 29, playing his home games at Chattanooga's cavernous Engle Stadium. But he still struggled in the majors, opening the 1958 season at Washington hitting .194. Before the year was out, Killebrew was sent to Class AAA Indianapolis and then all the way back down to Chattanooga. There he was reunited with first baseman–outfielder Bob Allison, who was having a banner season. Killebrew confessed that he considered this his last stand as a baseball player. He responded to the challenge by hitting .308 with 17 homers in eighty-six games. Just as important, a vacancy had been cleared at third base in the off-season with the trade of Eddie Yost to Detroit.

What followed was baseball's version of the ugly duckling becoming a swan. Playing his first full major league season, Killebrew made the All-Star team and tied for the American League lead with 42 home runs.

He was not eligible to win the AL Rookie of the Year award, but Senators fans weren't too upset by that. That award went to Allison, who hit 30 homers and drove in 85 runs. Killebrew had established himself as one of baseball's best power hitters. This estimation included some impressive individual blasts. He hit the first home run to clear the roof in left field in Detroit, off the Tigers' Jim Bunning. At Chicago's Comiskey Park, he belted a home run off the White Sox's Herb Score that struck a metal girder in the stands in left field so hard that it ricocheted all the way back to the shortstop position. The only season after 1959 that Killebrew failed to hit 30 home runs was 1965, when he missed almost two months with a dislocated elbow.

Overall, Minnesota's poor month was a total team effort; both its hitting and pitching ranked last in the American League. This general malaise even affected Oliva, who in three years in the majors had won batting titles in '64 and '65 and finished second to Robinson in '66. A career .318 hitter coming into the season, Oliva stumbled out of the gate, hitting only .222. The only Minnesota regular hitting better than .300 was shortstop Zoilo Versalles at .310. The starting pitching rotation of Jim Kaat, Dean Chance, Dave Boswell, and Jim (Mudcat) Grant combined for only two complete games. Chance was the only starter with an earned run average below 4.00, the capper being Boswell's 10.80. This was a shocking development considering the Twins boasted six experienced major league starting pitchers when spot starters Jim Perry and Jim Merritt were factored in. The team's two most effective pitchers were relievers Al Worthington and Ron Kline. Worthington was a thirty-eight-year-old journeyman right-hander who had begun his pro career in the New York Giants' organization in 1951. He had caught on with the Twins in 1964 and had appeared in sixty-five games during their pennant-winning season of 1965. He was coming off a 1966 season in which he had struck out 93 batters in 91 innings, but he admitted he had lost some movement on his pitches because of his age. The Twins thought the combination of Worthington and the thirty-five-year-old Kline gave them an experienced, deep pitching staff that would more than adequately compensate for the loss of hitting given up in the Chance acquisition.

WILHELM FUELS WHITE SOX

Speaking of bullpens, there was a familiar sight marching in from the home team's bullpen at Chicago's Comiskey Park, that of James Hoyt Wilhelm. About to celebrate his forty-fourth birthday in July, Wilhelm reached a milestone April 30 when he became the first pitcher to record one hundred career relief victories. Twelve of his teammates hadn't been born when the slow-talking North Carolinian had thrown his first professional pitch for Mooresville of the old North Carolina State League in 1942.

By 1951 Wilhelm still had not reached the majors, finishing his second full season with the New York Giants' Class AAA Minneapolis farm club. Through all of the years, Wilhelm never abandoned his allegiance to the "freak" pitch that he learned to throw as a high school pitcher back in Cornelius, North Carolina—the knuckleball. Not thrown at all with the knuckles, the pitch is pushed toward the plate with the fingertips. The lack of any kind of rotation causes an unpredictable flight pattern not easily traced by batter or catcher—or pitcher, for that matter. Another unique feature of the pitch is the lack of strain it places on a pitching arm. After nine years of throwing knuckleballs, Wilhelm wasn't ready to quit and return to the family farm. He reported to spring training with the Giants in 1952 coming off his first losing season (11–14 with the Millers) and a league-leading 210 innings pitched. The Giants were amply stocked with starting pitchers from the '51 team that dramatically made up a 14½-game deficit to the Brooklyn Dodgers and won the National League pennant on Bobby Thomson's "Shot Heard 'Round the World." Giants manager Leo Durocher liked Wilhelm's pitching and wanted to find a place for him on the pitching staff, so he suggested that Wilhelm become a reliever.

Thus belated, Wilhelm's incredible major league career began. As a twenty-eight-year-old rookie, Wilhelm pitched in seventy-one games, won the ERA title at 2.43 since he pitched 159 innings (the minimum requirement for qualifying for the title was 154), and finished with a 15–3 record. Only five other NL pitchers, all starters, won more games than Wilhelm. He pitched four more years for the Giants, including the '54 pennant winner that surprised Cleveland in the World Series. He was traded before the 1957 season to the St. Louis Cardinals, where he lost four of five decisions before being put on waivers during the final week of the season. Most baseball people considered him nothing more than a washed-up journeyman by then. The Indians released him in August 1958, allowing him to be claimed on waivers by Baltimore.

It was with the Orioles, and manager Paul Richards, that Wilhelm's tattered career was repaired. Richards made Wilhelm a starter again, and Wilhelm responded by winning another ERA title at 2.19 and going 15–11. In 1960 he contributed an 11–8 record as the Orioles finished second to the Yankees with the franchise's best record in sixteen years. With more young starting pitching arriving in Baltimore, Richards sent Wilhelm back to the bullpen for two solid seasons in 1961 and '62. Then came the blockbuster trade that sent Wilhelm, shortstop Ron Hansen, and a couple of youngsters—outfielder Dave Nicholson and third baseman Pete Ward—from Baltimore to Chicago for All-Star shortstop Luis

Aparicio and third baseman Al Smith. The trade was just part of an almost total makeover of the White Sox. Not only was Ward put in at third, Hansen at short, Nicholson in left, and Wilhelm made the bullpen stopper, but Tom McCraw became the new first baseman, J.C. Martin the new catcher, and the pitching staff added newcomers Gary Peters and Joe Horlen. This was a ballclub that manager Al Lopez thought could make a run at the Yankees, whose 1962 total of ninety-six victories marked a dropoff of thirteen wins. But while Chicago won ninety-four games in 1963 on the strength of the league's best pitching staff and with Wilhelm contributing twenty-one saves, the White Sox still were no match for New York and finished ten games out in second place.

The '64 White Sox were a game behind the Yankees with ten games to play, won their last ten games—and still finished a game out. The '65 White Sox were likewise frustrated despite the Yankee collapse, finishing second to Minnesota by seven games. Wilhelm kept his ERA below 2.00 both years and got off to a good start in 1966 under new manager Eddie Stanky until he fractured a finger on April 26. He was placed on the disabled list until mid-June and pitched only 89 innings all season, though he again kept his ERA under 2.00. Despite the injury, Stanky had no intention of so much as questioning Wilhelm's position as the king of the Comiskey bullpen. Wilhelm went into the '67 season owning major league career records for relief appearances (764), relief innings (1,428), and games finished (485) as well as the ninety-nine relief victories. Stanky knew that Wilhelm, no matter how old the arm, still owned the perfect disposition for a reliever; he could forget the last appearance, no matter how good or how bad.

It was Stanky's intention to virtually create an entire bullpen of Hoyt Wilhelms, starting with right-hander Wilbur Wood, who was picked up from Pittsburgh over the winter. Wood had been a starter through seven inconsistent seasons in and out of the majors with Boston and Pittsburgh. He had barely arrived at the White Sox's camp in Sarasota before Stanky pointed him toward the bullpen and Wilhelm began teaching him the fine art of the knuckleball. If Wood could just come close to emulating the success of Wilhelm and another right-handed reliever, Bob Locker, it would be difficult to come from behind in the late innings against Chicago.

For all of the good relief pitching that Stanky received early in the season, there was one defeat that particularly galled him in which he stuck with starter Gary Peters all the way. In a 3–3 game going to the bottom of the ninth inning at Washington on April 21, Stanky had Peters intentionally walk Cap Peterson to pitch to Ken (Hawk) Harrelson with the bases loaded and two out. Harrelson foiled the strategy by singling in the winning run. Stanky's postgame displeasure probably had less to do with not respecting the opposition—this was an improved Senators team under Gil Hodges, en route to its best April record since its expansion year of 1961—than with having his last move of the game backfire. "You blew this one," Stanky told his team. "And if we lose the pennant by one game, I want you to remember it."

THE RED SOX COLOR LINE

Of all the solid performances recorded by AL relievers, the strongest was turned in by Boston's Johnny Wyatt. In five appearances, Wyatt didn't give up a run in twelve innings, striking out twelve and giving up only six hits. This helped Boston to a surprising 8–6 start, leaving it only a game behind first-place Detroit at the end of April. Wyatt was a free spirit who was released after his first pro season in 1954 and spent 1955 pitching for the Indianapolis Clowns, a black barnstorming team. It took him seven years to make it to the majors. He became an All-Star with Kansas City in 1964 and was traded to the Red Sox two years later. With the Red Sox in 1967, he scribbled the word *THINK* on the first four fingers of his glove. On the fifth, he wrote *When in doubt, use fork ball.* Some American League batters suspected Wyatt used more than a fork ball. The assumption around the league was that Wyatt loaded up the ball with Vaseline.

The contribution of Wyatt, when added to that of Reggie Smith, José Tartabull, and George Scott, was arguably the greatest made to date to the Boston team by black and Latin players collectively. The Red Sox had been the last major league team to integrate when outfielder "Pumpsie" Green came up to the Red Sox in 1959, twelve years after Jackie Robinson broke baseball's so-called color line with the Brooklyn Dodgers. The Red Sox actually had Jackie Robinson in for a tryout in April 1945 along with two other black ballplayers—Sam Jethroe and Emory Wright. The tryout was the result of pressure being placed on the team by Boston city councilman Isadore Muchnick. The session at Fenway Park took place the same day that President Franklin D. Roosevelt died, which would have provided a convenient excuse if the ballclub wanted to brush the entire incident under the rug. At any rate, none of the players was signed by the Red Sox. Wendell Smith, the sports editor of a black newspaper in Pittsburgh and an active proponent of integrated major leagues, took the players to New York and arranged a meeting with the Dodgers' Branch Rickey. Jethroe, thirty-three years old at the time of his Red Sox tryout, ended up signing with the National League's Boston Braves, making his major league debut in 1950.

The Red Sox also had a chance to sign a whirlwind of a black ballplayer out of Alabama, a seventeen-year-old outfielder from Birmingham named Willie Mays. At the time, the Red Sox had an affiliation with the Birmingham Barons of the Southern League. Mays played for the Black Barons in the professional Negro leagues, and the Red Sox were given the right of first refusal on any of the players on the Black Barons. Tipped off to this highly touted prospect, the Red Sox sent Larry Woodall to Birmingham to watch him play. But Woodall, a Texan, didn't give Mays a serious look, and Mays signed with the Giants in 1950.

Pressure continued to build on the Red Sox throughout the fifties as more teams added black players. Robinson's presence with the Dodgers hastened integration in the National League. The Yankees, who were very careful whom to welcome into the grand pinstripe tradition, signed outfielder-catcher Elston Howard in 1950 and brought him up in 1955. When the Tigers purchased catcher Ozzie Virgil from the San Francisco Giants in 1958, the Red Sox were left as the last remaining all-white major league team.

With that came the unfortunate charge by some in baseball that the Red Sox were racist. Some were convinced it was an outgrowth of longtime club owner Tom Yawkey, an otherwise benevolent boss who happened to maintain a sprawling plantation in South Carolina during the off-season. George Scott, the hulking black power hitter from rural Mississippi, was among those who later discounted this theory, saying Yawkey was generous to him both on and off the field. Other critics of the Red Sox's racial makeup simply pointed to various personalities throughout the organization. Al Hirshberg, a Boston sportswriter, said he heard Mike Higgins, the Red Sox's manager through the late fifties, say, "There'll be no niggers on this ballclub as long as I have anything to say about it."

The Red Sox eventually included black prospects in their organization, among them Pumpsie Green and right-handed pitcher Earl Wilson, who had signed out of San Diego State in 1953 as a catcher. In his first minor league season, Wilson was spiked in the left hand and couldn't catch for a while. He spent that time throwing batting practice and was impressive enough to earn a look as a pitcher. The result was a hard-throwing right-hander who also could help himself at the plate.

Green and Wilson progressed through the Boston organization together, learning to deal with the tribulations that faced a black man playing alongside whites in Montgomery, Alabama, in the midfifties. Wilson pitched four seasons in the Boston system before sitting out the 1957 and '58 seasons because of military obligations. He reported to spring training in 1959 hoping to go straight to the majors, but both he and Green were sent to Minneapolis. Green was assigned to the minors only after the team had left camp in Florida and already begun heading north, falsely leading some to believe he had made the team. That compounded the racial pressure aimed at the club back in Boston, where civil rights activists were more intent than ever on having the Red Sox integrated. Green was called up at midseason to complete the integration of baseball, but he never developed into anything more than a marginal player. He played in 133 games in 1960 and hit .260 in '61. A year later he was sent to the Yankees. Wilson remained at Minneapolis in '59, where he finished with a 10–2 record and 129 strikeouts in 113 innings. He was brought up at the end of yet another losing season in Boston, appearing in nine games and splitting two decisions.

Wilson was returned to the minors in '61, spending the entire season at Seattle of the Pacific Coast League. But 1962 found him in the Red Sox's starting rotation, a position he held for the next five seasons. Only three months into his first full major league season, Wilson threw a no-hitter against the Los Angeles Angels. Despite realizing his dream of pitching in the majors, Wilson's years in Boston weren't altogether happy. Spring training in Winter Haven, Florida, brought back many of the racial obstacles Wilson had encountered playing minor league ball in the South. Assured by club officials that he would be treated no differently than his white counterparts, Wilson discovered he and the other black players on the Red Sox didn't have the same access to restaurants in which the team ate. Wilson wasn't prepared to simply sit back and accept this treatment as part of the price of playing in the majors, as Jackie Robinson was encouraged to do in 1947. Wilson made his displeasure known to team officials, which wasn't well received.

In mid-June 1966, Wilson was 5–5 with an ERA of 3.84. On June 13 Boston made a multiplayer trade with the Kansas City A's, acquiring pitchers Johnny Wyatt and Rollie Sheldon and outfielder José Tartabull in exchange for pitchers Ken Sanders and Guido Grilli and outfielder Jim Gosger. The Red Sox were in Cleveland when the trade was made. Wilson and roommate Lenny Green, a black infielder, didn't lose sight of the fact that the Red Sox had just added two more blacks to their roster. "Somebody's going to have to leave," Wilson told Green in their Cleveland hotel room the day after the trade. "There are too many of us here." The uneasy joking didn't progress much further before the phone rang. "Go ahead and answer it," Wilson told Green with a nervous laugh. "You know you're gone." It was manager Billy Herman, informing Wilson he had been traded to Detroit for white outfielder Don Demeter, who was hitting .212. As it turned out, Green's "call" came in October; he was released outright.

TIGERS JUGGLE OUTFIELD

The Tigers led the league in hitting through April '67 despite missing regular left fielder Willie Horton. He had originally hurt his left heel in an exhibition game in 1966 yet still managed to drive in more than 100 runs for a second consecutive season. But Horton aggravated the injury in spring training in 1967 and was forced to sit out the first month of the season. The Tigers turned to Gates Brown, who had been signed in the warden's office at the Ohio state reformatory in November 1959. A high school dropout in Crestline, Ohio, about seventy miles from Cleveland, Brown was sent to prison as a seventeen-year-old in 1958 for robbery and was sentenced to 10–25 years. At five feet eleven and about 225 pounds, Brown's favorite sport in high school was football, though his school days didn't last long. At age fifteen he spent seven months at the boys industrial school in Lancaster, Ohio. He returned to Crestline, but only briefly, before he was sent to prison.

Surprisingly agile for his size, Brown began playing baseball for the prison team that faced local competition—playing strictly a home schedule, of course. Brown played once a week through the summers of '58 and '59 before the prison's athletic director, Chuck Yarman, informed him of a plan. Yarman wanted to bring in scouts from a couple of major league teams to assess Brown's talent. Instead of grasping this as an opportunity to turn his life around, Brown greeted the proposal with skepticism. There had been plenty of inmates come through the system with athletic talent, Brown thought, so why were these people so convinced that he could make it as a major leaguer?

Representatives from the Indians, the Tigers, and the White Sox made the trip to the reformatory to watch Brown. The first team to lose interest was Chicago. With the field narrowed to Detroit and Cleveland, most sentiment leaned toward the "hometown" team, Cleveland. But Yarman believed Brown's future was with Detroit. He knew there were few black players in the Tigers' system and that the team would be under pressure to sign more black prospects. Yarman found a book with the measurements of Tiger Stadium and had the left-handed-hitting Brown concentrate on pulling the ball down the line and staying away from pushing the ball into what would be the spacious power alleys in Detroit. With the offer of a contract made by Tigers scout Pat Mullin, Brown was signed—and released from prison that fall. Beginning his pro career the following spring at Duluth-Superior in the Northwest League, Brown knew better than to even approach being a troublemaker again. The parole board told him in so many words that if he ever gave anyone reason to return him to prison, it was doubtful anyone but inmates and guards would see him for a long time. Brown assured his mother that if he didn't make it in baseball, it simply would be because he wasn't good enough.

Brown advanced steadily through the Tigers' farm system until he reached the big leagues late in the summer of 1963. He won the Tigers' left fielder's job in 1964, hitting .272 with 15 home runs and 54 RBIs. But he was displaced in '65 by Horton and spent the next two seasons as a peripheral player. He had a difficult time accepting being passed in the outfield rotation by newcomers like Jim Northrup and Mickey Stanley when he had been a starter a few years earlier. It played on his mind that he been usurped by two white players, though he didn't want to believe playing time could be based on race. Given a new life with the team in '67, thanks to Horton's injury, Brown responded immediately with home runs in each of Detroit's first two games at California. He started fourteen of the first fifteen games but cooled following his hot start, hitting .218 with the same two homers and seven RBIs in April.

TIGERS NO-HIT, YET WIN

Horton wasn't expected to return until at least a week into May, but he made an appearance as a pinch hitter April 30 in a Sunday doubleheader against the Orioles that was memorable for other reasons. Steve Barber, pitching in the opener at Baltimore's Memorial Stadium, was one pitch away from throwing a no-hitter. Only two weeks earlier, he had California no-hit going into the ninth inning but allowed a one-out double to Jim Fregosi. This time, Barber reached the ninth inning with a no-hitter despite control problems that saw him walk eight batters and get through only the fifth inning without allowing a base runner. But while Barber was mowing down the Tigers, the tension grew even greater because the Orioles were shut out for seven innings by Earl Wilson, the right-hander who had been the Tigers' most reliable starter all month. His accuracy that day extended beyond pitching; he had bet third-base coach Tony Cuccinello before the doubleheader that the day's crowd would be 26,500—and was short by only 384 customers.

The Orioles finally broke up the scoreless game in the bottom of the eighth inning beginning with a walk to Curt Blefary. He was sacrificed to second base by Woody Held. Orioles manager Hank Bauer then sent up Charlie Lau to pinch hit for the No. 8 hitter, catcher Andy Etchebarren, who had one of the two Baltimore hits. Detroit decided to intentionally walk Lau to bring up Barber and set up a double play that could get Wilson out of the inning. That strategy backfired when Wilson walked Barber, loading the bases with one out. Tigers manager Mayo Smith had Fred (The Bear) Gladding warming in the bullpen. Gladding had not been scored upon in four outings, earning a win and a save. But Smith allowed Wilson to pitch to Luis Aparicio. On Wilson's second pitch, Aparicio hit a low liner to right field. Al Kaline made the catch easily for the second out but couldn't throw to the plate in time to prevent Blefary from scoring the game's first run. Russ Snyder then was retired on a routine grounder, but the run gave the Orioles a 1–0 lead. Barber was three outs away from throwing a no-hitter.

Barber's control problems continued into the ninth inning, when Norm Cash held up on a check swing on a 3-and-2 pitch to earn Barber's eighth walk of the game. Barber was miffed by the call, certain that Cash had gone around. He was convinced he should be facing weak-hitting Ray Oyler, the Tigers' No. 8 hitter, with one out and nobody on. Oyler had been the only Tiger to hit the ball out of the infield against Barber, with a fly ball to the warning track in the third inning. After Dick Tracewski went in to run for Cash, Oyler also walked to put runners at first and second with no one out. Jake Wood was sent in to run for Oyler, and Wilson, the Detroit pitcher, was scheduled to bat. But Wilson was one of the best hitting pitchers in the majors at both pure hitting and situation hitting, and Mayo Smith didn't hesitate to send him up to try to move the runners up a base with a sacrifice bunt. Wilson did just that, bunting up the third-base line and forcing Brooks Robinson to make the play at first, sending Tracewski to third and Wood to second with one out.

One batter after allowing his pitcher to hit in the ninth inning with his team needing a run to tie, Smith turned around and pinch hit for his leadoff batter. He brought left-handed-hitting Dick McAuliffe back to the bench and sent up righty Willie Horton for his first at-bat of the season, a week earlier than expected. Horton wore an awkward-looking high-top shoe on his left foot to provide adequate support for his ailing ankle and heel. His task was to simply hit a long fly ball that could score Tracewski to tie the score. Bauer walked to the mound and reminded Barber not to walk Horton to load the bases. Barber assured Bauer he could strike out Horton and, sensing Bauer's uneasiness, said, "If you think it's bad there, you ought to be out here." Horton failed, popping up the ball meekly in foul territory near the plate, where it was easily caught by substitute catcher Larry Haney for the second out.

The crowd began to cheer wildly as Mickey Stanley made his way to the plate. Stanley had previously gone 0 for 2 with a groundout, a strikeout, and two walks. He looked at ball one, then watched strike one. He swung and missed at Barber's 1-and-1 pitch. With Barber only one pitch away from the no-hitter, Haney signaled for a fastball. Barber shook off the sign in favor of a change-up. Barber delivered, and the ball struck in the dirt in front of home plate, bounced up and hit Haney in the shoulder. The ball caromed back toward the mound, to Barber's right. Tracewski broke from third base for the plate on orders from Cuccinello, and Barber scrambled for the ball. Tracewski was well across the plate before Barber's throw, allowing the Tigers to tie the score at 1–1 despite not collecting a base hit. Plus, Wood had moved up to third base on the wild pitch, meaning the

Tigers would be able to also score the go-ahead on a sacrifice fly since there still was only one out. Bauer again headed for the mound, to replace Barber with veteran reliever Stu Miller. Barber received a thunderous ovation from the crowd as he walked to the dugout.

The first hitter to face Miller was Don Wert, a lightly regarded hitter. Wert responded by hitting a smash back up the middle. Luis Aparicio, Baltimore's shortstop, was able to run down the ball behind second base and get a glove on it. He tossed the ball to second baseman Mark Belanger for an attempted force on Stanley, but Belanger—who years later would earn a reputation as one of baseball's slickest-fielding shortstops—dropped the ball. Wood scored, and the Tigers, without a hit, snuck ahead, 2–1. Miller set down Kaline to close out the Detroit ninth.

Wilson didn't return to pitch in the bottom of the ninth despite being sent to bat in such a critical situation in the top of the inning. Instead, Gladding came in to try to notch his second save. In his eight previous shutout innings, Gladding had allowed only five hits and no walks. In this one he retired the heart of the Baltimore order—Frank Robinson, Brooks Robinson, and rookie first baseman Mike Epstein—in order, striking out Epstein to end the game. As if it were Gladding who pitched nine no-hit innings instead of one, the Tigers rushed the mound and mobbed him after Epstein struck out.

Barber was philosophical in the trainer's room following his latest no-hit near-miss, attributing his control problems to the fact that he had not pitched in a week. "I can't complain," he said, his tender left arm resting in a whirlpool. "After walking ten men, I was long overdue." Miller came into the trainer's room and cracked, "Takes you and me to come up with a no-hitter and lose." That was the first time two pitchers had combined on a losing no-hitter. Frank Robinson stopped by and told Barber, "Damn it, next time give 'em a hit in the first inning, will you?"

In the visitors' clubhouse, Tigers manager Mayo Smith scribbled his recollection of the improbable series of events from the ninth inning onto his lineup card and placed it in a cigar box. "I'm sending that off to Cooperstown," he bellowed. "That's where it belongs. I've never seen anything like that in thirty-five years in baseball, and I don't expect to see anything like it again." There were more reasons for the Tigers to laugh and joke after the second game, another victory. The sweep of the three-game weekend series left Detroit in first place by a half game over the Yankees as the month came to a close. The Orioles had to settle for a .500 month at 8–8 after spending ten days owning at least a share of first place.

Compounding the Birds' problems was the situation involving young Mike Epstein. The 1966 Minor League Player of the Year barely played during the early weeks of the '67 season. And when he played, he played poorly. He got into only six of Baltimore's first sixteen games, with only one hit and no RBIs to show for his first 11 at-bats. Epstein had a simple explanation for his feeble figures; he said he needed to play more. The Orioles didn't believe he had merited increased playing time—and thus began an angry standoff. The Birds of Paradise they were not for Mike Epstein, with no solution in sight.

A ROHRING DEBUT

While Epstein provided a prime case of frustration, the month's most unlikely hero was left-handed pitcher Bill Rohr of Boston. Until April '67, his pitching superlatives had been confined to his days at Bellflower High School in Garden Grove, California, where he threw three no-hitters. He was signed for a $40,000 bonus out of high school by the Pittsburgh Pirates in 1963 and sent to Kingsport, Tennessee. Red Sox personnel never saw him pitch in a game but were impressed enough with what they saw when he threw batting practice to draft him the following November. At six feet three and 155 pounds, he was so skinny his teammates nicknamed him "Six O'Clock." He was invited to spring training with Boston as a twenty-year-old in 1966 but was farmed out to Toronto. "I'll be back soon," he snarled upon learning of the demotion. "You'll hear of me again."

Thanks to a 14–10 season with the Maple Leafs in '66, he was right. Usually a slow starter, Rohr put together an impressive spring in 1967. He still wasn't sure of his short-term fate when, about ten days before the Red Sox broke camp, manager Dick Williams strolled up to him in the outfield during batting practice for a brief chat. In his next start, Williams told Rohr, he should try to increase his stint to five or six innings. That way, Williams explained, Rohr would be ready when the season opened. "Do you mean I'm going north with the club?" the disbelieving Rohr asked. Williams replied that Rohr not only was staying with the Red Sox but was a starter.

His first major league start came on a Friday afternoon at Yankee Stadium in the Yankees' home opener, pitching against Whitey Ford. Feeling the pressure, Rohr deemed it necessary to change road roommates from reserve catcher Bob Tillman to starting pitcher Jim Lonborg, who had opened the season earlier in the week by beating the Chicago White Sox. Rohr incessantly quizzed Lonborg about the Yankees' hitters, starting during dinner and going straight on into the night; Lonborg patiently and politely answered every question. Rohr dozed off and awoke early Friday morning, early enough that he knew he should be quiet and not disturb Lonborg. He sat quietly during the team bus ride to Yankee Stadium, realizing that he had not even seen this famed House That Ruth Built, much less was he prepared to begin his major league career there. He couldn't draw much comfort from his battery-mate because his catcher was Russ Gibson, a New Englander who was making his first major league start after spending ten years in the minor leagues.

The crowd included a couple of New Yorkers who were confirmed Red Sox fans—former First Lady Jacqueline Kennedy and son John Jr., the latter having the audacity to wave a Red Sox pennant. Rohr was staked to an early lead when Reggie Smith led off the game with his first major league home run. Rohr, meanwhile, eased through the New York lineup the first two times around without allowing a hit. The closest the Yankees came to getting a hit was in the sixth inning, when rookie out-fielder Bill Robinson lined a shot back off Rohr's left shin. The ball bounced over to third baseman Joe Foy, who turned the play into a "routine" 1-5-3 groundout. Boston manager Dick Williams, remember-ing how a similar shot off the foot of Dizzy Dean in the 1937 All-Star Game brought about the premature end of a Hall of Fame career, consid-ered taking Rohr out even with the no-hitter intact, but reconsidered. Foy gave Rohr more breathing room in the eighth inning with a two-run homer. In the press box, a Red Sox official called Rohr's parents in California to inform them of the events going on a continent away, leav-ing the line open for the remainder of the game.

The no-hit bid remained alive in the bottom of the ninth, and Gibson thought he could bear no more excitement, since he had himself singled twice off Ford. Gibson was particularly impressed that Rohr showed no fear, constantly heading back to the mound and delivering his best stuff. Tom Tresh opened the inning in dramatic fashion for New York by slash-ing a hard liner to left center that appeared destined to fall in for the first hit. But Boston left fielder Carl Yastrzemski ran back toward the fence, keeping his eye on the ball, and made an incredible leaping catch reminis-cent of a wide receiver in football. Even the partisan Yankee crowd let out a cheer, half out of appreciation for Yaz's dazzling play and half out of excitement that Rohr's no-hitter was intact. Rohr thought, "God, I owe it to Carl to pitch a no-hitter now."

Joe Pepitone was disposed of for the second out, bringing up veteran Elston Howard as New York's last chance for a base hit. In previously getting Howard out on two groundouts and one fly out, Rohr had not thrown him a curve ball. Williams came to the mound, prompting Rohr to think: "What the hell does he want? Leave me alone for about another minute, and we can all go in and talk about this all we want." With the Yankee Stadium crowd in a frenzy, Williams warned his rookie left-hander that Howard was a notorious first-ball hitter. Then he patted Rohr on the backside and returned to the dugout. Rohr's first pitch was a fastball that Howard swung at and missed. Rohr came right back with another fastball outside that Howard didn't offer at, evening the count at 1 and 1.

Rohr stuck with the fastball, coming across the letters for strike two. Only one strike away from the no-hitter, Rohr finally resorted to a curve ball but missed in the dirt. He came back with another curve on 2 and 2 that many of the Red Sox thought had broken across the plate for strike three to end the game. But home-plate umpire Cal Drummond never made the strike call, filling the count at 3 and 2. After not throwing a curve to Howard in three previous at-bats, Rohr threw his third consecutive curve to him. There wasn't much break this time, and Howard smashed the ball into right field, well in front of Tony Conigliaro for a hit.

The crowd reacted with a chorus of boos, some of the fans even throwing their rented seat cushions onto the field. Rohr didn't have much time to consider what had happened. He retired the next batter, Charlie Smith, on the first pitch to end the game. Amid the congratulations he received in the dugout from teammates, Rohr felt a hand grab his shoulder and turned around to face an FBI agent. The agent explained that Mrs. Kennedy and John-John wanted to meet Rohr. Moments later, the former First Lady and her son were in the visitors' dugout, asking Rohr to autograph a baseball. Rohr thought: "I should be the one asking for the autograph."

In the Yankees' clubhouse, Elston Howard remarked about the crowd's reaction to his breaking up the no-hitter. "That's my job, man," he said. "That was the first time I ever got booed at Yankee Stadium for getting a hit."

Rohr made his way down the long tunnel between the dugout and the clubhouse. When he made the left turn into the clubhouse, he was startled—and practically blinded—by the collection of television lights that were set up around his locker. After satisfying the media's demands, Rohr, the last player left in the clubhouse, made his way out to the team bus. Of all the emotions he felt during the historic day, none compared to what Rohr felt when he boarded the Red Sox's bus and was greeted by hearty applause from his teammates. Back at the hotel, there was a message for him left at the front desk by a man identifying himself as a talent agent asking if Rohr would appear on the popular "Ed Sullivan Show" the following Sunday night. Rohr considered this a prank until he answered the call—and accepted the invitation. He not only appeared on the show but further thrilled his parents by calling them in advance from Sullivan's dressing room.

Ironically, Rohr's next start also came against the Yankees, a week later in Boston. Rohr was just as nervous the second time around, and pitching coach Sal Maglie offered the following wisdom: "Just throw the same way against 'em that you did before." Sure enough, Rohr beat the Yankees, 6–0, and had a shutout going into the eighth inning. It was broken up by—who else—Elston Howard, with an RBI single off the huge "Green Monster" wall in left field. All Rohr had done was begin his big-league career with sixteen consecutive scoreless innings against the most storied team in baseball history.

3
MAY

LONBORG PROVIDES PITCHING Rx

Red Sox fans had reason for optimism in early May. Boston's hitting ranked second in the league, behind Detroit only. But more surprising, the Red Sox's pitching staff was third in the AL with a team earned run average of 2.91. This from a pitching staff that returned little experience in the starting rotation. Only three times during the opening month did a Red Sox starting pitcher go on to get a defeat. April ended with the Red Sox winning eight of fourteen games and standing third behind Detroit and New York as they embarked on a nine-game road trip through California, Minnesota, and Kansas City.

The trip began with Dennis Bennett throwing a six-hitter and hitting a three-run home run in a 4–0 victory over the Angels at Anaheim Stadium that inched the Red Sox within a half game of the Tigers. But the Red Sox were stalled the following night when Jim McGlothlin, an auburn-haired, freckle-faced right-hander, retired nineteen consecutive batters en route to a 3–2 victory. In the last of the three games at Anaheim, the Red Sox turned to Jim Lonborg, who at 2–0 was establishing himself as the leader of the Boston rotation despite being in only his third major league season.

The son of a professor at Cal Poly, Lonborg had majored in biology at Stanford with intentions of becoming a doctor and wasn't really interested in playing baseball after college. He played on a summer league team at Winner, South Dakota, sponsored by the Orioles in 1963. He actually became more interested in medicine that summer, spending part of his spare time in South Dakota watching a friend perform a hysterectomy. But when Lonborg agreed to sign the following year, he chose the Red Sox over the Orioles because he thought he could make it to the majors faster with Boston. The Red Sox made Lonborg agree to put his medical aspirations on hold until the club decided his pitching days were over.

Lonborg had risen to this status with Boston mostly on potential and on the lack of any other established starting pitcher in the organization. Lonborg, a right-hander, pitched only one minor league season, compiling records of 6–2 at Class A Winston-Salem and 5–7 at Seattle. In 1965 he pushed his way into Boston's starting rotation, joining Earl Wilson, Bill Monboquette, Dave Morehead, and Dennis Bennett. In his first major league game, he was done in by a series of cheap hits that eluded the Red Sox's less-than-dazzling infield. Manager Billy Herman came out to the mound and told Lonborg: "That's the worst exhibition I ever saw." To which the embarrassed Lonborg replied, "I'm sorry." Herman, confused by Lonborg's answer, rebutted: "I don't mean you. I mean the infield!"

Lonborg struggled to a 9–17 record and 4.47 ERA on that team, which lost one hundred games. In 1966 his year began ominously. He lost to Baltimore on Opening Day on a two-out balk with the bases loaded in the ninth inning. He finished 10–10—no Boston starter compiled a winning record—with an ERA of 3.86. Teammates who pitched alongside Lonborg in the minors and in his early years with the Red Sox didn't recall his stuff being particularly impressive or overpowering. But Lonborg turned a critical corner on August 7, 1966, when he was shelled at Detroit in the first game of a doubleheader, 9–2. Lonborg lasted all of a third of an inning, giving up four runs on four hits and a walk. The loss dropped his record to 5–8 and had Lonborg fearing a demotion to the minors. Billy Herman sent Lonborg to the bullpen for the second game. Boston was trying to protect a 7–6 lead with two outs in the bottom of the tenth inning of the nightcap when Herman summoned Lonborg as Boston's fifth pitcher of the game, to face left-handed-hitting Dick McAuliffe.

Herman's instructions to Lonborg were simple: Bear down and don't let the guy do anything except hit the ball on the ground, and don't give in to him! Sure enough, McAuliffe rolled a grounder to shortstop Rico Petrocelli to end the game. Lonborg, consumed by a combination of elation and relief, headed straight for his locker and cried. A better-than-average fastball and some faith—from both without and within—had produced his shining baseball hour to date. That winter in Venezuela, Lonborg worked on his slider and change-up. He also worked on that new outlook toward challenging hitters. Teammate Dick Egan dared him to begin the season by knocking down Luis Aparicio, the Baltimore shortstop who was a national hero in Venezuela. Deck Aparicio, Egan said, and I'll buy you all you can eat. Down went Aparicio, and out came the boos from the stands. Aparicio saw Lonborg smile, realized there was an ulterior motive for the knockdown, and simply grinned back. That was the first time Lonborg intentionally knocked down a hitter.

Lonborg took the mound in the finale of the series at Anaheim in early May coming off his most impressive start of the season. He had shut out Kansas City on six hits while striking out thirteen and walking none. Through eight innings against the Angels, Lonborg allowed only a leadoff single in the seventh inning to Jim Fregosi. With Mike Andrews tagging California starter Nick Willhite for a fifth-inning home run to left field, Lonborg was only three outs away from a second consecutive shutout, this one a one-hitter. José Cardenal led off the California ninth with a harmless grounder that shortstop Rico Petrocelli handled for the first out. Fregosi followed with his second hit, a single to right field. That brought up Jay Johnstone as the tying run. Johnstone didn't exactly manhandle Lonborg, but he managed a ground single to center that sent Fregosi to third base.

Those among the Anaheim Stadium crowd of 8,880 who had not yet headed home suddenly came to life. Lonborg was pitching with the tying run only ninety feet from home, yet he had not yet been hit hard. Because of that, there was little reason for Lonborg to acknowledge the pressure of the moment. There was little reason to feel that sense of desperation that he felt in August 1966, when Dick McAuliffe stood at the plate in an at-bat that Lonborg feared might mean a ticket back to the minors. So Lonborg continued to try to play with the Angels' batters instead of challenging them. Rick Reichardt hit another grounder between Petrocelli and Andrews to score Fregosi to tie the score and send Johnstone to third base. That brought up Jimmie Hall, a left-handed hitter with power. Red Sox manager Dick Williams had Hall intentionally walked, electing to take his chances against another lefty, rookie Don Wallace, with the bases loaded and one out. The move paid off as Wallace, who had entered the game late as part of a double switch, shanked a pop into foul territory down the left-field line that Carl Yastrzemski squeezed in his glove for the second out.

The game came down to Lonborg pitching to the Angels' Buck Rodgers, a gritty catcher. Instead of going after Rodgers with a fastball, Lonborg threw a curveball that broke low and into the dirt in front of home plate. Boston catcher Russ Gibson dropped to his knees to block the ball. The pitch struck the dirt in front of the plate, bounced up off Gibson, and headed back toward the mound. Gibson, unaware that he had blocked the ball, turned and began running toward the backstop. At that point, Johnstone broke for the plate. It was only after Johnstone had started homeward that Lonborg broke for the orphaned baseball that lay in the grass about twelve feet in front of the plate. By the time Lonborg reached the ball, Johnstone had crossed the plate to give an Angels team that had huffed and puffed its way to four routine singles all night a 2–1 victory.

Losing two of three games at Anaheim established a pattern the Red Sox carried throughout the road trip. By the time they headed home from Kansas City on the night of Wednesday, May 10, the 3–6 trip had left them below .500 at 11–12 and in sixth place, 4½ games out.

BOOMER TIME FOR TIGERS

The Tigers and White Sox, meanwhile, had begun to distance themselves from the rest of the pack. Detroit, riding a five-game winning streak, owned a half-game lead over Chicago, winner of six straight. Additionally motivating to the Tigers was the return of Willie Horton to regular duty in left field. Even with a collection of hitters featuring former AL batting champions Al Kaline and Norm Cash, there was a presence about Willie Horton that couldn't be duplicated in the Tigers' dugout. He was Detroit's most dependable power hitter, nicknamed "The Boomer." Kaline and others liked to parade through the dugout in the late innings and proclaim that it was "Boomer time," trying to inspire Horton to provide a crucial homer. "Boomer time" in 1967 officially began in the sixth inning on May 10, when Horton, making his fifth start of the season, delivered his first home run. It followed a walk to Kaline and provided the winning margin in a 4–2 victory at Cleveland.

Even with Horton's triumphant return to the home-run column, there was a melancholy tone to the day for many of the Tigers. One of the early-season projects for Mayo Smith was to see if veteran right-hander Bill Monboquette, forty, could still pitch in the big leagues as a reliever. His career had plunged dramatically from the days when the Massachusetts native realized his boyhood dream by signing with his beloved Red Sox. But in 1967 he seemed detached from his achievements with Boston—making the All-Star team in 1960, throwing a no-hitter against the White Sox in 1962, winning twenty games in 1963. In 1964 Monboquette had slumped to 13–14 and, for the second consecutive season, allowed the most hits of any American League pitcher. In '65 Monboquette had led the majors with eighteen losses. That fall he was traded to Detroit for outfielder George Thomas and infielder George Smith. But with the Tigers in 1966, Monboquette managed to pitch only 103 innings, the fewest since his rookie season eight years earlier. He finished 7–8 with a career-high earned run average of 4.72. There was little reason to believe he could contribute much, if any, in 1967 to a Detroit team that was considered in need of only fine tuning. Monboquette had no chance to break Detroit's solid starting rotation, and the Tigers' deep bullpen gave him little opportunity to showcase what he could do as a reliever. His first appearance of the season came in a mop-up situation on April 16, getting in one inning in an 11–7 loss to close a doubleheader at Kansas City. He pitched another inning six days later when the cause appeared lost against Minnesota.

And that was it. There were younger pitchers at Toledo of the International League who needed to be seen against big league hitters. So on May 10 in Cleveland, Bill Monboquette returned from a day trip to the movies—watching *Casino Royale* with teammates Dick Tracewski and Larry Sherry—to discover a message in his room to call manager Mayo Smith. Monboquette, fearing the worst, returned the call to learn he was officially being released as of May 15. The Tigers had no need for a forty-year-old who pitched only two innings in a month. Monboquette dejectedly returned home to Massachusetts, hopeful that some major league team would call him.

WHITE-HOT SOX

As hot as the Tigers were, the White Sox were even hotter. A sweep of a Sunday doubleheader against California on May 14 gave them a ten-game winning streak, the longest in the league to that point. Coupled with Boston's sweep of Detroit, the White Sox enjoyed a lead of 1 1/2 games over the Tigers. The four-game sweep of the Angels sported the White Sox's familiar brand. It began on a Friday night with the bunching of two of three total hits together in the fifth inning to produce the game's only run. Joe Horlen pitched into the ninth inning to improve his record to 4–0. On Saturday afternoon it took Chicago 10 innings to score, but the result was the same. A sacrifice fly by pinch hitter Smokey Burgess scored pinch runner Walt Williams to give Jim O'Toole his first AL victory on a two-hitter. In the Sunday doubleheader, the White Sox virtually erupted for victories of 4–2 and 3–1. In the second game, Gary Peters limited the Angels to one hit, a second-inning home run by former White Sox first baseman "Moose" Skowron. Further examination of the winning streak reveals what made the 1967 White Sox tick. As a team, the Sox hit all of .211 in the ten games and scored only 38 runs. Conversely, Chicago allowed only 12 runs. To date for the season, the White Sox boasted an incredible 2.06 ERA after five weeks, led by Horlen's 0.90. The best batting average among Chicago regulars was Ken Berry's .280.

With such poor hitting, the White Sox needed all the help they could get to win. And management gave them all it could. The approach amounted to: if we can't hit, neither will anybody else. For one thing, the game balls were stored in a dark, dank area of Comiskey Park; the moisture made them relatively soft and harder to hit for distance. Some opponents went so far as to accuse the White Sox of actually freezing the baseballs. Detroit pitcher Hank Aguirre once complained to the home-plate umpire that the ball was downright cold. Many pitchers said the ball felt damp. Cal Hubbard, the American League's umpire-in-chief, was once dispatched to Chicago to investigate how and where the White Sox stored their baseballs, but nothing was proven. In addition, the White Sox maintained the playing field to their advantage, fully within league rules. The grass in front of home plate was watered down so much that the water would often squish about halfway up a fielder's shoes. This was done because the White Sox featured plenty of sinkerball pitchers and their infielders weren't always the best at covering ground. Hence, a wet infield would slow down grounders, allowing Chicago infielders to make more plays.

The first-place White Sox also amassed surprisingly low numbers at the Comiskey Park turnstiles. Even after coming home riding a seven-game winning streak, only 24,132 fans paid to see the three-day, four-game series. And while baseball attendance in April and early May often is held down by poor weather, the White Sox had to be embarrassed at drawing an average of only 7,465 to their first ten dates. Crowds at White Sox home games had grown smaller regularly since 1960, when the team came off a pennant season to draw a franchise-record 1.6 million fans. By 1966 the total had slipped to 990,000. Management was puzzled by the team's lack of drawing power. Sure, there were the handicaps of playing in aging Comiskey Park, opened in 1910 and the oldest park in the majors, and of the deteriorating South Side neighborhood that might have kept some Sox fans away. Still, the White Sox had outdrawn their crosstown rivals, the National League Cubs, in every season expect one since 1950. White Sox owner Arthur Allyn was eager to move his team into a new stadium. After he announced the July 24 exhibition game in Milwaukee against the Twins, talk grew that if the city of Chicago didn't help him move into new digs, Allyn would take his team north to Milwaukee.

FINLEY AND THE A's

Another American League surprise by mid-May was the Kansas City Athletics. On May 16 they hoisted themselves up over the .500 mark for the first time since the earliest days of the season and into third place. This was foreign terrain for a franchise that had not tasted a winning season since 1952, when it was located in Philadelphia. For one of the few times since the team moved to Kansas City in 1955, there was legitimate hope that the A's could at least finish in the middle of the pack. KC fans weren't pleading for a pennant; they simply wanted a respectable ballclub. They had inherited the worst team in baseball (51–103) after the 1954 season, when Arnold Johnson, owner of the Kansas City Blues minor league team, bought the Philadelphia A's and moved them to Kansas City.

Kansas City had embraced the team despite its faults. The city had been saddled with the tag of being a great minor league town for the better part of the century. Fans had flocked to see the Blues of the American Association. The Kansas City Monarchs of the old Negro National League also were a rich part of the city's baseball heritage. Jackie Robinson played for the Monarchs in 1945 before moving into the Dodgers' minor league system. Satchel Paige pitched seven years for the Monarchs before joining the Cleveland Indians in '48. Ernie Banks spent two seasons in Kansas City before getting his break to join the major leagues with the Cubs.

Johnson's Blues were a minor league affiliate of the New York Yankees, and it was with the help of Yankees owner Dan Topping that Johnson was able to acquire the A's. (Among the also-rans in the bid to buy the team was an insurance man from Chicago named Charles O. Finley, whose main link to baseball was being a batboy for the Birmingham Barons when he grew up in Alabama.) Johnson hastily renovated and expanded Blues Stadium from 17,500 seats to 30,611 just in time for Opening Day 1955. Former President Harry Truman, a Missourian, threw out the first pitch. Despite finishing sixth in the eight-team league, the new Kansas City A's placed second in the AL in attendance, drawing close to 1.4 million people. And another million poured in during 1956, even though the Athletics dropped back into the basement.

As the decade wore on, two constants marked the Kansas City Athletics' existence. One was the penchant for finishing at or near the bottom of the American League. Another was a curious relationship with their AL reciprocals, the powerful Yankees. Remember that the A's could trace their very existence in Kansas City to the accommodating Yankees. Johnson maintained a friendly relationship with the New York brass to which he once was subservient as a minor league affiliate. During his five years as owner of the Athletics, Johnson made ten deals with the Yankees. Those swaps often helped make the Yankees richer on the field and helped the A's pay their bills. Among the young prospects sent to New York, most in exchange for aging veterans, were infielder Clete Boyer; outfielder Hector Lopez; and pitchers Ralph Terry, Ryne Duren, and Bobby Shantz. There was another young outfielder who was considered to have great power who spent less than two seasons in Kansas City before making the move to the Yankees. Roger Maris hit 16 home runs for the

A's in 1959, just two seasons before he reversed those numerals to become baseball's all-time single-season home-run king.

Johnson died in March 1960, and the American League operated the team that season instead of hurriedly seeking an immediate buyer. The A's finished last and saw attendance drop below eight hundred thousand. The club was offered up to the highest bidder and, on December 19, became the proud property of Charlie Finley. After failing in his bid to buy the A's in 1955, Finley had turned his attention to other franchises. He made a pitch for the Chicago White Sox in 1958, only to watch the Comiskey family sell the team to Bill Veeck; he also looked into the availability of the Detroit Tigers. When the American League voted in 1960 to expand from eight teams to ten for the 1961 season, Finley's mouth watered at the prospect of operating the new team planned for Los Angeles. He even was set to name Casey Stengel, recently deposed by the Yankees, as his manager. But the LA rights instead were awarded to Gene Autry, the "Singing Cowboy," who actually arrived at the league meetings in St. Louis hoping to land the radio rights to the team, not the team itself. Finley again rode off empty-handed. With the auction of the A's, Finley finally was a major league owner—though some Athletics fans may have been skeptical of that term being used to describe the level of ball they had watched in recent years.

There was fear in Kansas City that the team's new absentee owner had no interest in the town, that he planned to pack up the team like a bunch of lamp shades and end tables and cart it off, just as Arnold Johnson had done to bring the team to Kansas City in the first place. The Athletics' lease for the ballpark, since renamed Municipal Stadium, extended through 1963. Finley, upon taking over the team, tried to allay such fears. "My intentions are to keep the A's permanently in Kansas City," he said. Ironically, in his zealous efforts to prove his conviction to the city, he eliminated a clause in the franchise paperwork that would have allowed him to move the team if it failed to draw at least 850,000 fans. The A's would rarely even come close to that figure in their first few seasons under Finley, seasons in which the team remained shackled near the bottom of the standings.

It didn't take long for Finley's eyes to wander. His first season as owner of the A's had not even finished before he weighed the merits of moving the team to Dallas, a spurned suitor in the first round of expansion that didn't yet have an adequate stadium. Again, in the spring of 1962, Finley canvassed his fellow AL owners at a league meeting in New York about relocation and acknowledged examining three cities—Dallas, Oakland, and San Diego—the latter two with new stadiums on the drawing boards. A month later Finley asked the city of Kansas City to build a new baseball stadium. He also talked with Bill Cunningham, an official with the new Oakland–Alameda County Coliseum, about bringing the A's to the Bay Area in '62 or '63. As the lease on Municipal Stadium wound down in 1963, Finley continued to explore other options and was even assisted financially in his stadium safari by AL president Joe Cronin. He talked with Horace Stoneham, owner of the San Francisco Giants, about sharing Candlestick Park until the new Oakland stadium was ready.

In January 1964, with his lease in Kansas City having expired, Finley shook Kansas City with the announcement that he had signed a lease agreement for his team to play in Louisville. At the news conference, he joked that the interlocking "KC" design on the team caps could be retained if the team were called the Kentucky Colonels. Finley's AL peers failed to recognize the humor in all of this; they voted nine days later that Finley would forfeit ownership of the franchise if he relocated without the required league approval—which he knew he couldn't receive. Like a man begrudgingly returning to his wife after proclaiming his intention of divorce, Finley signed a new four-year lease to stay in Kansas City through the 1967 season. He was further angered that while Kansas City refused to shell out cash to build him a new stadium, it was more than happy to spend $625,000 to build pro football's Kansas City Chiefs a new practice field, training headquarters, and office complex. Finley traveled to Oakland during the summer of 1966 to view firsthand the construction of the Coliseum and returned that fall to watch the first game played there by the Oakland Raiders of the American Football League. By this time, Finley had also gained some interest in Seattle.

While Finley was failing to put a winner on the field, he didn't lack effort in original ideas to get fans into the ballpark. He introduced a mule as the new team mascot. He installed a mechanical bunny below field level near home plate to pop up and deliver a new supply of baseballs to the home-plate umpire. He turned the hillside just beyond the right-field fence into a home for a flock of sheep. He outfitted his team in garish, gold-colored vest tops and pants to go with kelly green caps, socks, and undershirts. On the field, Finley could afford to try more novelties, since there was little chance of endangering the team's already awful position in the standings. In 1965 he had versatile shortstop Bert Campaneris play all nine positions in one game. That same year, he also brought back Satchel Paige—the best estimates being that the former Negro League pitching legend was fifty-nine years old—to start one game.

Finley wasn't afraid to stick his nose in the day-to-day operations of the ballclub. It wasn't unusual for him to call the clubhouse from his Chicago office to deliver some dictum on how the team should be handled that day. One time when the A's were playing in Cleveland, he went to the trouble of calling the visitors' clubhouse and having the Indians' broadcast of the game placed next to the receiver. It would have seemed simpler to call Kansas City and listen to the A's announcers. By calling the clubhouse, Finley achieved a Big Brother presence, though his players were for the most part in the dugout during the game. Managers were an expendable commodity for Finley. When Alvin Dark took over the team beginning the '66 season, he became Finley's seventh manager in seven seasons.

The A's finished last in '64 and '65, but a seventh-place finish in '66 and an influx of new, young talent actually gave Kansas City new hope for 1967, the final year of Finley's KC lease. Maybe the Athletics could reach the first division, and support for the team could give Finley reason to stay in Kansas City. The A's had put together one of the best young pitching staffs in the majors. Jim Nash, twenty, was coming off a 12–1 finish with a 2.06 ERA in 127 innings. Jim Hunter, twenty, had won seventeen of nineteen decisions the two previous seasons and was seen by Finley as the potential star of the staff. That's why Finley, upon signing Hunter out of high school in rural North Carolina, concocted a story about Hunter running away from home, then returning with some catfish that earned him the nickname "Catfish." Lew Krausse, twenty-three, had been signed as an eighteen-year-old for $125,000 in 1961 and pitched a three-hit shutout nine days after his high school graduation. He led Kansas City in victories in 1966 with fourteen. There also were Johnny (Blue Moon) Odom, twenty, and Chuck Dobson, twenty-three. Ace reliever Jack Aker, practically the old man of the team at twenty-six, led the league in '66 with twenty-six saves and served as the team's representative to the players' union. Pitching wasn't the only source of optimism. Campaneris led the league in stolen bases for the second consecutive year in '66 with 62. And Finley had tapped a gold mine with Arizona State University, signing third baseman Sal Bando and outfielders Rick Monday and Reggie Jackson. Monday, the No. 1 pick in baseball's initial amateur draft in 1965, won the starting right-field job in 1967.

But although the A's opened the season playing some of the best baseball since the team relocated in Kansas City, the antics of their owner still commanded much of the attention. To the team's already odd uniforms, Finley added gold batting helmets in replacement of the green ones, and the A's became the first team in baseball to wear white shoes. The latter was more than many baseball purists could stand. When Kansas City opened the season by beating Cleveland, Indians manager Joe Adcock filed a complaint with the league office, claiming that the new shoes were a distraction. Cleveland outfielder Leon Wagner described the new outfits as "tutti-frutti." Whatever flavor the A's were, their better baseball was more palatable to Kansas City fans. And they were in third place, even though their young pitching staff was struggling along with the worst team ERA in the league.

MINNESOTA'S MOUNDMEN

But the epitome of a struggle on the mound belonged to veteran Minnesota left-hander Jim Kaat. The 1966 American League leader in victories (25) and innings pitched (305), Kaat got off to a horrific start in 1967. When he was knocked out after 2⅓ innings against Chicago on May 22, it marked the ninth time in as many starts that Kaat had failed to finish a game. His record was 1–5, his earned run average 6.26. Until this time, Kaat had enjoyed a marvelous career. A relatively small youngster in high school, he was turned down by the scouts and never really considered playing baseball as a career. He attended Hope College in Michigan, grew tremendously, and was signed in the summer of 1957 by the Washington Senators. Growing to six feet five and 220 pounds, Kaat worked his way onto the team's starting rotation by the time it moved to Minnesota in 1961 and made more than thirty starts each year from '61 through '66.

The timing of his '67 collapse couldn't have been worse, considering his outspoken criticism the previous October of Twins manager Sam Mele for his decision to fire pitching coach Johnny Sain. Critics in the stands and the press box wondered whether Kaat's performance was in any way related to his unhappiness with Mele, who brought in Early Wynn as his new pitching coach. Whereas Sain would treat a struggling pitcher like a maze that needed to be solved, Wynn thought the way to cure every pitcher's ills was through increased hard work. A slumping pitcher heard that he wasn't working hard enough, wasn't running enough. The solution was to don a rubber sweat jacket and run until he dropped. Or march off to the bullpen for some extra throwing. Kaat wasn't about to panic, believing he had pitched much better than his record indicated. But in late May, Wynn convinced Mele to drop Kaat from the starting rotation, to banish him at least temporarily to the bullpen, where he could straighten himself out. Kaat was replaced in the rotation with another lefty, Jim Merritt, who had an ERA of 1.75 but had pitched only 10⅓ innings in six appearances over the first five weeks of the season.

The Twins couldn't have asked for a better start from their key winter acquisition, right-handed starter Dean Chance. After eight starts, Chance had a 6–1 record with four complete games, two shutouts, and an ERA of 2.19. He carried these numbers back to California in late May for his first appearance against his former team. Chance overpowered the Angels for eight innings and barely missed his third consecutive shutout in the Twins' 7–2 victory. With a record of 7–1, Chance had accounted for half of Minnesota's victories.

For Wilmer Dean Chance, the opportunity to play on a pennant winner meant more than being recognized as the best pitcher in the American League. He already had captured the highest honor a major league pitcher could achieve when in 1964 he was named the Cy Young Award winner for both leagues (winners for each league weren't established until 1967) while pitching for the Angels.

Chance had started out in the Orioles' organization, signing out of high school in Wooster, Ohio. He was signed in 1959, the same year Baltimore signed a hulking first baseman out of Miami named John (Boog) Powell. The Orioles had their eye on Powell early in his high school career and anticipated having to spend more than $100,000 of bonus money to sign him. But Powell went through a terrible slump during his senior year that lowered his value. With some of the money available that was originally earmarked to sign Powell, the Orioles were able to sign a couple of other prospects, including Chance.

He began his pro career well, going 10–3 in sixteen games with a 2.94 ERA that summer at Bluefield of the Appalachian League. In 1960 he was promoted to Fox Cities of the I.I.I. League—Illinois, Iowa, and Indiana—where he played for a crusty little guy named Earl Weaver and went 12–9 with a 3.13 ERA. But when the American League held its expansion draft to stock the new Los Angeles Angels and Washington Senators for the 1961 season, the Orioles left Chance unprotected—against Weaver's wishes. Chance was claimed by the Angels.

The move was the big break that Chance needed, though his first year in the Los Angeles organization yielded an unimpressive 9–12 record and 3.66 ERA at Class AAA Dallas–Fort Worth. Chance was brought up to the Angels that September—and never returned to the minors. As a rookie in 1962, he immediately moved into the starting rotation and became the top winner (14) on the second-year team that stunned the experts by finishing third in the league.

While Chance may have been the Angels' best pitcher, he wasn't their best-known. That distinction went to another rookie, a tall, dark-haired, twenty-six-year-old left-hander named Robert (Bo) Belinsky. It was Belinsky who convinced the Angels they could play with the big boys when he no-hit the Orioles on May 5, 1962, in only his fourth major league start. Confidence was something that Belinsky didn't lack. While growing up in Trenton, New Jersey, he was accustomed to challenging any and all comers at a local pool hall. When he signed with the Angels, he held out before even signing because he objected to a portion of the contract.

Belinsky parlayed his success on the field and charisma off the field to become one of Los Angeles' most popular sports celebrities. He earned much of his fame by dating Hollywood actress Mamie Van Doren. Chance and Belinsky often would be treated to a night on the town by newspaper columnist Walter Winchell, whose presence at a table meant there was no need for the waiter to bring the check.

Belinsky and Chance became an integral part of a team that needed an identity to combat the immense popularity of the crosstown Dodgers. Chance was more than happy to slap an arm around a rookie like Rick Reichardt and show him the ropes around LA. Meanwhile, Chance became an even better pitcher, peaking in 1964 with the Cy Young numbers of 20–9 and a 1.65 ERA, while Belinsky had difficulty approaching his early heroics. Chance became the ringleader of the regular card games that were a necessary diversion on a team that, as the only AL team west of Kansas City, logged an incredible number of hours in the air. Pinochle and gin rummy were Chance's games—he never touched poker—and Jimmy Piersall and Fred Newman were among his regular card compatriots.

Angels catcher Buck Rodgers thought Chance wasted a tremendous amount of his talent, referring to him as having a million-dollar arm and a ten-cent head. With Chance needing to throw one more strike against Minnesota's Zoilo Versalles to pitch a no-hitter, Rodgers called for a slider, knowing that Versalles was a good fastball hitter. Chance shook him off and winked. The wink, Rodgers realized, was Chance's way of alerting him that a spitball was coming. Chance had virtually no control of his spitball; hence, he rarely threw it. Yet a spitter was on the way with a no-hitter on the line. Versalles singled up the middle. Another time, Chance needed to retire the Yankees' Tom Tresh for a 1–0 Angels victory. Tresh was a notorious fastball hitter. With a 1-and-2 count, Rodgers signaled for a breaking pitch; Chance shook him off. Rodgers put down the same fingers; Chance again shook him off. Rodgers begrudgingly called for a fastball. Tresh crushed it, hitting a tying home run. Rodgers marched to the mound, where he was berated by Chance for not calling for the breaking pitch a third time. "You knew I wanted the breaking pitch," Chance snapped. Rodgers soon learned that Chance liked to have control of the situation. If Rodgers called for a slider on 3 and 2, Chance invariably would walk the batter. If Rodgers called for a fastball on 3 and 2 and Chance would shake it off and OK a slider, Chance would get the slider over the plate.

While Chance developed close bonds with many of his California teammates, he didn't shed too many tears when he learned of the trade to Minnesota. He grew weary of pitching for a team whose hitting couldn't be counted on regularly. In winning twenty games in 1964, Chance set a major league record by winning six games by the score of 1–0. Of course, Chance almost never helped out his own cause. He was arguably the worst hitter in baseball, claiming poor sight in his left eye as the culprit. He set a record in 1964 for strikeouts by a pitcher—while batting, that is—when he fanned 58 times.

In Minnesota, Chance joined forces with another free-spirited pitcher, Dave Boswell. An example of the Boswell sense of humor was the time he couldn't resist spooking a ballpark attendant who was painting the advertising signs on the outfield wall at the Twins' spring training park in Orlando. Boswell stood in the outfield along with other players shagging flies during batting practice. He picked up a ball while standing about twenty feet from the painter and proceeded to heave it as hard as he could at the wall, within a few feet of the painter. Just before the ball crashed into the wooden fence, Boswell let loose with a blood-curdling scream of "Look out!" At which the terrified painter immediately abandoned the tools of his trade and leaped off the ladder.

Boswell and Chance provided a stark contrast to Twins reliever Al Worthington, a devoutly religious man who regularly organized Sunday prayer meetings. Worthington often asked Chance to come to the meetings but was politely rebuffed. One week Worthington lined up Baltimore Colts football star Mike Curtis as a guest speaker and, hoping to have a big crowd, pleaded with Chance to attend. Chance told Worthington that if he woke up in time, he would come. Worthington, sensing a breakthrough, told Chance he would come and get him. Not wanting to embarrass Worthington, Chance agreed to come.

Chance arrived and saw Boswell, each silently responding with looks that said, "What are *you* doing here?" During the meeting, Worthington asked everyone to bow his head. He then noted that everyone in the group had sinned, and those who needed help should raise their hands. After the meeting ended, Boswell came straight over to Chance and shook his hand. Chance was puzzled, and Boswell explained: "Those hypocrites. When the guy asked if anybody there needed help, I peeked. Dean, you were the only guy in the room that had his hand raised."

THE OLD AND THE NEW

As Chance continued to excel for the Twins, one of the game's premier left-handers of the fifties and early sixties was nearing the end of his career. Whitey Ford had come to spring training with the Yankees at age thirty-eight, having pitched only 73 innings in 1966. A consistent winner for New York beginning with his 9–1 record as a rookie in 1950, Ford had pitched the past few years while troubled by pain in his left shoulder and elbow. He underwent two shoulder operations in 1964 and wouldn't consider any further surgeries. The '67 season began encouragingly enough with a 2–2 start. But the excruciating pain persisted in Ford's left arm. He lasted only three innings in a 14–0 loss to Baltimore on May 12. Yankees manager Ralph Houk rested Ford until May 21 at Detroit. In that game, Ford gave up a run in the bottom of the first and, more important, realized he no longer was capable of throwing the ball with anything on it. At the end of the inning, he matter-of-factly walked to the dugout, calmly told Houk to get someone else ready to pitch, and removed himself from the game. He continued on into the clubhouse, undressed, and showered. As he dressed, Ford began scribbling a note as team publicist Bob Fishel came into the clubhouse. Ford said, "I guess I won't see you for a while." To which a confused Fishel replied, "What do you mean?" Ford answered, "I'm going to the airport and go home." Ford finished writing the note and placed it in Houk's locker. The message said simply: "I've had it, Ralph. I'm going back to New York. I'll call you tomorrow."

With that, a sixteen-year career that had yielded 236 victories—plus ten more wins in eleven World Series—came to an end. On the flight back to New York, Ford's mind wandered amid the memories of the great seasons and great times that were the powerhouse Yankee teams. On so many flights during the Yankees' heyday, Ford and Mickey Mantle had talked about the great golf courses they would play after they retired—Pebble Beach, Firestone, Augusta. But such pleasant daydreaming didn't last long. Those times seemed so long ago; this was a totally different Yankee team, and Whitey Ford found nothing difficult about quitting. He spent much of the flight realizing he was out of work and wondering what he was going to do to earn a living.

While Ford had decided his career was over, the Yankees still insisted he undergo yet another examination of his tattered left elbow upon his return to New York. Team physician Sidney Gaynor determined there was a spur on the elbow. Ford, whose career-high annual salary was $78,000, hoped the team would bend major league rules and leave him on the disabled list for the rest of the season, allowing him to collect his full salary. Instead, general manager Lee MacPhail told him he would receive two weeks' severance pay. All these years, Ford thought, had come to this. Then again, the Yankee organization never was known for sensitivity. Veteran Yankee broadcaster Red Barber was fired following the 1965 season as a result of his request during the waning days of the season that the TV cameras pan the empty seats at Yankee Stadium. The official announcement of Ford's retirement was made May 31. He actually was second in the AL in earned run average at 1.64 when he quit. When Ford was honored at Yankee Stadium,

Mantle watched the ceremony from the steps of the dugout and felt as bad for himself—realizing his own retirement couldn't be delayed much longer—as he did for his longtime buddy.

Another Yankee who struggled early was Bill Robinson, the rookie outfielder acquired from Atlanta. Robinson had gotten past the talk of being a black Mickey Mantle and thought he was over the elbow injury that occurred during winter ball. But Robinson really wasn't ready for the majors. He was fighting to keep his average above .150 in late April, with no runs batted in following his two-run homer on Opening Day in Washington. By mid-May he had lost his starting job in right field to Steve Whitaker. By Memorial Day, his average had plummeted to .111, and he was still without another RBI.

The game that Robinson had loved to play for so long had turned on him, had become an enemy to fear. At home games Robinson would race from his position at game's end so he could shower, dress, and get out to his car before the ruthless fans from the upper deck had a chance to confront him. He often found the paint on his car scratched. Other times, fans threw rocks at his car. Robinson couldn't leave his troubles behind on the short drive from the Bronx to his apartment in the suburban town of Teaneck, New Jersey. His wife, Mary, often found him inconsolable. He brooded, trying in vain to relax by listening to music, but he often spent much of the day worrying about whether he was going to fail again that night at Yankee Stadium. On the road, Robinson found little comfort in his roommate, Al Downing. It wasn't that Downing was unsympathetic. But Downing was afflicted with a form of narcolepsy, or sleeping sickness, and spent much of his time away from the ballpark on the road sleeping.

Meanwhile, the world champion Orioles pushed within five games of first-place Chicago on May 27, good enough for third place, but still had not solved the problem of what to do with Mike Epstein. He had appeared in only nine games, serving as a pinch hitter and occasional first baseman when Boog Powell was nursing an injury. When the Orioles prepared to cut down their roster on May 10, Epstein was called in to see the Orioles' brass and was informed by general manager Harry Dalton that he was being shipped back to Rochester. "Like I told you," manager Hank Bauer reminded him, "we're not going to break it up."

Epstein left the meeting totally disillusioned. He had done everything the organization asked of him for two seasons and had performed beyond expectations. When he considered returning to the minors, only negatives entered his mind. A minor league pitcher could make a name for himself by firing a fastball a little bit too far inside and plunk a big name like Epstein on the elbow. All it took was one hard slide into second base to end the chance of returning to the big leagues. All it took was a season in which he didn't equal his superlative totals from 1966, and the skeptics would say Epstein was a fluke.

So Epstein did the unthinkable—at least, the unthinkable for 1967. The rookie walked out. He told Dalton he had no intention of returning to Rochester. With Dalton assuring him he was making the wrong decision, Epstein set off for Stockton, California, his wife's hometown. Virtually every day for three weeks, Dalton called and Epstein assured him this was no idle stunt, that he was through with baseball and was making plans to return to the University of California to attend law school. Epstein even received a call from Sid Gillman, coach of the American Football League's San Diego Chargers, who remembered the Mike Epstein who was a starting fullback as a sophomore in college and was curious to see what kind of football player he still would make. Since the Orioles refused to use him, Epstein would consider coming back to baseball only if Baltimore traded him. Epstein went so far as to call his lawyer in late May and tell him to prepare to sue major league baseball, claiming that he was being denied the opportunity to make a major league living based on his past record.

The matter was settled May 29, when Epstein was sent to the Senators in a trade that also included an exchange of left-handed pitchers—Frank Bertaina going to the Senators with Epstein for Pete Richert. Washington was seeking consistent hitting out of first base, where the platoon of right-handed-hitting Ken Harrelson (.226) and lefty Dick Nen (.189) was one of the weakest positions on the team. But even the trade didn't initially convince Epstein he should return to baseball. He was depressed at the thought of leaving the Orioles for the Senators, who were synonymous with losing. But friends convinced him that the major leagues was the major leagues, no matter what the address. It was only after a long phone conversation with Senators manager Gil Hodges that Epstein decided to return to baseball.

Memorial Day was the backdrop for the first crucial confrontation of the AL season, first-place Chicago taking a half-game lead into Detroit for a holiday doubleheader against the second-place Tigers. A crowd of 40,798 watched the Tigers sweep their way to a lead of 1½ games over the White Sox by scores of 4–2 and 4–3. The spotlight shown brightest on Detroit reliever Fred Gladding. "The Bear," with his hardened stare coming through a pair of thick eyeglasses, picked up saves in both games, allowing one hit and one walk overall in 3⅓ innings. For the season, Gladding had pitched 20⅓ innings without giving up a run in thirteen appearances, while earning eight saves. His pitching had a great deal to do with the Tigers leading the league. At six feet one and 225 pounds, the bespectacled Gladding was an imposing figure to face from sixty feet six inches away. He picked up his nickname in the minor leagues thanks to a teammate named Gabby Wytucky, who thought Gladding looked like a bear that was stomping around a berry patch. Gladding grew up only minutes outside of Detroit, idolizing Tigers pitchers Virgil Trucks and Dizzy Trout. Gladding even emulated Trout's habit of carrying a red bandana. Gladding signed with the Tigers in 1956 and was a starting pitcher throughout his minor league career, only beginning to pitch in relief upon reaching Detroit late in the 1961 season. Gladding was a mainstay of the Detroit bullpen the three previous seasons, appearing in an average of forty-six games. He was strictly a power pitcher until new pitching coach Johnny Sain helped him develop confidence in his breaking ball during spring training.

4
JUNE

BOSOX, YAZ MAKE THEIR MARK

By June 1 the sweet season of Red Sox rookie pitcher Bill Rohr had begun to turn sour. He had not won another game after the back-to-back complete game victories over the Yankees in his first two starts. After losing at home to the Twins, 4–0, on June 1, Rohr's record stood at 2–3. His ERA had gone from 0.50 after the two Yankee wins to 4.58, and only once had he lasted more than five innings. Particularly damning in the latest loss was a walk to Twins pitcher Dean Chance. Manager Dick Williams had lost his patience with Rohr, who was getting ready to serve two weeks of military reserve duty, and was prepared to alter his starting rotation, since he was more confident than ever that the Red Sox were close to competing with the Tigers and White Sox. Rohr was frustrated that pitching coach Sal Maglie offered little or no help. Maglie's idea of coaching Rohr was to tell him how he would have pitched to a Willie Mays or a Stan Musial. Rohr would listen as best he could, then simply walk away.

Williams needed to improve his bench and starting rotation. Red Sox vice president Dick O'Connell provided the tools through two trades completed during the first week of June. First, Boston sent relief pitcher Don McMahon to Chicago for infielder Jerry Adair on June 3. The next day, O'Connell packaged a couple of reserves, veteran outfielder Don Demeter and young first baseman Tony Horton, and sent them to Cleveland for Gary Bell, a right-handed starting pitcher. Neither acquisition on its own looked like the kind of steal that would produce a pennant. Adair, thirty, had hit only .204 in twenty-eight games with the White Sox. But he was an excellent defensive player who could play second baseman or shortstop and was capable of playing third base. He originally signed in 1958 with Baltimore for a $40,000 bonus out of Oklahoma A&M and became recognized as one of the American League's best defensive infielders. Dick Williams was with the Orioles when Adair came up—his teammates called Adair "Casper" because of his light complexion—and always considered him one of the best infielders in the majors. Adair was traded from the Orioles to the White Sox during the '66 season, missing out on the World Series. With the trade to Boston, many people around the league pitied Adair for being traded from a sure pennant winner for the second consecutive year. The Red Sox could part with McMahon because Johnny Wyatt was almost untouchable coming out of their bullpen. Chicago needed relief help because right-hander Dennis Higgins had to be placed on the disabled list with a detatched retina.

Bell had not pitched particularly well for the Indians, going 1–5 with a 3.71 ERA. But Williams was convinced Bell could go out and give him a good seven innings on a regular basis. And O'Connell went so far as to say Bell would keep the Red Sox in the pennant race. In Horton, the Red Sox were cutting loose a player who had been considered one of the top prospects in the organization only a few years earlier.

Bell didn't try to conceal his elation at being traded, saying, "Getting out of Cleveland was like getting out of prison." Wyatt put the trade's impact on the pennant race in his own unique perspective, noting that "there's a lot of cotton yet to be picked." Williams planned to place Bell and Lee Stange into the starting rotation. Rohr, who didn't count against the team roster while serving in the army, would be sent to Toronto upon his return to try to work out his problems.

While the Red Sox were trying to hone the fine edges of their attack, there was no questioning who was the heart of their ballclub. Carl Yastrzemski finally was putting together the kind of season that Red Sox fans had hoped for since he came up in 1961, burdened with the tag of being the next Ted Williams. Never really considering himself a power hitter, Yaz reached mid-June already within reach of his best home run season in the majors. His 14 homers were second in the league behind the 18 hit by Baltimore's Frank Robinson. His 40 RBIs were third behind Robinson's 53 and Al Kaline's 41. At .326, he trailed only Kaline (.335), Robinson (.335), and Minnesota rookie Rod Carew (.330).

The difference in the Yastrzemski who had hit between 15 and 20 homers a year and the '67 version who looked like he might smack 40 was an off-season program that improved both his muscles and mind. He worked out at the Colonial Country Club, just outside Boston in the town of Wake-field, Massachusetts, under the supervision of a former Hungarian Olympic coach named Gene Berde (pronounced *Bird*-ee). An exercise smorgasbord of rope climbing, weight lifting, sprinting, and other drills made Yastrzem-ski realize just how relatively out of shape he was. By the time he was ready to head to Florida in February, Yastrzemski was rejuvenated mentally and physically by Berde's rigorous athletic gauntlet. He was convinced he could be a pull hitter and not be intimidated by Fenway Park's cavernous right-center power alley. Maybe, finally, he could satisfy the expectations of Boston's demanding fans even if he wasn't the next Ted Williams.

In 1939, the year Ted Williams broke into the major leagues, Carl Yastrzemski Jr. was born on the eastern end of Long Island, the son of a potato farmer. Carl Sr. was the best baseball player for the Bridgehampton White Eagles, an amateur team sponsored by a Polish-American fraternal club, and Carl Jr. became the team's batboy. The local little league wasn't formed until young Carl was twelve. Then, with him pitching and playing shortstop, the team won the Long Island championship. He continued to star in Babe Ruth League play and for Bridgehampton High School, where he hit .500 over his four seasons and also threw a no-hitter. Baseball wasn't the only sport Yastrzemski excelled at; as a senior basketball player, he set the Long Island record by scoring 628 points in twenty-two games.

A Red Sox fan from Long Island named Arthur Susskind wrote to Joe Cronin, then general manager of the Red Sox, about a slugger with a long Polish name that he couldn't spell. One of the first scouts to spot Yastrzemski's baseball prowess was Boston's Frank (Bots) Nekola. Nekola first noticed Yastrzemski as a sixteen-year-old infielder with a good arm and an average glove. But what really caught Nekola's eye was the swing—perfectly level. The batting stance was somewhat awkward—bending from the waist to get a better look at the pitch, bat held high and far back, the front right shoulder hunched forward slightly and the front foot pulled around touching the inside of the batter's box. The kid said his hitting hero was Ted Williams, but at the plate he resembled Stan (The Man) Musial of the St. Louis Cardinals, who was the closest thing the National League had to offer in batting excellence to Williams.

This, Nekola concluded, was the swing of a future major leaguer. The Red Sox were one of fourteen major league teams that tried to sign Yastrzemski out of high school as an infielder, but he decided to accept a baseball scholarship to Notre Dame (one of only three the Irish offered that year). He enrolled in the School of Commerce and played freshman ball in the spring of 1958. When he returned to South Bend that fall, the Red Sox were more determined than ever to sign him. When Yastrzcmski came home on Thanksgiving break, Nekola brought Yaz and his parents to Boston to meet with Cronin. Yastrzemski was offered a bonus reportedly worth $100,000 to sign, and the opportunity to become Boston's regular second baseman within only a few years. College would have to wait; Yaz signed.

He began his pro career in 1959 at Raleigh of the Carolina League, playing second base and shortstop. His batting average of .377 not only led the league but was the best in the league in eleven years. Not considered a power hitter, Yastrzemski hit 15 home runs and drove in 100 runs. More than half of his homers were hit over Raleigh's imposing right-field wall, which had a 386-foot power alley. There was another large number to consider; Yastrzemski committed 45 errors, the most of any infielder in the league. But the hitting far outweighed the fielding, and Yastrzemski was the runaway choice as the league's most valuable player. With the minor league year ending almost a month before the major league version, Yastrzemski was brought to Boston in mid-September and shown off as a coming attraction to the Boston media. Said Johnny Murphy, the Red Sox's farm director: "You'll have to see him to appreciate what a fine prospect this Yastrzemski really is." During batting practice before a game against the Yankees, Yaz hit two balls into the bullpen in deep right field.

But instead of staying in Boston in September, Yastrzemski was dispatched to Minneapolis, where Gene Mauch's Millers were playing in thc American Association semifinal playoffs. Yastrzemski delivered a game-winning single against Omaha, to which Omaha manager Joe Schultz responded by protesting the game, since Yastrzemski never played for Minneapolis during the regular season. The game had to be replayed, but Yastrzemski was allowed to play in the league finals against Fort Worth (he hit .389) and in the subsequent Little World Series against Havana, the International League champion. Yaz was somewhat disappointed the following spring at not moving up directly to the Red Sox, but, at age twenty, realized he was being handled properly. At Minneapolis in 1960, he struggled early, blaming his troubles on the increased traveling in Class AAA that might find the Millers busing to Houston, Omaha, and Dallas on the same trip. He hit .400 during the final two months to finish at .339, five points behind league-leader Larry Osborne of Denver. Yaz actually led the batting race with two games to play and went 4 for 9, only to have Osborne finish 8 for 10. He hit seven homers and knocked in 69 runs. Most important, he moved to the outfield, where the Red Sox decided his future was. And Red Sox manager Mike Higgins made it known late in the '60 season that he planned to have twenty-one-year-old Carl Yastrzemski in the starting lineup the following year.

On Opening Day 1961, Yaz stood in left field at Fenway Park, within the shadow of the famed Green Monster. Figuratively, he also stood in the shadow of Ted Williams, who had played that same eccentric left field for so many years. Just to add some whipped cream atop this delectable comparison, Yaz was outfitted with uniform No. 8, one notch below Williams's famous No. 9. Yastrzemski wasn't thrilled that writer after writer interrogated him on the subject of following the Splendid Splinter. "Yes, it irritates me," he replied. "There's no comparison." And that wasn't meant with any disrespect.

Yaz first encountered Williams that spring in Florida, where Williams assessed his talents by saying, "You're all right. Just don't let them mess around with you." Yastrzemski was penciled in as the No. 3 hitter in the batting order but got off to a slow start, hitting in the low .200s for much of the first half of the season. Yaz asked Higgins one day if he could skip batting practice and come to the ballpark late because he was hitting so poorly. Higgins agreed but the next night called Yastrzemski into his office to assure him his starting position was safe despite his struggles. Yastrzemski finished strong, as he had the previous year in Minneapolis, using a .386 surge over the last two months to close his rookie year at .266 to go with 11 home runs and 80 RBIs. In 1962 he began to hit better against left-handers and play more aggressively in the outfield. The results: 19 homers, 94 RBIs, a .296 average, and league highs for outfielders in assists and errors. Yastrzemski believed his new style of defense could actually cancel out some of the errors if a base runner was afraid to take the extra base and relaxed on a ball that he eventually booted.

Yastrzemski continued to progress as a hitter. He won the AL batting title in 1963 with a .321 average. Two years later he led the majors with 45 doubles while hitting .312 with a career-high 20 home runs. During the '65 season, he was hospitalized for nine days when a hard slide into second base resulted in some broken ribs and an injured kidney. While in the hospital, Yaz was visited by team owner Tom Yawkey. It was then that Yawkey confided that he dearly wanted to win just one more pennant and that he believed Yastrzemski was the player who could lead the Red Sox to that goal. Yastrzemski didn't need any extra incentive, but a bond was formed on that hospital visit that inspired him to want to do even better for Yawkey. On the day before the '66 season began, the Red Sox voted Yaz as their captain.

But Yastrzemski couldn't make Boston a winner by himself. The losing continued, and with it a parade of managers. Higgins was replaced after the 1962 season by Johnny Pesky, who was fired during the 1964 season. Yastrzemski was dragged into a controversy during Pesky's regime when, at a winter banquet, he paraphrased Pesky's own admission that the manager was among those who made his share of mistakes during the previous season. This was interpreted as needless sniping by Yastrzemski. Yaz once begged out of a game, telling Pesky he had an upset stomach. It was Pesky whose stomach was churning when he learned Yaz went that night to a fried chicken restaurant. Billy Herman got to manage one full season, delivering one hundred losses in 1965, and was dismissed in the dying days of the '66 campaign.

Then came 1967, when the combination of Yastrzemski's own hot start, Dick Williams's new attitude, and the further maturing of young talent yielded the Red Sox's best start in years. Yaz was hot and only needed a slight spark to really ignite. That spark was provided in early June while the Red Sox were in Chicago to play the White Sox, who had fallen behind Detroit and into second place. Sportswriter Doug Gilbert of the *Chicago American* asked White Sox manager Eddie Stanky his opinion on who should make the American League All-Star team. When discussion turned to Yastrzemski, Stanky offered the following succinct assessment: "Yastrzemski's an All-Star from the neck down."

Even from Stanky, who made a habit of verbally baiting opponents both as a player and a manager, these words were particularly combustible and capable of blowing up in the faces of the White Sox. Yastrzemski was incensed by Stanky's comment and proceeded to make Stanky swallow his words. In the subsequent Thursday afternoon doubleheader, Yaz went 6 for 9 and helped Boston rally from a 2–0 deficit in the second game to earn a split. As Yastrzemski rounded third base in his home run trot, he tipped his cap to Stanky.

THE SHOT HEARD 'ROUND KC

The Tigers built their lead over the White Sox to two games on June 6 with a doubleheader sweep at Kansas City. In Detroit's opening 11–1 victory, A's pitcher Lew Krausse absorbed most of the damage. He was pounded for ten hits in eight innings, including a towering home run in the eighth inning by Tigers pitcher Earl Wilson that landed on the runway to the scoreboard in center field. Kansas City's frustrations mushroomed during the second game, decided by a 7–1 score, beginning when Detroit's Dick McAuliffe stole home against "Blue Moon" Odom on the front of a double steal. The Tigers led, 6–1, in the seventh inning when Odom knocked down McAuliffe at the plate. McAuliffe dusted himself off and grounded out to first baseman Ramon Webster. But on his way back to the Tigers' dugout, McAuliffe made a remark in Odom's direction. Odom and McAuliffe exchanged more words, and players from both dugouts swarmed onto the field. No one was injured; the closest thing to a fight was a Tigers reliever taking a poke at Kansas City's Ozzie Chavarria. But it took eight minutes to restore order and continue play after angry fans pelted the field with paper cups.

Well before the second game ended, Krausse headed back to his Kansas City in-season residence, the Bellerive Hotel. Krausse liked to routinely blow off a little steam by firing a .38 caliber pistol out the window into a vacant lot outside his room. What made the shot in the dark that night different was that Krausse had changed rooms that day, which he forgot. The bullet, instead of landing harmlessly below, entered the offices of the Phillips Petroleum Company and nearly struck a cleaning woman. Making matters even more complicated was the fact that Phillips was going through a strike, and the police considered the shot an act of intentional violence. The next morning investigating officers traced the shot to Krausse's window and confronted the young pitcher. He was shaken by what had happened, admitted his involvement, but convinced police he meant no harm.

A's owner Charlie Finley was not amused by the episode. He had signed Krausse in June 1961 as a $125,000 bonus baby, in part because Krausse's father had been a scout in the Athletics' organization. Not to say young Krausse didn't have the credentials to merit such a contract; he pitched eighteen no-hitters in high school and semipro ball growing up in Chester, Pennsylvania. Two teams, including the A's, offered him the chance to pitch for them immediately in the majors. The catch was that the other team was the Houston Colt 45s, who wouldn't be joining the National League until 1962. Krausse didn't take long to show the A's, and the rest of the American League, what he could do. Only a few days after signing, he shut out the LA Angels, 3–0. But Krausse's promising start didn't last long. Pitching coach Ted Wilks decided Krausse needed to master another pitch, and the result was a sore elbow. Krausse pitched in twelve games as a rookie, struggling to a 2–5 record, giving up 49 hits and 46 walks in 56 innings. He spent most of the next four seasons in the minors until he made Kansas City's starting rotation in 1966 and compiled a 14–9 record and 2.98 earned run average. But '67 began disastrously for Krausse, the blowout loss to Detroit dropping his record to 3–8. Being single and one of the free spirits on the team, Krausse had pushed himself toward the end of Finley's plank. With the shooting incident, he unwittingly had used up his last chance before being used as the owner's personal scapegoat.

THE ANGELS DISAPPOINT

Plenty of California Angels fans believed Bill Rigney had used up his last chance as manager when a doubleheader sweep by Baltimore on June 6 left the Angels twelve games under .500 and 12½ games out of first place. It was the largest deficit of the season for the Angels, who had occupied last place since late May. But Rigney received a vote of confidence from general manager Fred Haney, who had acknowledged a lack of spirit and intensity in the ballclub in late May, when the Angels first tumbled into the basement. On one May night at Anaheim Stadium, it required the persistent organ playing of Shay Torrent to drown out the booing of the crowd.

The Angels' primary problem was scoring runs, though they were getting good production out of the power hitters they had acquired from Minnesota—Don Mincher (10 home runs, 28 RBIs) and Jimmie Hall (7 home runs and 15 RBIs). The experiment of starting young Paul Schaal at third base wasn't working out; he was hitting .182. Bobby Knoop, the dependable All-Star second baseman, was hitting .202. Things didn't improve much throughout the lineup, from catcher Buck Rodgers (.208) to outfielders Jay Johnstone (.213) and José Cardenal (.213). Most of the Angels' pitching problems were in their starting rotation. The right-handed relief tandem of Minnie Rojas and Bill Kelso had a combined record of 6–5 in making a combined forty-three appearances. But George Brunet, the No. 1 starter since the trade of Chance, hadn't won a game since beating Detroit on Opening Day. At 1–9, Brunet led the league in defeats and appeared headed for a 20-loss season. Marcelino Lopez had opened the year as California's No. 2 starter but was lifted from the rotation after three lackluster starts. Sinkerball specialist Fred Newman probably would have been a help, but he underwent shoulder surgery after the '66 season and wasn't expected back until the second half of the season at the earliest. Veterans Jack Sanford and Lew Burdette didn't quite have it anymore, and rookie Jorge Rubio didn't quite have it yet. On the positive side was the emergence of pitcher Jim McGlothlin. The twenty-three-year-old right-hander led the league in ERA at 1.21, had a 5–1 record, and had not allowed an earned run in throwing three complete games his last three starts. And there was rookie Rickey Clark, who got a spot start against the Yankees in late April and remained in the rotation despite a 2–6 record. In an attempt to bolster the rotation, the Angels traded left-hander Nick Willhite to the Mets on June 9 for righty Jack Hamilton, who had a reputation for throwing the spitball.

A FRANCHISE AND A FIRING

Management wasn't as forgiving in Minnesota for the Twins' shortcomings. A team that was expected to push for the league lead stood at .500 on the morning of June 9 at 25–25, having given up four runs in the ninth inning of the previous night's game to lose to Cleveland, 7–5. In the Indians' ninth, Twins manager Sam Mele allowed right-handed reliever

Al Worthington to pitch to four left-handed pinch hitters. That resulted in two singles—one in which Fred Whitfield lined the ball into right field because first baseman Harmon Killebrew was playing runner Leon Wagner on the bag—and a walk.

Armed with what he considered a managerial oversight that couldn't be ignored, Twins owner Calvin Griffith decided to dismiss Mele the next afternoon before the Twins' home game that night against the Orioles. No firing of a manager is easy despite the modern acceptance of its inevitability, but the situation was made even more awkward because of Mele's personal circumstances. Mele was a longtime Massachusetts resident, and his wife and five children always remained behind until after the school year, then came out to spend most of the summer with him. The day of the firing happened to be the day Mele's family was joining him in Minnesota. His thirteen-year-old son, Steve, was visiting with him in the manager's office when Mele was summoned to Griffith's office. There, Mele was told the players were no longer responding to his leadership, that he particularly had lost touch with many of the veterans. Griffith assured Mele that he always would have a job in the Twins' organization if he wanted.

This was no idle statement made by Griffith. Unlike many of the major league owners, for him baseball was a family business. His uncle, Clark Griffith, was a major league player before the turn of the century and began his relationship with the franchise, the original Washington Senators, as manager from 1912 to 1920. From that point he took over control of the ballclub as president and owner. Young Calvin learned the baseball business at his side. Clark continued to operate the team on a daily basis until his death at age eighty-five in 1955. The nephew tried to copy his uncle, with the objective of operating a successful business on and off the field. That proved difficult when other teams were backed with much more money. While the team was debt-free when Clark Griffith died, the Senators' inability to compete for the best available new talent doomed the franchise to also-ran status in the American League.

On advice from his uncle, Calvin Griffith made it a point never to enter the clubhouse. That was the players' sanctuary, his uncle told him, and it would mean nothing but trouble to frequent the players' turf. This didn't mean Griffith remained aloof from his players. On the contrary, he often made road trips with the team and looked forward to informal chats with players in a hotel or over breakfast. He believed it was important to know his players and their families personally, as if he were the owner of the corner five-and-dime.

Indicative of the team's fate was that it could win the pennant in 1933 and attract only 437,533 fans at home. That was the last year the original Senators won a pennant while in Washington, and they rarely were even in contention for the next quarter century. Other troubled franchises such as the Philadelphia A's, Boston Braves, and St. Louis Browns relocated in the early fifties. Griffith didn't seriously consider such a move, but it wasn't for lack of opportunity. He often was visited by representatives of Minnesota's Twin Cities, who were eager to bring in a major league team after years of successfully supporting top minor league clubs of the Giants (in Minneapolis) and the Dodgers (in St. Paul). There was even talk in 1958 that the Dodgers, facing the prospect that Los Angeles voters would prevent them from building their planned Dodger Stadium in Chavez Ravine, would bolt the LA Coliseum after one season and move to Minnesota.

Griffith was offered $10,000 to showcase the Senators in Minnesota for an exhibition game against the Philadelphia Phillies. He couldn't accept fast enough, since there were times when the Senators couldn't earn $10,000 for a three-game series at St. Louis or Philadelphia. Griffith quietly explored other prospective homes for his team in the late fifties, visiting Seattle, New Orleans, and Toronto. Los Angeles also intrigued him greatly, but he still wasn't prepared to abandon Washington. He was spurred into making a decision when the majors committed to their first expansion as a means of appeasing cities that threatened to form a third major league, the Continental League.

The catalyst for the proposed new league was twofold. Major league baseball had operated with the same sixteen franchises since the beginning of the century. While some new cities were embraced with franchise shifts, there remained many areas that were frustrated at their inability to become part of the major leagues. Second, there was an active group in New York determined to bring back a National League presence following the exodus of the Giants and Dodgers to California after the 1957 season. The New York group was rebuffed in its attempts to return to the NL, primarily because the city had not solved the problem that prompted the California moves in the first place—inadequate facilities. The New York group then decided that if it couldn't get back in the NL, it would then help form another league. New York attorney Bill Shea headed a four-man group that sought out sites for the new Continental League, which named former Dodgers executive Branch Rickey as its president. The Continental League soon announced it would place teams in New York, Houston, Minneapolis–St. Paul, Denver, and Toronto.

This pushed the majors into action regarding expansion, hopeful that the addition of new teams early in the sixties would head off the first challenge to the major league setup since the old Federal League died after the 1915 season. Both the National League and the American League targeted making definitive expansion plans at joint meetings of the leagues in October 1960. Each league figured to add two teams. Each league figured to devote one of those teams to canceling out the other's strongest territory. While the NL looked at returning to New York, now owned by the Yankees, the AL wanted dearly to tap the Los Angeles market that the Dodgers had already found so lucrative.

There were NL people enamored with placing a team in Houston, with its thriving economy and plans for the first domed stadium. Some were particularly intrigued with skipping New York in favor of an all-Texas expansion to Houston and Dallas–Fort Worth. Officials representing the latter, which operated a Class AAA team for the Kansas City Athletics, were anticipating joining Los Angeles in the American League's expansion plans.

The National League moved first, on October 17, 1960, with the announcement that New York and Houston would begin play in 1962. That left nine groups—Los Angeles, Dallas–Fort Worth, Minneapolis–St. Paul, Toronto, Buffalo, Oakland, Seattle, San Diego, and Denver—hoping to land the anticipated two AL spots. But there were two other variables. The Kansas City A's remained up for sale following the death of owner Arnold Johnson, and there was some question about moving the A's.

And there was Calvin Griffith. Twice he had considered moving the Senators, only to be turned down. His fellow owners cited their desire to maintain a team in Washington, though none of them wanted to be there themselves. But the dilemma of leaving Washington abandoned could be solved through expansion. A group of Washington-area investors, led by General Pete Quesada, made it known it would love to operate a team in the capital if the Senators skipped town. Still, opposition to the Senators' move existed, and Griffith again was turned down on the first vote on the morning of October 26 at an owners' meeting at the Savoy-Hilton Hotel in New York.

During a lunch break, Griffith was asked by Yankees owner Dan Topping, an influential force in the league, just how serious he was about relocating the Senators. "That's the only way I can stay in baseball," Griffith said. Topping told him not to worry, that he would get Griffith the votes necessary. On the next vote, Griffith was granted permission to take the Senators to Minnesota. Expansion franchises were subsequently awarded to Los Angeles and Washington. And since the new American League teams would begin play the following spring, a year ahead of their National League counterparts, there would be no void in the nation's capital at all.

The Quesada group was officially approved less than a month later. The ownership question regarding the new Los Angeles Angels was more complicated. Former major leaguer Hank Greenberg, an executive with the White Sox, had originally showed interest in acquiring the franchise and playing in the Los Angeles Coliseum, where the Dodgers were playing until their new stadium would be ready in 1962. Greenberg wanted to sign a two-year lease with the Coliseum, but that was blocked by Dodgers owner Walter O'Malley. The issue of the Angels' ownership was tabled for the next AL owners' meeting in December 1960 in St. Louis. By then Greenberg's interest had waned. Gene Autry, the former "Singing Cowboy" of motion picture fame, went to the meeting in St. Louis with the intent of signing up the Angels on his Los Angeles radio station, KMPC, because the Dodgers had just left for another station. Autry not only landed the Angels' broadcasts, he landed the entire team for $2.5 million. Autry himself might have had a career as a pro athlete. Growing up in northern Texas and southern Oklahoma, nineteen-year-old Gene Autry was offered a contract by the St. Louis Cardinals' Tulsa farm team. But Autry's job as a railroad telegraph operator offered more financial security, and Autry turned down Tulsa.

Fame came to Autry for his ability to simultaneously sing, play guitar, and sit astride a horse. Encouraged to take his musical skills to New York by a stranger who turned out to be Will Rogers, Autry sold more than a million copies of "Silver-Haired Daddy of Mine" in 1930. He became a country-and-western star, though many children got their first taste of his singing by listening to "Rudolph the Red-Nosed Reindeer." His rodeo show crisscrossed the country, though Autry tried to book the tour in Madison Square Garden each October perchance to catch a World Series game.

The new American League franchises were stocked at a subsequent meeting in December 1960. Each of the eight existing teams had to provide a list of fifteen players available for the expansion draft, knowing they would lose eight players each at a cost of $75,000 per player to the new teams. Many of the players were aging journeymen, others young prospects. Los Angeles struck it rich with a couple of youngsters who became the core of its team throughout the sixties. Off the Red Sox's list, they selected eighteen-year-old shortstop Jim Fregosi, who hit .267 at Alpine of the Sophomore League in 1960. Off the Tigers' list, they grabbed twenty-two-year-old catcher Bob (Buck) Rodgers. He had labored five years in the Detroit system. With the Angels, he put together a solid season at Dallas–Fort Worth in 1961 and came up to the major league club that September for good.

With the transfer of the Senators, Minnesota fans were elated to be joining the major leagues, and preferred inheriting an existing team— albeit a loser since 1945—to starting from scratch with an expansion franchise. There actually were some very positive signs as the Senators became the Twins and were relocated to Metropolitan Stadium in suburban Bloomington, Minnesota, south of Minneapolis. The '60 Senators had finished fifth among eight teams, the club's first escape from the cellar since 1955, and the team boasted some encouraging young talent led by Harmon Killebrew and Bob Allison. Right-handed pitcher Camilo Pascual from Cuba also was developing after plenty of patience on management's part. His statistics for 1954–58 included a record of 28–66 with an earned run average of 4.66. But in '59, Pascual finished 17–10 with a career-best ERA of 2.64, second-best in the American League.

The Twins were instant heroes in Minnesota, which also landed a National Football League franchise—the Vikings—the same year. Manager Cookie Lavagetto was immediately given a new car by a local auto dealership and hosted his own radio show. The '61 Twins finished seventh in the ten-team league, but the attendance of 1.2 million was the best in franchise history. Four years later, after Sam Mele replaced Lavagetto as manager, the Twins completed their metamorphosis by rewarding their new fans with a pennant.

Success didn't change Griffith's philosophy about operating a baseball team frugally. That meant personal contract negotiations with each player, an exercise that Griffith found stimulating. On the occasions when Griffith did knuckle under and open the vault a little wider, he made it clear to the player not to expect a penny more than what was negotiated. His players joked that Calvin Griffith had an eleventh commandment—thou shalt not allow a game to be postponed because of rain, allowing the fans to return home with rain checks.

This miserly reputation was spread throughout baseball. Relief pitcher Ron Kline wasn't thrilled about coming to the Twins from Washington during spring training in 1967. Kline held out and even spent the time visiting the Senators' camp in Pompano Beach, Florida. He finally reported to the Twins in Orlando after two weeks, and Griffith rather routinely greeted him and asked him if there was anything he could do for him. "Yeah," Kline snapped. "Trade me. I didn't like you before I knew you, I don't like you now, and I'm never going to like you." Kline nicknamed Griffith "The Toad," and his new teammates joined in the fun by also calling Kline "Toad."

Changing managers was one of the parts of the baseball business that Griffith never learned to accept. One of the few times he violated his own rule about visiting the clubhouse was when he came to announce a change of managers. While Griffith knew that Mele wasn't the reason the Twins weren't near the top of the standings, he knew firing him was the best way to shake up the ballclub.

Mele was an intensely loyal employee. He had spent four of his eleven major league seasons with Griffith's Senators. In 1958 he was able to end a playing career that had bottomed out in the minors by landing a job as a scout for the Senators. He became a coach under Lavagetto later that season and replaced Lavagetto as manager of the Twins in 1961. Mele often incurred the wrath of fans who wanted slumping veterans pulled from the lineup, but he hated to embarrass players who had contributed so much to the team's past success. When the '63 Twins only equaled the win total from the previous season, Mele accepted a pay cut from Griffith. With the collapse of the Yankees in 1965, the Twins seized hold of the AL for a year. Mudcat Grant and Jim Kaat formed an effective nucleus to the pitching staff. Harmon Killebrew was one of four players to hit more than 20 home runs, though he missed much of the season due to injury. Tony Oliva won his second straight batting title, and Zoilo Versalles provided enough glue to hold things together to be named the American League's Most Valuable Player. In the '65 World Series against the Dodgers, the Twins swept the first two games in Minnesota, lost the next three at Los Angeles, then returned home to even the Series in Game Six before being shut out in the finale by Sandy Koufax.

Mele was approached the following winter by Ed Short, general manager of the White Sox. Al Lopez was retiring after managing the White Sox for nine years, and Short offered Mele a two-year contract to come to Chicago. Mele wasn't satisfied with the salary he was making in Minnesota and told Short he would take the job but that he had to talk to Griffith before signing a contract. Mele told Griffith it looked like he was taking another job, that he deserved more money than he was making with the Twins. Griffith asked Mele what he thought he was worth. Mele told him, and Griffith told him he could have it. Maybe Mele could have played both sides of the issue and tried to get Short to up his ante. But out of loyalty to Griffith, Mele accepted the raise and the new contract through the 1967 season and called Short to tell him he wouldn't be joining the White Sox.

Only a few months later, at the All-Star break in '66, Griffith fought back the urge to fire Mele. The Orioles were running away with the pennant. Mele was aware that discontent among the players might sway Griffith into making a change. Mele had said upon taking the job in June 1961 that he wouldn't publicly criticize any of his players, but players complained in '67 that Mele was quick to point a finger at them. One player summed up the situation by saying it sounded like Mele was 16–0 and the players were 0–16. Veteran catcher Earl Battey often relayed the general text of player meetings to Mele, though individuals weren't specified.

Despite such warnings, Mele was jolted when Griffith called him in on the morning of June 9. He agreed that his managing against the Indians could be seen as a last straw but maintained that the only thing he would have done differently was play Killebrew off the bag on Whitfield's at-bat. Mele left the meeting telling Griffith he would have to think about whether to stay with the organization. The first person Mele ran into after the meeting was, fittingly, Billy Martin. Mele told him he had been fired, and the two blubbered, as they had six years earlier when Martin was released.

Mele's successor was forty-three-year-old Cal Ermer, who almost cried when told of the shakeup. Ermer had managed the Twins' Denver affiliate since 1965 and was in Indianapolis that morning when informed of the move. He arrived in Bloomington at 6:30 P.M., almost two hours after Griffith announced the managerial change at a news conference. Ermer was another longtime Griffith man, actually starting his managerial career at age twenty-three when he went from infielder to manager of the Senators' farm team at Charlotte in 1947. Ermer's major league playing career consisted of one game for the Senators at the end of the '47 season. He returned to Washington's minor league system for another four years, the last two as a full-fledged player-manager. He managed three different teams in the organization—helping to develop much of the talent on the current Minnesota roster—to first-place finishes before earning the job with the big club. Ironically, the Denver team he left behind had a record that was worse than the Twins'—22–24.

Mele's tenure with the Twins ranked third in the majors at the time— only the Dodgers' Walter Alston and the Angels' Bill Rigney had been with their clubs longer—and Griffith made a point of saying a Twins manager never again would be hired for more than a season at a time. He added that Martin, who had no managerial experience, never was considered for the position. Griffith immediately put Ermer on the spot by declaring: "We've got the personnel with the Twins to win the American League pennant." For all of the midseason managing changes that had been made in baseball history, no American League team had won a pennant after changing managers in midstream. And the Twins' first game under Ermer wasn't an indication that a change in leadership was all the team needed: Baltimore knocked out Dean Chance in the fifth inning and routed Minnesota, 11–2.

TONY C's BOOMING BAT

The Twins did begin to turn things around under Ermer, the Angels suddenly showed life, and other events began to unfold around the league that tightened the AL race. One such critical game was played June 15, when the fourth-place Red Sox played host to the first-place White Sox after splitting a doubleheader the previous day. The teams were scoreless through ten innings before Chicago punched across a run in the eleventh against Johnny Wyatt, who came on to pitch in the tenth inning when starter Gary Waslewski had to leave because of back spasms. Walt Williams led off the inning with a double. Boston then expected Don Buford to try to bunt Williams over to second base and sent George Scott charging in from first base to field a bunt. But Buford swung away and smacked a hard shot down the first-base line; Scott snared it for the first out. Williams then scored on a two-out double by Ken Berry to give Chicago the 1–0 lead, but Scott's clutch defensive play allowed the Red Sox to come to bat in the bottom of the eleventh trailing by one run instead of two.

White Sox pitcher John Buzhardt set down Carl Yastrzemski and Scott for Boston's first two outs before Joe Foy kept the Red Sox alive with a single. That brought up Tony Conigliaro, who was just getting hot after beginning the season cold. In the first fifty-two games, Conigliaro had hit only two home runs to go with 15 RBIs and a .262 batting average. But going into the series finale against the White Sox, Conigliaro had doubled his home-run total from the previous five games. While Yastrzemski was in the top five in the league in home runs, RBIs, and batting average, it appeared the Red Sox would need Conigliaro—one of the AL's top power hitters in his first three seasons—to come through if they had any hopes of challenging for the league lead. With the game on the line, Conigliaro swung wildly at the first two pitches. But Buzhardt couldn't put Conigliaro away and extended the count to 3 and 2. On the payoff pitch, Conigliaro connected and sent the ball sailing over the Green Monster and into the net—his third home run in six games—to beat Chicago, 2–1. Conigliaro's habit on home runs was to round the bases with his head down. This time, he rounded third and just happened to raise his head—to see the entire population of the Boston dugout eager to greet him at home plate. The victory, coupled with the Twins' 6–4 win over the Tigers that day at Bloomington, vaulted Boston and Minnesota over Baltimore and into a third-place tie, four games behind the first-place White Sox and 2½ games behind Detroit.

If there was a Boston player who challenged Yastrzemski for the affections of the Red Sox fans, it was Conigliaro. He had numbers; he was the youngest player ever to lead a league in homers when he did it in 1965. He had charm: Brash and good looking, Conigliaro became something of a heartthrob when he attempted to become a combination ballplayer and rock singer. He recorded songs such as "Play the Field" and "When You

Take More Than You Give," titles that never made anyone forget Elvis Presley. He also had the bloodline, which was particularly important to the parochial Red Sox fan; he was born in the Boston suburb of Revere, moved to east Boston at age nine, and played his high school ball just north of the city in Lynn at St. Mary's High School. His father, Sal, was the superintendent of a tool and die factory in Lynn and drove Tony and his younger brother, Billy, to and from school each day. Tony pitched and played shortstop, nearly hitting .600 as a senior and attracting attention from fourteen ballclubs.

In 1962, Conigliaro's high school senior season, Red Sox scout Milt Bolling was told to choose one of three prospects for a $20,000 bonus that was available. The final decision came down to Conigliaro and a slick-fielding shortstop in Pittsfield named Mark Belanger, and Bolling selected Conigliaro. He was brought to Boston for an informal workout after signing and was so nervous that he couldn't hit the left-field wall, no less hit over it. He began to show a penchant for injuries soon after turning pro. Even before reporting for his first spring training, he broke a thumb when he was hit by a pitch thrown by an uncle. The injury cost him the batting title of the New York–Penn League; he hit .363 at Wellsville with 24 home runs and 74 RBIs but didn't get the required number of plate appearances to qualify for the title.

Conigliaro reported to spring training with the Red Sox at Scottsdale, Arizona, in 1964 and drew the attention of Ted Williams, who was making his annual spring trip to help with the Boston outfielders. Williams was hitting fungoes and dared Conigliaro to grab one particular liner. "I'll buy you a Cadillac," Williams said. Conigilaro made the catch over his shoulder but didn't press Williams on the Cadillac issue. Why should he? He was driving a Corvette Sting Ray at the time. Bill Crowley, the team publicist, was crossing his fingers that Conigliaro could make the team. The Red Sox hadn't drawn a million fans to Fenway Park since 1960, and it wouldn't hurt to have a nineteen-year-old, good-looking power hitter from Lynn on the ballclub. Conigliaro looked like a decent bet to come north with the Red Sox despite his age, and his position on the roster was clinched when veteran outfielder Gary Geiger began the season on the disabled list with a bleeding ulcer.

Conigliaro didn't let up and even beat out Roman Mejias for the starting center fielder's job on Opening Day at New York. When the Red Sox opened their home season against Chicago, Conigliaro hit the first pitch he saw from Joe Horlen over the Green Monster. Still living at home, Conigliaro hit .290 with 24 home runs as a rookie. He was outspoken, not afraid to verbally back himself into a corner. He prepared to bat against the Angels' Bob Lee in Los Angeles by reciting his 11-for-14 record against Lee the previous year in the minors. Conigliaro hit a harmless pop-up and returned to the dugout to a merciless chorus, reminding him that he now was 11 for 15 against Lee. Conigliaro fumed but said nothing. He came up against Lee in the bottom of the ninth with the Red Sox trailing by a run and the bases loaded with two out. Conigliaro socked a game-winning grand slam and smuggly reported upon reaching the dugout: "That's 12 for 16."

On another occasion, Conigliaro was fined $250 by manager Johnny Pesky for missing curfew in Cleveland. He homered the next day and then asked Pesky: "Does that help?" The manager replied, "Hit four more, and we're even." On Conigliaro's next at-bat, he was hit by a fastball thrown by Pedro Ramos and suffered a broken arm. While he was sidelined at home with the broken arm, Conigliaro earned $800 from several speaking engagements. His popularity aside, there were times when Conigliaro was booed at home during his rookie season. "The hell with the fans," he said within the sanctuary of the clubhouse. Yastrzemski, acquainted with Conigliaro's plight, quickly stepped in and offered some advice: "They're paying your salary. Don't try to fight them."

Pesky wanted to try to curb Conigliaro's youthful enthusiasm off the field on the road and in 1964 had him room with journeyman infielder Dick Williams. Conigliaro continued to lead an active social life, and while Williams didn't rat on him, he did tell Pesky at the All-Star break that the leash on Conigliaro needed to be tightened. It's not that Williams had it in for Conigliaro—to the contrary, he likely would have followed the same course had he been in Conigliaro's circumstances—but he thought things had to be brought under control for the good of Conigliaro and the ballclub. On the next road trip, Pesky caught Conigliaro breaking curfew and fined him $1,000. Conigliaro immediately accused Williams of turning him in, and their relationship cooled from that point on. Pesky didn't last the season as Red Sox manager but did offer the following prediction regarding Conigliaro: "If he takes care of himself and doesn't get hurt too often, he can be another Joe DiMaggio, good for forty or more homers a season." Pesky was noting that Tony C was shelved with injuries five times in 1964, when he hit 24 home runs. Conigliaro led the AL with 32 home runs in 1965 at age twenty, the youngest player to accomplish that feat, with his batting average falling to .269 but his RBI total increasing from 52 to 82. The following year, Conigliaro hit .268 with 28 home runs and 93 RBIs.

The day after Conigliaro's dramatic eleventh-inning homer, just the right set of circumstances caused the AL standings to compress even further. The Red Sox went to Washington and dropped a doubleheader to the Senators, the Twins were beaten in ten innings by Cleveland, the Yankees and White Sox were rained out in Chicago, the Tigers and A's had a doubleheader rained out in Detroit, and the Angels went into Baltimore and swept the Orioles to extend their winning streak to five straight and nine of the last ten. California's hero was outfielder Woodie Held, just acquired from Baltimore for disappointing-pitcher Marcelino Lopez. Held hit a home run in each game as the Angels won, 2–1 and 5–3. The standings read thusly after the games of June 16, with only two games separating third place from ninth place:

Chicago	33–23	—	Kansas City	29–31	6
Detroit	32–25	1½	Baltimore	28–30	6
Minnesota	30–29	4½	New York	28–30	6
Boston	30–30	5	California	30–33	6½
Cleveland	29–30	5½	Washington	27–35	9

One reason the Angels were able to climb back into contention was the pitching of Jim McGlothlin. The twenty-three-year-old had won a position in California's starting rotation at the beginning of the season almost by default. By mid-June he had established himself as the ace of the staff. When he shut out Cleveland on June 22, McGlothlin improved his record to 7–1 with a league-high five shutouts and an earned run average of 1.41. This included a miraculous stretch of four consecutive complete games in which he didn't give up an earned run and recorded three shutouts. With McGlothlin leading the way, the Angels had retooled their starting rotation with fellow youngsters Clyde Wright (twenty-four) and Rickey Clark (twenty-one) and boasted the second-best team ERA in the league behind the White Sox.

At the plate, first baseman Don Mincher was doing his part to justify the Chance trade. Mincher was leading California in home runs (12), runs batted in (34), and batting average (.294). But Mincher and Jim Fregosi were the only Angels regulars hitting better than .250. Manager Bill Rigney gave Paul Schaal more than enough time to prove he could be the everyday third baseman. But through 200 at-bats, Schaal was hitting an anemic .193 with only 11 extra-base hits. That prompted the trade with Baltimore to get thirty-four-year-old infielder Woodie Held, who was hitting all of .146 at the time of the deal. Outfielders Jimmie Hall and Rick Reichardt were aiding Mincher in the power department, combining for 19 home runs. But Reichardt was hitting .241 and Hall .230.

THE BONUS BOYS

The fact that Reichardt was on a pace to hit in excess of 20 home runs wasn't lost on some AL fans. For Reichardt, reaching that milestone would provide the opportunity to silence some of the baseball people who had been skeptical of his receiving a reported $175,000 bonus when he had signed in 1964 after his junior year at the University of Wisconsin. Remember that only a handful of major leaguers were receiving annual salaries of $100,000. Reichardt was coming off a season in which he was named college baseball's player of the year. Scouts saw a gifted hitter who led the Big Ten Conference in batting as a sophomore and who also possessed power. He was a versatile athlete who also played wide receiver, led the Big Ten in receiving as a junior, and played in the Rose Bowl. In fact, Reichardt arrived at Wisconsin on a football scholarship, had hoped to participate in basketball and track, and initially turned to baseball as a means of getting out of spring football practice.

And Reichardt could figure more than an ERA. His father was a doctor, and he was studying premed and psychology. After his junior year, he was being wined and dined by high-profile figures from most major league teams. Suffice it to say the Madison campus was abuzz when Reichardt popped in at one of the local restuarants with none other than Stan Musial, representing the Cardinals. The Dodgers had Reichardt flown into Los Angeles for contract discussions. But Reichardt unwittingly aggravated the Dodgers by checking into the Continental Hotel, which happened to be owned by Angels owner Gene Autry. So much for serious talks with the Dodgers.

Even without the Dodgers, the Reichardt auction moved on apace. One after another, teams dropped from the running. There was a lot of sentiment in Wisconsin for Reichardt to stay home and sign with the Milwaukee Braves. But not only did the Braves fail to make a competitive bid, they even asked Reichardt if they could release an inflated figure to the press. The bidding eventually came down to similar offers from the Angels, Cardinals, Yankees, and A's. Reichardt originally wanted to sign with the Yankees but chose the Angels because he liked the chance of making an impact with an expansion organization and also liked the idea of playing in new Anaheim Stadium, which was scheduled to open in 1966. (Fittingly, it was Reichardt who hit the first home run at the Big A.) After Reichardt made his decision, A's owner Charlie Finley came back with the highest offer yet, but Reichardt stood firm.

Word of the deal shook baseball, which to date had allowed a survival-of-the-fittest mentality to exist. The teams with the most money generally could sign the best players. For years, the Yankees and Dodgers were able to keep their ample farm systems stocked. An attempt to legislate equality of some measure came in the fifties, when teams were required to keep players receiving signing bonuses of $30,000 or more on the major league roster for two years. The Reichardt signing accentuated fears that big money would take control of the game. Baseball executives soon after instituted an amateur player draft, similar to the college drafts that were being used in pro football and basketball.

Reichardt then headed into baseball with the stigma of being the "bonus baby" who changed the game. The bonus itself didn't go very far. Reichardt gave some of the money to the university, to the Wisconsin football and baseball staffs, to his father, and to the attorney who helped him dot the i's and cross the t's on his first contract with the Angels. After paying taxes, there wasn't much left over. Reichardt hit .292 in thirty-four games for Quad Cities of the Class A Midwest League and .286 in twenty-three games with Hawaii of the Pacific Coast League. He closed the year playing eleven games with the Angels, with six hits in 37 at-bats.

Reichardt was up in the majors to stay late in the '65 season, a year in which the "bonus baby" played for the major league minimum of about $12,000, after spending most of the year at Hawaii. In 1966, the year the Angels moved to Anaheim, Reichardt was fourth in the AL in batting in early August. But he was troubled by severe headaches and high blood pressure. Doctors discovered that the source of his affliction was a kidney disorder. He had a kidney removed and missed most of the rest of the season, finishing with 16 home runs, 44 runs batted in, and a .288 batting average.

There remained many Reichardt doubters, those who never accepted his huge signing bonus. Many of his toughest critics wore Angels uniforms. It didn't help Reichardt's acceptance that he was a well-educated player in a profession populated primarily by people who never attended college. He had college acquaintances in many of the league cities and therefore didn't hang out until the wee hours with his teammates. He wasn't a part of the clubhouse ritual of comparing tales of womanizing. Even Reichardt's penchant for showing a college-style enthusiasm was frowned upon by many of the veterans.

Some of his teammates made no effort to hide from Reichardt their disdain for him, what he received, and what he represented. Men who scraped and sweated to remain in the majors were enraged when Reichardt, whose signing bonus exceeded their career earnings, downplayed a loss by saying, "It's just a game." He blamed defensive lapses on his "active mind." After struggling in the outfield one blustery day in Cleveland, Reichardt described the wind as "diametrically opposed." This friction helped solidify the thought in Reichardt's mind that, indeed, he was blowing in one direction while most of his teammates were blowing the opposite way. One such teammate was the guts of the Angels, All-Star shortstop Jim Fregosi. He was hard on the young players in general and seemed to save his most stinging wrath for Reichardt. Since

Fregosi was highly respected throughout baseball and was a particular favorite of team owner Gene Autry, this conflict became the greatest intangible obstacle that Reichardt faced. Many players who did empathize with Reichardt's plight didn't defend him openly because that would have meant crossing Fregosi. Ironically, Reichardt found an emotional outlet when he developed a friendship with Dean Chance, the team's ranking fun-seeker. Reichardt believed there was a connection between his playing his best ball while rooming with Chance and was disappointed personally as well as professionally when Chance was traded to Minnesota.

With the furor over Reichardt's bonus, baseball adopted the amateur draft for high school and college players. The incredible expectations placed upon Reichardt were then shifted to Rick Monday, the talented outfielder from Arizona State University who became baseball's first No. 1 draft pick in 1965 when he was selected by Kansas City. Monday had played only one varsity season, hitting .359 with 11 home runs and 49 RBIs as a sophomore to help the Sun Devils win the College World Series.

Monday had starred at Santa Monica (California) High School and nearly signed out of high school with the Dodgers. His mother was torn between wanting her son to attend college and to play with her beloved Dodgers. Monday was given the chance to work out with the Dodgers' rookie league team. He was taken with the pudgy coach running the workout—pitching batting practice, catching, hitting fungoes, seemingly doing everything.

The coach was Tom Lasorda, and he was determined to get Monday's name on a Dodger contract. He invited Monday and his mother to his home after practice and preached his Dodger gospel. Thus began an almost comical cycle of events: Monday's mother would pick up the pen, apparently ready to sign, then put it down and state a reason why her son should go to college. Lasorda would then up the offer. This verbal volleying included Mrs. Monday's "demand" for something above and beyond Rick's normal salary. Lasorda, ashen-faced, couldn't imagine what she would ask for. She wanted autographed pictures of Sandy Koufax and Don Drysdale. Lasorda agreed to get the pictures, and the negotiations continued. Finally, Mrs. Monday said college was too important to pass up, and she put down the pen for good. Lasorda delivered the photos anyway.

Other teams had expressed interest in Monday, and it actually was a Pirates scout who recommended him to Arizona State coach Bobby Winkles. He had fractured a foot while playing freshman ball and followed that with a poor season of summer ball in Alaska. But his sophomore stats and overall physical potential made him one of the names considered for the No. 1 pick. Aside from receiving numerous inquiring phone calls from teams and prospective agents, Monday heard from a number of attorneys who said he should consider suing baseball. The draft is illegal, they told him, and he should be able to bargain for the highest offer like Rick Reichardt. This was the last thing that a nineteen-year-old who had always dreamed of playing in the major leagues wanted to hear.

About midway through the college season, Monday was told by A's scout Art Lilly that Kansas City, owner of the first pick, intended to pick him. Despite Charlie Finley's image, Monday was encouraged. He knew the team needed help badly, and his path to the majors could be a quick one. This draft day produced no glitz and glamour; when Monday was picked, he was sitting in the stands at Omaha's Rosenblatt Stadium during the College World Series.

Monday played well at Lewiston of the Class A Northwest League in '65 and Mobile of the Southern League in '66. At Mobile he was reunited with Arizona State third baseman Sal Bando, who had been a year ahead of him in school. Strangely, Monday was made the leadoff hitter at Mobile. This wasn't the doing of manager John McNamara, but of Finley himself. The A's owner didn't want to be embarrassed by his No. 1 pick not putting up impressive numbers, so he wanted Monday to get as many at-bats as possible.

At Mobile, Monday hit .267 with 23 home runs and 72 RBIs. Still, Monday experienced many of the frustrations that haunted Reichardt. For some fans, he couldn't do enough. If he went 4 for 5, well, that's what a No. 1 pick should deliver. McNamara was a consoling figure, assuring Monday that he wasn't expected to perform superhuman feats. Monday and Bando were called up to the A's for the final month of the '66 season, piling in their car in Mobile and driving straight through to Kansas City. They arrived at about 7:00 A.M., welcomed by A's coach Bobby Hofman. They were told to get a room, get settled . . . and get to the ballpark for a 10:00 workout. Welcome to the majors, boys.

At spring training in '67, Monday received a different kind of welcome from Ken Harrelson. At an exhibition game, Harrelson matter-of-factly mentioned to the rookie that there were between "thirty and thirty-five thousand" people in the stands. Monday knew full well the park seated only about six thousand. "Betcha a dollar," Harrelson said, and Monday eagerly accepted. Harrelson then noted that his bottom figure was thirty, just plain thirty, not thirty thousand. And Monday was out a dollar. Later that day, Harrelson told Monday, "I'll run you fifty yards for a buck." Monday again accepted, confident of victory in the race. When Monday took off, Harrelson simply stood up. Monday jogged back expecting to even his day's bets. But Harrelson said, "I said I'd run you for a buck, and I did. I just ran *you* for a buck." Frustrated, Monday handed over another dollar. Monday got the last installment of Harrelson's lesson a few days later. He received an envelope in the mail. In it were two dollar bills and an unsigned note that read: "Welcome to the major leagues."

The Angels had their problems being welcomed into the majors. As Los Angeles' AL expansion team in 1961, they played their first season in small, antiquated Wrigley Field, which housed the old LA Angels of the Pacific Coast League. The crosstown Dodgers relocated from the LA Coliseum to beautiful Dodger Stadium in 1962, and the Angels moved in as tenants for the next four seasons. They even used the Dodgers' private airplane on the road. They moved out to bustling Orange County in 1966 and carried with them to Anaheim two predicaments. Despite having their own shiny new stadium, the Angels still were second-class citizens when compared to the Dodgers, probably the best-known team in baseball behind the Yankees. There even were some Orange County residents who saw the arrival of the Angels only as the reason for a tax increase. And while Orange County was a popular destination for new California residents, these newcomers often retained allegiance to their old teams. It wasn't surprising for the Yankees or White Sox to challenge the Angels for the loudest cheers received at Anaheim Stadium.

This isn't to say the Angels were Southern California's baseball lepers. To the contrary, the quick development of the team—the best of major league baseball's four expansion teams of the early sixties—couldn't help but draw plenty of support. The original Angels won seventy games and finished eighth, ahead of Kansas City and the expansion Senators. With five players hitting 20 or more home runs, their 189 home runs were second in the majors only to the Yankees team that boasted the greatest one-year, one-two punch of Roger Maris (61) and Mickey Mantle (54). The '62 Angels rose all the way to third place, finishing only ten games behind the champion Yankees and five games behind second-place Minnesota. And while the Angels fell back to eighty victories and ninth place the next season, they were the one expansion team that achieved respectability almost immediately.

Respectability was fast looking unattainable for the '67 Athletics despite the rosy spring forecasts. By late June the A's had dropped near the bottom of the AL. The same Kansas City fans who in March believed their team might challenge for the first division were dreading yet another last-place finish. Earlier in the month, they tried to bolster their hitting by buying first baseman–outfielder "Hawk" Harrelson, whom they had traded to Washington a year earlier. Harrelson was made expendable in

Washington by the trade that brought the Senators first baseman Mike Epstein. Combined for the A's and Senators in 1966, Harrelson had hit .237 with 12 home runs and 50 RBIs. In twenty-six games with Washington in '67, Harrelson had hit only .203 with three homers and 10 RBIs.

Kansas City's poor performance was, as usual, reflected in poor attendance. That only poured more fuel onto the rumors that Charlie Finley would uproot his team at the end of the season, taking it to Oakland or Seattle. All of this made playing for the A's an unenviable task. The players didn't blame the fans for not supporting a losing lame duck. Still, they were relieved when the A's went out on the road, and their play was more relaxed.

But there was another battle—a more important long-term battle off the field—that Kansas City was determined to win. In a June 27 election, voters in Jackson County, Missouri, Kansas City's home county, were asked to approve a $43 million bond issue for the construction of a two-stadium sports complex. While other cities like Cincinnati and Pittsburgh were getting ready to build multipurpose stadiums to house both their baseball and football teams, Kansas City was prepared to build separate stadiums for the A's and the Chiefs. The baseball fans of Kansas City thought if the bond issue received the required two-thirds margin for passage that Finley's seven-year itch would subside and he would see the wisdom in leaving his team put.

The bond issue was approved by about 68.9 percent of the county voters, meaning the winning margin was about six thousand votes. Finley wasn't even in town to follow the vote. On election day he elected to remain at his home in LaPorte, Indiana. The significance of his absence—and his refusal to comment on the election results when asked by reporters—wasn't lost on Joe McGuff, sports editor of the *Kansas City Star.* "Finley's silence plus his refusal to deny any of the rumors concerning possible franchise moves has convinced most people here he will attempt to move," McGuff wrote. "It was hoped approval of the sports complex would produce a change in Finley's attitude, but his initial reaction was disappointing."

F. ROBBY, KALINE SIDELINED

The same day that Kansas City hoped it had secured its long-term baseball future, the 1967 AL race was altered by injuries suffered by the top two hitters in the league—Baltimore's Frank Robinson and Detroit's Al Kaline. Robinson was threatening to become the first major leaguer to repeat as a Triple Crown winner. Only Kaline and Carl Yastrzemski appeared to have much of a chance to catch him in any of the three categories. Robinson was leading in batting with a .337 average, followed by Kaline at .328, and Yastrzemski at .327. In home runs, Robinson was second with 21, one behind Harmon Killebrew. Robinson and Killebrew were tied for the RBI lead at 59, followed by Kaline and Yastrzemski at 53.

Robinson and the Orioles were at home on June 27 to play the league-leading White Sox. Chicago was the hottest team in the AL, winning seven of its last ten games to build a 4½-game lead over second-place Detroit. Baltimore, conversely, had been unable to put together any kind of respectable winning streak, had fallen three games under .500, and was only three games out of the cellar. The previous night the White Sox had scored twice in the top of the ninth to win, 5–4. Chicago had the bases loaded with one out when pinch hitter Jim King appeared to hit into a game-ending double play on a sharp grounder to first baseman Boog Powell. But Baltimore catcher Andy Etchebarren was knocked down by White Sox runner Tom McCraw barreling into the plate, and the relay back to first wasn't in time to get King. The Orioles were convinced McCraw slid out of the baseline to impede Etchebarren and that King should have been called out at first base on McCraw's interference, ending the inning. Instead, the play stood, and Ken Berry followed with a single to score what proved to be the winning run.

Robinson was still angered by the McCraw episode the following night when he needed to break up a possible double play at second base in the fourth inning. But when Robinson slid hard into second baseman Al Weis, he was struck just above the left eye by Weis' knee and knocked unconcious. Weis also was seriously injured, and it seemed almost out of context, with two ballplayers strewn on the ground, that Ken Berry raced in from right field before time was called, picked up the ball, and tagged out Robinson. All that was known at the time was that Robinson had suffered a mild concussion.

That Robinson's injury was traced to his aggressiveness wasn't out of character. He had maintained an almost angry demeanor on the field throughout his twelve years to date in the majors. He had picked up that attitude learning the game in his native Oakland and maintained it through his early years with the Cincinnati Reds, where he was named National League Rookie of the Year in 1956 and NL Most Valuable Player in 1961. Despite his success through the years, he refused to let up, refused to concede that any part of the ballpath didn't belong to the runner. And when Robinson was traded to Baltimore in December 1965 for starting pitcher Milt Pappas, Robinson had new motivation for proving himself all over again. All he did was win the Triple Crown, lead the Orioles to a surprising world championship, and become the AL's MVP.

Kaline's emotion-fed injury, though, was atypical. His style was one of grace, of a fluid swing that enabled him to become the youngest player to win a batting title when he captured the '55 crown as a twenty-year-old. It was this effortless play that even convinced teammates years later that Kaline wasn't "putting out" as much as he should, that he could have become one of the biggest names in baseball history had he showed more determination.

Kaline had to overcome a debilitating bone disease to develop his baseball skills while growing up in a modest home in south Baltimore. He was born with osteomyelitis, which wasn't diagnosed until he was eight years old, when his left foot swelled badly one day when he and some friends were jumping out of box cars parked in the railroad yard near his home. Doctors determined that some bones had to be removed from Kaline's foot because they were decayed. Kaline's foot then continued to grow but in a deformed manner, with his toes bunched together. He ran with only his big toe and little toe touching the ground. A second operation was performed to insert a piece of metal to try to help his balance.

The foot problems didn't quell Kaline's love for baseball. He liked to visit the vacant lot just down the street, where the utility workers often played softball, and run the bases when the men's games were over. Kaline's affection for baseball was fueled by his father, Nick, who worked in a broom factory, and two of his uncles, Bib and Fred. While Kaline's father worked, his uncles often shuttled him from game to game each summer, when the gawky kid was playing in as many as three amateur leagues. Kaline put together an incredible career at Baltimore's Southern High School. He hit .333 as a freshman, .418 as a sophomore, .469 as a junior, and .488 as a 5-foot-10, 160-pound senior.

The Tigers first noticed Kaline during his sophomore year, when they scouted Southern High to evaluate another player. Ed Katalinas, Detroit's eastern scout, returned to watch Kaline the next two seasons and filled out his final report on one of the blue forms reserved for the Tigers' top prospects. Katalinas told John McHale, the Tigers' farm director, that Kaline should be the club's top signing priority, and McHale gave him the go-ahead. Major league rules at the time prohibited a player from signing until the day after his high school graduation. Kaline was scheduled to graduate on June 17, 1953, and Katalinas, like many scouts then, approached the day with an increasing sense of paranoia, fearing that somehow, some way, another team was poised to steal Kaline out from under his nose at the eleventh hour. Katalinas asked Kaline's parents if it would be all right if he came by at 12:01 A.M. on June 18 to discuss contract details. Kaline's mother, a cleaning woman with failing eyesight, didn't share the scout's sense of urgency and told him Al planned to go out on a date after the ceremony and it would suffice for Katalinas to simply drop by the next morning around ten. Katalinas returned at the prescribed hour, half expecting to find Kaline having signed with another team. (Kaline actually did turn down offers from two other teams that exceeded the $30,000 deal he signed with Detroit. He nearly signed with the Red Sox, but they turned their attention at the last minute to signing infielder Billy Consolo. And Washington was eager to sign Kaline. Senators scout John Martin had been critically injured in an automobile accident driving home from watching Kaline. According to Sherry Robinson, Washington's farm director, Martin's last words before dying in a hospital were: "Sign Kaline." Kaline was fond of the Senators, the closest major league team to his home, but Washington wasn't willing to make a competitive offer. The Senators were the only major league team that didn't even offer him a Class AAA contract.)

Katalinas hit it off well with Kaline's father early in the "recruitment." The two of them hammered out the final deal in the living room while Kaline and his mother talked in the kitchen. The fine print required the Tigers to deliver $15,000 cash on the spot and pay Kaline $15,000 for his first season. With the bonus money, Kaline paid off the mortgage on his parents' brown row house and also financed an operation that saved his mother's eyesight.

The total figure was important because major league rules then required any player signed for at least $30,000 to remain on the major league roster for at least a year. The rule was introduced to prevent baseball's wealthiest teams—namely, the Yankees and Dodgers—from stockpiling the best amateur talent. Eighteen-year-old Al Kaline was headed straight for the Detroit Tigers, though he did tell Katalinas it would be a few days before he could join the team because he wanted to fulfill his obligation to play in an amateur state tournament. Katalinas begrudgingly agreed, then watched in horror as Kaline passed out during the second game of a doubleheader because of the heat.

With the Tigers playing in Philadelphia, Katalinas personally drove Kaline and his father right to the team's hotel. They arrived just as the Tigers' bus was getting ready to leave for Shibe Park to play the Athletics. With one suit of clothes to his name, Kaline checked into the hotel and hurriedly made his way back to the bus, where manager Fred Hutchison was breaking one of the unwritten rules of the game by holding the bus—for a rookie, no less. Kaline was so scared when he got on the bus that he stood on the drive to the park, fearing he would sit in the wrong place. Pitcher Teddy Gray, the Tigers' player representative, invited the teenager to come sit next to him; it was the only time Al Kaline was the last player on the Tigers' bus.

Kaline got to bat 28 times in thirty games in 1953, hitting .250 with one home run and two RBIs. He settled in as a regular outfielder the following season, hitting .276 in 138 games. But it was the 1955 season that established Kaline as one of baseball's top hitters. In only his second full major league season, Kaline collected 200 hits and hit .340 to win the AL batting title by 21 points over Cleveland's Vic Power. He also had a surprisingly successful power year, finishing fourth in the league with 27 home runs and fifth in RBIs with 102. He earned the reputation of being a stellar outfielder. He threw out Cleveland's Dale Mitchell trying to stretch a single into a double—from a sitting position in right field. As the years went by, Kaline added other defensive highlights. In a game against the White Sox, he threw out runners at second base, third base, and home plate. Mickey Mantle hit a long drive to right field in Yankee Stadium that Yankees announcer Mel Allen was so sure was out of the park he called it the game-winning homer. The men tending to the visiting clubhouse were listening to Allen's broadcast and braced themselves to greet a downcast Tigers team. The players instead arrived excited and ecstatic because Kaline leaped above the wall and robbed Mantle of the home run.

Kaline became a fixture on the AL All-Star team in the early sixties. The hitting, the fielding: it all came so easy. But that also became a problem for Kaline, especially because he and the Tigers weren't able to deliver Detroit fans their first pennant since 1945. Tigers fans couldn't understand why Kaline couldn't hit .340 every year. And management feared that Kaline's grace on the field would be interpreted by the fans as indifference. They wanted Kaline to get his uniform dirty, to prove to the fans and the press he was giving everything he had on the field. He often became sullen, which only made matters worse when he got into a batting slump. The left foot that was surgically repaired when he was a youngster still had not completely healed, and Kaline regularly had the Tigers' trainer rub down the foot to ease the pain. There were times when he wished he would be traded away from Detroit. Mantle and Whitey Ford once told Kaline a deal was close that would bring Kaline to the Yankees for a package of players headlined by first baseman "Moose" Skowron. But Skowron was sidelined soon after by a broken wrist, and if such a deal ever was in the works as Mantle and Ford suggested, it never came off.

Kaline arrived at spring training 1967 proclaiming he was physically fit and wasted little time proving this by scoring all the way from second base on a wild pitch during a Grapefruit League game. He made it a point to avoid attending a World Series game, promising himself that the first Series game he saw would be one that he was playing in. Kaline was coming off a season in which he equaled his career high in home runs (29) and, though never considering himself a power hitter, was within 28 of the club career record of 306 set by Hank Greenberg.

Until the night of June 27, he was putting together the kind of season that might yield his first Most Valuable Player award, especially with Frank Robinson apparently sidelined with the concussion suffered that night in Baltimore. Kaline came to bat in the sixth inning against hard-throwing Indians left-hander Sam McDowell with Cleveland holding a comfortable 6–1 lead. Having gone 0 for 2 previously in the game, Kaline again was unable to do anything and struck out. The usually sedate Kaline suddenly began to seethe because he was unable to score a runner from third base with less than two outs—against a lefty, no less. He walked back to the dugout and, instead of simply slipping his bat back into the concrete back rack as he had done on every occasion since joining the Tigers twelve years earlier, he violently rammed in the bat. His hand slipped momentarily, and his right hand slammed into the concrete.

Kaline was in great pain, and though he was unaware of the extent of the damage, he could see that the knuckle on his right pinkie finger was knocked out of joint. He tried for a couple of minutes to pull the knuckle back into place while sitting in the dugout but failed. Finally, he grabbed the team trainer and quietly retired to the training room. The finger was broken, and Kaline was told he needed to be placed in a cast all the way up to his elbow. The Tigers finished the game, an 8–1 Cleveland victory, by moving Jim Northrup to center field to replace Kaline in right and bringing in Mickey Stanley to play center.

The verdict on Kaline's condition was made official the following day. He was placed on the twenty-one-day disabled list, which probably would keep him out of action until mid-July. To fill Kaline's vacancy in the outfield, the Tigers acquired veteran outfielder Jim Landis from the Houston Astros in exchange for Larry Sherry, a little-used relief pitcher. To fill Kaline's spot on the roster, Detroit promoted infielder Lenny Green, Earl Wilson's former roommate with Boston, from Toledo.

With the White Sox having built their largest lead of the season at 5½ games, Kaline feared his implausible outburst might have finished off the Tigers' chances of winning the pennant. He laid in a hospital bed the next morning feeling more embarrassment than pain. "Of all the dumb things I've ever done," he said, "this has got to be the dumbest." Kaline was chided immediately after the incident by teammates like Dick McAuliffe and Jim Northrup, who playfully instructed him in the fine art of venting one's frustrations without breaking one's bones. But overall, this wasn't a laughing matter in the Detroit clubhouse. When Kaline dressed out for games to watch from the dugout in subsequent days, he was greeted by an almost overwhelming silence from his teammates. Not even Norm Cash, the clown prince of the Tigers, was willing to knock Kaline while he was down. Kaline couldn't stand this treatment and decided he would be more comfortable if he spent the remainder of his stay on the disabled list watching games from the press box.

The loss of Kaline wasn't the only major problem facing Detroit. Veteran left-handed pitcher Mickey Lolich was enduring the worst losing streak of his major league career. When he was knocked out after only $3^2/_3$ innings by the Yankees on June 25, he had lost seven consecutive decisions, his record dropping to 5–10. Lolich had failed to complete a start since the May 19 victory over the Yankees that left him 5–2. Four times in the next eight starts he failed to last through four innings.

Lolich's dilemma was a mystery to all concerned—manager Mayo Smith, pitching coach Johnny Sain, and Lolich himself. At 6 feet 1 and 207 pounds, the pot-bellied Lolich struck a pose hardly befitting a professional athlete. But for all of the jokes about Lolich's portly build, there was no belittling the ability contained in his left arm. Lolich was the kind of pitcher who could warm up with only about ten pitches. He was difficult to catch, not always able to match his velocity with adequate control. He relied on the movement of his pitches, often throwing a hard sinker with his catcher setting up on the far edge of the plate. Early in his career, critics usually cited his weight when things were going bad and tried to run him into shape as a means of reversing his fortunes. The fact was Lolich was in shape, as far as his pitching was concerned; he simply was large.

Lolich first spent most of a season in the majors in 1964. It was an impressive debut—an 18–9 record, 3.26 earned run average, and 192 strikeouts compared with only 64 walks in 232 innings. While carving out a spot in the Tigers' starting rotation each year since, he had been unable to improve on his '64 accomplishments. But even with the 5–10 record and eight-game losing streak, Smith's confidence in Lolich never wavered. Lolich was only pulled from the starting rotation when he was required to meet his obligations to the military reserves.

Meanwhile, in Baltimore, the injury to Frank Robinson proved to be just as serious as Kaline's broken hand. Robinson awoke the morning after to discover he had double vision. He spent the next month out of lineup, the Orioles replacing him in right field with little-used Sam Bowens.

5
JULY

The Orioles entered July with the second-best batting average in the league, yet they were mired in eighth place, five games under .500. That pitching staff which had looked untouchable in the '66 Series had come unraveled. Baltimore's most consistent starting pitcher was rookie Tom Phoebus, who was 7–3 with three shutouts. Jim Palmer, who led the '66 Orioles with fifteen victories, was shelved with arm problems. Dave McNally, a thirteen-game winner in 1966, was sputtering along at 4–5 with a 5.35 ERA that was the worst among regular AL starting pitchers. Wally Bunker, a ten-game winner in '66, had failed to complete any of his first fourteen starts and was 2–4 with a 4.09 ERA. And there was Steve Barber, also a ten-game winner in '66. The man who somehow lost a no-hitter to Detroit in April was 4–9, his ERA bloated at 4.08, and his walks at a league-high 61 in 75 innings.

In the first move made by Baltimore that began to dismantle a team that a few months earlier was considered a budding dynasty, the Orioles sent Barber to the Yankees for cash, minor league first baseman Ray Barker, and two players to be named later. Without getting a quality starting pitcher in return, a signal was sent that the Birds, trailing by ten games on July 1, weren't confident of jumping back into the pennant race.

TAKING STOCK

The Orioles' struggles were contrasted by the success enjoyed by the White Sox, who took a 5 1/2-game lead on July 1 by winning at Detroit to even the series between the teams going into the third and final game. In fact, the city of Chicago basked in the glory of having both the White Sox and the Cubs—who had not finished in the first division since 1946—in first place. Nobody was planning for a Windy City Series, but each team gave every indication it was solid enough to at least remain in the pennant race most of the year. White Sox manager Eddie Stanky boldly made public the confidence he had in his ballclub: "If we're within a couple games of the lead at the All-Star break, we'll take the pennant."

There had been plenty of major league pennant races—and even a few pennants—for Stanky to draw experience from. In eleven years as a major league second baseman, Stanky had the distinction of going to the World Series three times within five years . . . each time with a different team—the Brooklyn Dodgers (1947), the Boston Braves (1948), and the New York Giants (1951). A feisty ballplayer, Stanky endured eight years in the minors before earning the starting job at second base for the Cubs during spring training 1943. He hit .245 as a rookie but was traded the following June to Brooklyn, where he became an All-Star. But it was with the Dodgers that Stanky found himself asked to accept what he considered the unthinkable in the name of the team—play baseball alongside a black man. When Jackie Robinson was promoted to the Dodgers in the spring of 1947 to play third base, Stanky didn't mince words or hide his feelings for his new teammate. "I don't like you," Stanky told Robinson, "but we'll get along because we're teammates." Indeed, Stanky later came to Robinson's aid when Robinson was being taunted by some of the Phillies. They played together only one season because Stanky was dealt to Boston the following spring in a trade that allowed the Dodgers to move Robinson to second base.

For Stanky it was a case of leaving one pennant winner for another. He played two seasons for the Braves, beginning with the '48 pennant winners, then two more for the Giants, where his double-play partner was shortstop Alvin Dark. One of the last things Stanky did on the field in his two seasons with New York was leap on the back of Giants manager Leo Durocher after Bobby Thomson hit his dramatic home run to win the '51 NL playoff series against Brooklyn. Stanky became player-manager of the Cardinals two months later at age thirty-four. He managed St. Louis for four seasons, never finishing higher than third place, and was dismissed two months into the '55 season. His term in St. Louis featured an incident involving Robinson, who had become a perennial All-Star and paved the way for other blacks to begin filling rosters of most major league teams. In 1953 Robinson accused Stanky—who once defended him against bigots—of yelling racial slurs at him from the Cards' dugout.

Stanky wasn't eager to remain in major league managing after being fired by the Cardinals. He worked in various capacities for a couple of teams and turned down five major league managing offers before taking over the White Sox in 1966. Likewise, Stanky wasn't Chicago's first choice to succeed Al Lopez. The White Sox were turned down by Mayo Smith, who accepted an offer from Detroit a year later, and Sam Mele, who elected to remain in Minnesota only to be fired in June 1967. Even with the decade-long layoff from major league managing, Stanky was only the tenth-oldest skipper at age forty-eight. But there was a perception that the years had mellowed him. "I don't like the word mellow," he snapped soon after his hiring. "It reminds me of a piece of fruit that's gone soft."

As the White Sox settled in atop the AL in July '67, it was their hitting that was soft, though their .240 team batting average was respectable enough to rank fourth in the league. Chicago was sixth in runs scored and ninth in home runs. And for a league-leading team, the White Sox's lineup was relatively unsettled. The closest things to constants were center fielder Tommie Agee and third baseman Don Buford. Agee, the 1966 AL Rookie of the Year, led the team in homers with 10 and stolen bases with 22 and was tied with Tom McCraw for the club lead in RBIs with 32. Buford had 16 stolen bases and had improved his defense tremendously. Maybe it was his new glove, a Ted Williams model he bought from Sears.

McCraw's power numbers—nine homers and 32 RBIs—were deceiving in that he collected three home runs and eight RBIs in one game. Al Weis had lifted his average from .155 as the everyday second baseman in 1966 to .245 in '67, but was lost for the season with the knee injury that occurred in the collision with Frank Robinson. Defensive specialist Ron Hansen (.209) went virtually unchallenged at shortstop. Rookie catcher Duane Josephson was hitting close to .300 in late May when he went out of the lineup for more than a month with a thumb injury. With Josephson unavailable, J.C. Martin (.230) did most of the catching, with assistance from Gerry McNertney.

The outfield was unsettled around Agee. Pete Ward began the year as the regular left fielder but often gave way to Walt Williams and also subbed for McCraw at first and Buford at third. Ken Berry, the club's most dependable everyday hitter (.275), opened the year in right field but was shuttled between right and left by midseason. In early July he had to be rested occasionally because of headaches. Berry was an indicator of how the White Sox didn't blindly hope that they could hit their way to victory. During batting practice, Berry would work voraciously on his fielding—diving for balls, working on his technique for climbing the outfield fence. A wide receiver in high school who originally attended Wichita State University on a football scholarship, Berry often called upon his instincts as a receiver to play the outfield. Veteran Jim King (.200) couldn't hold down the right-field job. Even with the White Sox's lead building, general manager Ed Short was eager to acquire more power. With many positions remaining fluid, he could afford to look for both an infielder and an outfielder.

Those seeking impressive figures from Chicago needed to look no further than the White Sox's pitching statistics, which, as expected, were the best in the league. Chicago's team ERA was an incredible 2.35; California was a distant second at 3.11. The White Sox boasted three of the top five AL starters in ERA with Joe Horlen (10–1, second to California's Jim McGlothlin at 2.17), Gary Peters (10–4, third at 2.32), and Tommy John (6–5, fifth at 2.43). And there was hardly a weak link in the bullpen. Hoyt Wilhelm had allowed only 31 base runners in 36 innings; his ERA was at 0.75 in nineteen appearances. Wilbur Wood, Wilhelm's able student in the science of mastering the knuckleball, had a 1.04 ERA in twenty-one appearances. There also was Bob Locker, the team leader in appearances with thirty-two to go with a 2.11 ERA, and Don McMahon, the June acquisition from Boston in the Jerry Adair trade, who overall with the Red Sox and White Sox had a 2.13 ERA in twenty-three games.

During the week before the All-Star break, Red Sox star pitcher Jim Lonborg met with writer William Craig to do an interview for a story that was published in *The Saturday Evening Post* in early September. Lonborg impressed Craig, his interests in subjects such as medicine and Beethoven proving him to be more than the prototype ballplayer. When discussing his more aggressive pitching style in 1967, Lonborg quoted Aristotle: "Passion dulls the reason of all mankind." Lonborg's passions included skiing, and he told Craig he planned to take a ski trip to Lake Tahoe during the off-season. Craig would write: "He knew that he could break a leg and ruin his career. But he was unperturbed by the thought. It would not happen."

The All-Star break arrived in mid-July with Chicago owning a lead of two games over Detroit and 2½ games over Minnesota. California, which had been 12½ games out and 12 games under .500 on June 6, rode a six-game winning streak to move into fourth place, 4½ games out with a record of 45–40. The only other team in the league with a winning record was Boston, in fifth place and six games out at 41–39. The Red Sox led the league in batting at .252, but doubters still were out in full force, expecting Dick Williams's team to drift back into the second division during the second half of the season and finish where so many Boston teams had finished for decades.

Almost as common as a Red Sox swoon was the team's penchant for festering in its own crises. It appeared another loomed on the horizon surrounding George Scott. The second-year infielder could hit consistently, hit for power, and also wield a surprisingly effective glove at first base considering his linebacker-like build. But Scott seemingly couldn't remain in Williams's favor. Williams was incensed by Scott's failure to carry out his directives. He once benched Scott for striking out too often and said talking to him was like talking to cement. Twice in one month, Scott cost the Red Sox runs when he was ruled out for leaving third base too soon on sacrifice flies. He was benched once for not hitting to right field. And on July 9, during the opener of a doubleheader split at Detroit, Scott was shown the pine for not running out a routine pop-up that eventually dropped in and would have been a base hit.

Despite the occasional mental vacuums, it was difficult not to like Scott. He always had a good word and, even in his own times of professional crises, managed a smile. As a six-foot-two, 205-pound senior in high school at Greenville, Mississippi, Scott had starred in baseball, football, and basketball. He turned down football-scholarship offers that included Michigan State University to sign with the Red Sox in 1962 as an infielder. It was at Pittsfield of the Class AA Eastern League in 1965 that Scott earned his ticket to the majors. He was voted the league's most valuable player, winning the league's triple crown with 25 home runs, 94 RBIs, and a .319 batting average. Scott had moved around the infield early in his pro career, playing third base, second base, and shortstop despite his size. But at Pittsfield in '65, Scott divided his time between third and first. He made the Red Sox coming out of spring training in 1966 and eventually settled in at first base as Joe Foy established himself as Boston's everyday third baseman.

As of the '67 All-Star break, Scott had missed only two games and was hitting a solid .288 with 10 homers and 40 RBIs. The Red Sox were getting solid hitting from all but two positions. Rookie center fielder Reggie Smith was struggling after beginning the season filling in at second base for Mike Andrews. The International League batting champion in 1966, the switch-hitting Smith was hitting only .222. But Williams maintained confidence in the player who had played so well for him at Toronto and left him in the lineup. And there was catcher, where Mike Ryan, Russ Gibson, and Bob Tillman combined to hit .219

with three homers and 30 RBIs. The overall hitting strength of the team allowed Boston the luxury of using catchers strictly for defensive purposes, but Williams still was eager to get a veteran catcher with some pop in his bat, maybe one that was familiar with handling a pitching staff during a pennant race.

One of the biggest individual surprises of the first half of the season was Minnesota rookie second baseman Rod Carew. Installed as a starter in spring training, Carew was fifth among AL hitters at the All-Star break with a .313 batting average.

Carew had been born on a train in Panama, named after the doctor who had to be summoned from the train's white seating section to perform the delivery. Carew's father, Eric, worked for the Panama Canal Company. His mother, Olga, was a maid. The five Carew children all slept in the same room. Rod's first primitive experience with baseball came at age seven, with a broomstick and tennis ball. At eleven he was hospitalized for six months with rheumatic fever. The combination of sickliness and a quiet, timid personality didn't set well with his father. Rod once walked away from a fight, only to have his father order him back to duke it out. He complied, realizing the only option was to be punished by his father. Rod's favorite role model was an uncle, Joseph French, a physical education teacher who helped hone Rod's baseball skills. The Carews moved from Panama to New York City when Rod was fifteen. He wasn't able to play high school baseball because he worked after school in a neighborhood grocery store. That didn't stop him from playing sandlot games at Macombs Dam Park near Yankee Stadium. It was there that Carew's sweet swing was spotted by Twins scout Herb Stein, and Carew was signed in 1964.

There was no question that the Twins had accepted Cal Ermer as their leader and were prepared to play their best during the second half of the season. Ermer's calm demeanor was a departure from the disciplined approach of Sam Mele, but Ermer also proved early on he could put his foot down. Only a few weeks after taking over, Ermer defused what could have been a potentially damaging confrontation between Tony Oliva and Ted Uhlaender. There had been some good-natured ribbing on the team bus after a win at Cleveland on June 18, but some of the racial joking by Uhlaender, an irreverent Texan, irked Oliva. A shouting match ensued, but Ermer intercepted the two players and dressed them down outside the bus, telling him to save their aggression for the opposition. He also held a team meeting at the hotel and prevented the situation from building any kind of momentum.

The first half of the season had been something of a rollercoaster ride for the Tigers. They played the first month minus their regular left fielder, Willie Horton, arguably their best power hitter. Since June 27, They had played without Al Kaline, their most consistent hitter and best player over-all Mickey Lolich had lost 10 of 15 decisions. Their three best starters—Lolich, Earl Wilson, and Denny McLain—owned the three worst ERAs on the ballclub.

Yet the Tigers had hung around the top of the standings since early May, even owning first place for most of early June. Manager Mayo Smith must have thought that with a healthy hitting attack and a starting rotation that was as reliable as his bullpen, the Tigers could easily erase their two-game deficit.

In the second division, Cleveland, which was picked by some to contend, was 40–42 after being swept by Washington on the last day before the break. The Indians were blessed with one of the best pitching staffs in the AL and led the league in strikeouts. But their four main starters—Sam McDowell, Luis Tiant, Sonny Siebert, and Steve Hargen—were only a combined 27–25, although all of them except McDowell had ERAs of less than 3.00. At the plate, Cleveland didn't have that one "go-to" guy who could pick up a team. Third baseman Max Alvis and second baseman Larry Brown were the only players who had enough at-bats to qualify for the batting lead and were hitting above .250. And if the Indians were hoping thirty-three-year-old Rocky Colavito could duplicate some of his past home run magic, that assumption was way off base. Colavito came into the '67 season having hit 20 or more homers each year for eleven seasons. He won the major league home run title by hitting 42 back in 1959 during his first tour of duty with the Indians and hit a career-high 45 with Detroit two years later. He returned to Cleveland from Kansas City after the '64 season, led the AL in RBIs in 1965 with 108, and kept hitting for power in '66 with 30 home runs. But going into the '67 All-Star break, Colavito had played in only fifty games and hit five home runs with 18 RBIs.

Baltimore trailed Cleveland by a game. With the pitching problems and the injury to Frank Robinson, there were few positives to point to from the first half of the season. The odd thing was that the Orioles weren't far off statistically from their 1966 performance. Even with the revamped pitching staff, the team ERA was 3.29, ranking fourth in the league. In 1966 their ERA was 3.32, fourth in the league. While hitting nine points below what they hit in '66—.249 compared to .258—the Birds were on a pace to come within 30 runs of what they scored in '66.

But a nine-game deficit will take its toll on a team's psyche. It even extended to the front office, where, for whatever reason, the receptionist at the Orioles' offices stopped using the phrase "world champions" when answering the telephone.

New York, Washington, and Kansas City appeared worthy of their standing as the bottom three teams in the league. The Yankees had little speed and shaky pitching to go with Mickey Mantle's 16 home runs. The season had become a nightmare for rookie outfielder Bill Robinson, who was hitting only .169 with eight RBIs in 136 at-bats. Elston Howard had been reduced to a part-time player. Tom Tresh never recovered from a spring knee injury and limped into the break with a .201 batting average. The Senators, out of the cellar only thanks to the sweep of Cleveland, were last in hitting and pitching. Their only legitimate hitting threat was burly Frank Howard, who had grabbed the home-run lead with 24 and had driven in 53 runs. Senators starting pitchers had managed to finish only ten games. The A's had no power (35 home runs, only 11 more than Frank Howard), and their young pitching wasn't coming through, with the exception of Catfish Hunter, who was 8–7 with a 2.63 ERA. Jim Nash, expected to be the star of the staff following his remarkable rookie showing of 12–1 and a 2.06 ERA the previous year, was 9–8 with an ERA of 3.52. And there was Lew Krausse, leading the league in losses with twelve and an ERA of 4.68 that was the poorest among AL pitchers who had thrown enough innings to qualify for the ERA title.

Mickey Mantle was chosen to play in the All-Star Game for the twelfth time and was thoroughly embarrassed by his selection. His performances had dropped drastically following the '64 season, a year that also marked the last of five consecutive Yankee pennants. The move to first base had not gone well. He begrudgingly accepted the club's decision to shift him there, believing it would mean less wear on his battered legs. In the back of his mind, he was bitter that the Yankees wanted to squeeze every last year out of him. Then again, he wanted to play as long as he could.

In the closing days of his career, Mantle had become a shadow of what he was when he arrived in the major leagues at the age of nineteen in 1951. Back then, he was a balanced package of power and speed. But that was almost immediately chipped away at when Mantle suffered the first of many serious injuries. It occurred during the '51 World Series against the New York Giants, when another gifted rookie outfielder, Willie Mays, hit a drive into the gap in right center. Mantle sprinted after the ball and at the last minute realized he was on a collision course with center fielder Joe DiMaggio. He abruptly changed direction but in the process caught his right foot in one of the rubber outfield drains. His right knee was badly twisted, and Mantle was taken to a local hospital.

He was escorted to the hospital by his father, "Mutt," who had proudly left his job as a mine worker in Oklahoma to watch his boy play in the World Series. When their cab arrived at the hospital, Mickey unconsciously shifted his weight onto his father to steady himself. His father immediately collapsed under his son's weight and fell to the sidewalk. Mickey was startled by the event and soon learned its tragic roots. "Mutt" Mantle had Hodgkin's disease, a fact he had successfully withheld from Mickey for more than a year. "Mutt" Mantle was dead within a matter of months at the age of thirty-nine. Mickey was crushed by the loss of his greatest friend and cheerleader. And since other men in the Mantle family had died at relatively young ages, Mickey would live for years with the fear that he, too, might not live long.

Mantle approached each game with incredible zeal, and he didn't slow up much away from the field with buddies Whitey Ford and Billy Martin. But he didn't allow injuries or hangovers to keep him from playing. In becoming one of baseball's greatest stars, Mantle won the Triple Crown in 1956 with a .353 batting average, 52 home runs, and 130 RBIs. It was only the incredible output of the '56 season that began to convince Yankee fans that Mantle was worth savoring. Up until that point, he couldn't appease New Yorkers. Maybe it was his manner, the stoic determination that prevented him from displaying emotion to the crowd. The young Mickey Mantle was often booed and jeered at Yankee Stadium.

By the mid-sixties, Mantle was a different ballplayer. A steady stream of injuries had sapped him of much of his speed. And with the gradual breakup of the Yankees, many of his friends had left the ballclub. He and Ford and Martin and Yogi Berra had thought of themselves as the "little brothers" during the glorious fifties. By the mid-sixties, Mantle felt like the "old brother," a feeling that only grew worse when Ford suddenly retired in June. Yet ironically, as Mantle's achievements diminished the fans' adoration for him grew. It was difficult to question the drive of a man who appeared in the lineup day after day though his legs had to be wrapped extensively for him to make his way out onto the field.

At the All-Star break in 1967, Mickey Mantle was tied for fifth place in the American League with 16 home runs, to go along with 35 RBIs and a .260 batting average. It wasn't a complete surprise when he was picked as an All-Star reserve by his former outfield mate, Orioles manager Hank Bauer. Mantle had rarely put much stock in All-Star games, and the '67 edition at Anaheim Stadium was no exception. Most of the ballplayers arrived in California on Monday, July 10, the day before the game. But even on the morning of the game, Tuesday, July 11, Mantle was still at his off-season home in Dallas, the exclusive Preston Trails Country Club. Only that afternoon did he board a flight to Los Angeles, arriving at the stadium after the AL stars had taken infield practice. Said Bauer: "Glad you could make it."

He didn't stay long. With the National League leading, 1–0, in the fifth inning, Mantle pinch-hit for Angels pitcher Jim McGlothlin and was struck out by Ferguson Jenkins of the Cubs. Mantle bid his teammates adieu, showered and changed, and left. A police escort delivered him to nearby John Wayne Airport, and he took a helicopter back to Los Angeles International. He took a flight home to Dallas while his AL teammates took the NL into extra innings, 1–1. Mantle's buddies at Preston Trails were still watching the game—which the NL won in fifteen innings, 2–1—when Mantle came strolling in the door.

BOSOX EXORCISE GHOSTS

By the morning of Sunday, July 23, the American League had been distinctly separated into haves and have-nots. With Boston and California getting hot after the All-Star break, the top five teams—Chicago, Boston, California, Detroit, and Minnesota—all were within two games of each other. There then was a five-game gap separating the contenders from the sixth-place Senators.

Most significant, the Red Sox had come out of the break winning nine of ten games, including the last eight in a row. This allowed Boston to move from fifth place to second. The Red Sox moved within a half game of the first-place White Sox, even equaling Chicago in the loss column at forty. The Angels were the only other contender with a winning record since the break (7–4) as they rose to third place, 1 1/2 games behind the White Sox.

White Sox management decided it needed to do something to add some hitting to the ballclub. What Chicago came up with was thirty-six-year-old Ken Boyer, the seven-time National League All-Star third baseman whom St. Louis unloaded on the Mets two years earlier. Boyer came over to the White Sox having played fifty-six games for the Mets, hitting .235 with three home runs and 13 runs batted in. The White Sox were hoping to rediscover the semblance of a right-handed bat that had produced 272 homers over thirteen seasons.

In Cleveland that Sunday afternoon, the Red Sox rode the complete-game pitching of Jim Lonborg and former Indian Gary Bell to a double-header sweep of the Indians, 8–5 and 5–1. For Lonborg, this provided more evidence that he had become one of the best pitchers in baseball. His record improved to 14–3, the latest victory giving him a 5–0 record in his last six starts. When Tony Conigliaro gave Lonborg a 2–0 lead with a first-inning home run, it meant Tony C, at age twenty-two, was the youngest player to hit 100 major league home runs.

Even with the sweep, the Red Sox failed to gain ground on the White Sox, who won a pair at Kansas City that same day. But it couldn't be ignored that Boston had won ten consecutive games for the first time since 1951. The Red Sox were a complete ballclub, winning with dependable starting pitching, a deep bullpen, and hitting both for average and power. Their weakness to date was getting the upper hand against the AL's other contenders. With a 52–40 record, they were only 18–20 against the other four first-division teams while going 34–20 against the five clubs with losing records. Boston sports columnist Harold Kaese sat in the press box after the Sunday sweep and wrote, "The Red Sox should win the pennant easily. The question is not if, but by how much." The players weren't ready to take such a public stand, but they boarded their flight home from Cleveland confident they wouldn't fall by the wayside during the second half of the season as had so many previous Boston teams.

Red Sox fans apparently also believed this team was different. There were times when heartbroken Red Sox fans met their fallen heroes at Logan Airport in an attempt to soften the blow of another season lost. Such was the case in 1949, when thousands were drawn to the airport after the Red Sox lost the last two games of the season at Yankee Stadium to lose the pennant to the Yankees by a single game. This time, between five thousand and ten thousand fans mobbed Logan to welcome home the hottest team in baseball, a team that bore little resemblance to the one that in spring training had been rated a 75-to-1 shot to win the pennant. As the plane taxied down the runway toward the United Air Lines terminal, the pilot warned the Red Sox to be prepared to be greeted by some well-wishers. That hardly prepared them for the horde of fans that made it virtually impossible for them to deplane. As the players gawked out the windows at the crowd—larger than the delirious mob that greeted the Beatles on their first visit to Boston a year earlier—some of the players joked that they should offer the fans Conigliaro as a sacrifice to spare the rest of the team from suffocating adulation. As it was, a group of state patrolmen formed a flying wedge to enable the Red Sox to get out of the plane without incident and into their cars. When Dick O'Connell later learned that the fans were tipped off to the team's arrival by the Red Sox's radio announcers, he tactfully informed the announcers that such information no longer could be disclosed.

Being one-half game out of first place in July wouldn't have created such a stir in Chicago or Detroit. For many years in New York, it would have been grounds for questioning the worth of the manager. But this was

Boston. This was the Red Sox. In the preceding forty-eight seasons, the Red Sox had claimed only one pennant. Thirty of those years saw them compile losing records, eight of those worthy of last place.

But it seemed that Red Sox fans were hurt less by what their team was than by what their team could have been through the years. This had been a powerhouse franchise for the first twenty years of American League play, winning six pennants by 1918. Known as the Puritans when the AL was formed in 1901, Boston was the American League's first representative to the World Series in 1903 and beat Pittsburgh. After Boston's National League team changed its nickname from the Red Stockings to the Braves in 1907, the Puritans filled the sartorial vacancy by becoming the Red Sox. Baseball's winningest pitcher, Cy Young, won 193 games in a Boston uniform from 1901 to 1908. The Red Sox returned to the top in 1912, playing in new Fenway Park, named for the surrounding area. For what it's worth, Fenway Park opened the same day the *Titanic* sank. To conform to the land available, the new ballpark featured a left-field fence that was only about 320 feet from home plate. In consequence, the left-field wall stood 37 feet high; it was made of concrete and metal and painted green. Thus was born the "Green Monster."

The 1912 Red Sox were led by "Smokey" Joe Wood, a fireballing twenty-two-year-old who finished 34–5 with an earned run average of 1.91. Wood had won thirteen consecutive games when he was matched against the "Big Train," Walter Johnson of Washington, winner of a record sixteen consecutive games earlier that season, on September 6. Maybe the most ballyhooed single regular-season game to date, the local newspapers matched Wood and Johnson in a "tale of the tape" reserved for a heavyweight championship fight. Wood won the showdown, 1–0, and went on to tie Johnson's mark. In the 1912 World Series, the Red Sox beat the New York Giants when Giants outfielder Fred Snodgrass dropped a fly ball in the tenth inning of the seventh and final game. Wood broke a thumb in the subsequent spring training and was never the same again, pitching with Boston through 1915. The Red Sox added another world championship that year, boasting the era's best outfield in baseball: Tris Speaker, Duffy Lewis, and Harry Hooper.

While Boston fans easily recognized the talent of that marvelous outfield combination, they were oblivious to the hatred between Speaker and Lewis. Part of the disagreement grew out of a team prank in which many of the players shaved their heads on a whim while on a road trip going into steamy St. Louis. Lewis's hair failed to grow back naturally afterward. This embarrassment was compounded by Speaker's propensity for routinely flipping Lewis's cap off his head in front of the fans during batting practice. Lewis finally had enough of this stunt one day at

Fenway Park and angrily warned Speaker: "You do that again, and I'll kill you." Speaker accepted the dare, and Lewis flung a bat at him, striking him hard enough across the shins that he had to be helped into the clubhouse. The extent of their interaction after that usually was confined to calling for fly balls hit between them.

The bumbling business tactics of club owner Joe Lannin led to the trading of Speaker to Cleveland on Opening Day of 1916. Speaker had been given an $18,000 raise two years earlier during the major leagues' bidding war with the Federal League. But when the upstart league folded after the 1915 season, Lannin tried to cut Speaker's salary by $8,000. Speaker held out during spring training and was sent to Cleveland.

Speaker, who had hit better than .300 in each of his six full seasons with Boston, only became a bigger star in Cleveland. In 1916, his first season after the trade, Speaker led the AL in hitting with a .386 average. Four more times he hit better than .375 during the next nine years. The Red Sox continued to prosper without him, repeating as AL champs in 1916—and beating Brooklyn in the World Series—before Lannin sold the team that December to theater entrepreneurs Harry Frazee and Hugh Ward. Boston returned to the Series in 1918, helped by a young right-handed pitcher named Babe Ruth, to beat the Chicago Cubs. Ruth not only compiled a pitching record of 13–7 but also led the majors in home runs with 11.

Ruth became baseball's biggest sensation in 1919, when he was converted to an outfielder. He hit the unthinkable number of 29 home runs, about 12 percent of all the home runs hit in the league. But the team overall was eroding, falling to sixth place. To make matters worse, Frazee faced mounting debts. He still owed Lannin from his purchase of the ballclub, and he also was losing money in the theater business. With that financial backdrop, Frazee agreed on December 26, 1919, to sell Ruth to the New York Yankees, who had never won an AL pennant. The deal was actually twofold: Yankees owner Colonel Jacob Ruppert agreed to give Frazee $125,000 for Ruth and also provided him with a loan of approximately $300,000. The sale wasn't announced until January 6, 1920, and prompted the expected polarized reactions from baseball fans in Boston and New York. While Frazee had obtained enough capital to continue forward in theater, producing *No, No, Nanette* for one, he also had shifted the balance of power in baseball to the Yankees. As Ruth became arguably the best-known figure in the history of American sports and helped establish the Yankees with parallel greatness that lasted into the midsixties, the Red Sox were relegated to also-ran status. Frazee sold the team in 1923. Disinterest in the team developed to the point that the paid attendance in 1932, with the team compiling a club-record 111 losses, was a meager 182,150. Across town that year, a mediocre Boston Braves team attracted more than 500,000.

A reversal of the Red Sox's fortunes began on February 25, 1933. That's when "boy millionaire" Tom Yawkey bought the team. As a young-ster he was adopted by his uncle, lumber businessman William Hoover Yawkey, one of the richest men in Michigan and principal owner of the Detroit Tigers. It was common to find young Tom playing on the grounds of the family's summer home in southern Ontario with one of the most feared hitters in baseball, the Tigers' Ty Cobb, who would have been invited over for Sunday lunch. While Yawkey cut a slight, unassuming figure, his background did include athletics. He played second base dur-ing his last two years at the Irving School in Tarrytown, New York. Yawkey graduated from Yale but contradicted the rich-kid stereotype by working in a lumber camp in Wisconsin, a copper mine in Arizona, and a coal mine in West Virginia.

One of Yawkey's first significant decisions as Red Sox owner was to order the renovation and expansion of Fenway Park following the '33 season. Construction was nearly completed three months before Opening Day 1934 when a four-alarm fire virtually destroyed what had been ac-complished. But all was restored in time to begin the season, with a plaque imbedded into the brick wall of the stadium alongside Jersey Street proclaiming the "new" Fenway Park. Yawkey added a twenty-three-foot screen to the left-field wall in 1936. This was meant to provide protection not for left-handed pitchers—balls into the screen still were home runs—but for the shopkeepers on Lansdowne Street behind the wall. They often were made aware of the baseball exploits of the day by the abrupt entry of baseballs through their front windows.

Much of the park retained the flavor of the thirties and forties into the late sixties. That included a manually operated scoreboard on the facade of the Green Monster when most stadiums had converted to elec-tronic boards. About an hour before game time, a couple of scoreboard boys would emerge with a ladder through a door just to the left of the main board that featured the essential information for that day's Red Sox game. Loaded down with the proper metal cards, they would fill in the numbers corresponding to that day's pitchers at Fenway, the proper name of the visiting team—the word *BOSTON* was permanently affixed in the spot reserved for the home team—and similar information for the other games of the day. The numbers pertaining to the current inning and score of each game were subbed out from inside the scoreboard, where the board boys operated in a relatively dark and stifling atmosphere.

Through the years, Yawkey was content to remain in the background. His standard ballpark attire was khaki pants, a white, short-sleeved shirt, a brown windbreaker, and hush puppies. He idolized his ballplayers, treating them with respect and benevolence. He often arrived at the park hours before game time and took the field himself, accompanied by stadium workers. He knew most of his employees on a first-name basis, all the way down to the ushers. He once explained this interest by saying, "Perhaps I thought I had to get an insight into what makes them tick, what they think. My dad told me I could learn something from everyone in the world. I try to."

The Red Sox prospered through much of the late thirties and forties. Yawkey acquired AL home-run champion Jimmie Foxx from the Philadelphia A's after the 1935 season, and Foxx slammed 198 homers for Boston over the next five years. He was traded to the Cubs in 1942 but not before watching the early maturation of a spindly youngster from San Diego. Ted Williams joined the Red Sox in 1939, hitting .327 in 149 games. Combining determination and discipline, he became arguably the game's greatest hitter, collecting 2,654 hits and six AL batting titles over nineteen seasons. Opposing teams were so certain that the left-handed-hitting Williams would pull the ball into right field that they devised a special defensive shift against him. The shortstop played over where the second baseman usually played, the second baseman played closer to first base, and the third baseman was stationed directly behind second base. The apex of Williams's brilliant career was his .406 batting average in 1941, the first time a major leaguer had hit .400 since 1930 and a feat that remained unequaled fifty years later. The "Splendid Splinter" helped Boston end a twenty-eight-year pennant drought in 1946 before the Red Sox lost the World Series to the Cardinals. Boston fans were teased in 1948, when the Red Sox lost a playoff to Cleveland, and in 1949, when the Red Sox blew a one-game lead over the Yankees with two to play by dropping consecutive games at New York.

The Red Sox went into decline in the early fifties and had a penchant for crossing paths with some of baseball's most tragic figures. Jimmy Piersall was a talented hitter and outfielder who crossed over the line of being colorful on the field. One day while playing the St. Louis Browns in 1952, Piersall stood on first base and began flapping his arms and yelling "Oink! Oink! Oink!" to distract pitcher Satchel Paige. Browns catcher Clint Courtney noted afterward that he thought Piersall was "plumb crazy," which proved to be an accurate assessment. Piersall was institutionalized later that season.

Another ill-fated Red Sox player was Harry Agganis, who had all the makings of a hometown hero. He signed with the Red Sox after starring as a quarterback for Boston University. He played a season and a half for the Red Sox, leaving the lineup in June 1954 because of a pulmonary infection. Within a few weeks, Agganis died of a blood clot at age twenty-five. And there was Jackie Jensen, a college football hero who developed into one of the AL's great stars of the late fifties, winning the Most Valuable Player award in 1958. But after winning his third AL RBI title in 1959, Jensen announced he was retiring because of a fear of flying. He returned in 1961, only to quit again for good after the season. In the meantime, the Ted Williams saga came to an end. His greatness on the field was contrasted with a frosty relationship with both the fans and media in Boston. That was encapsulated on the final day of his career, when he homered in his final at-bat at Fenway Park but declined to tip his cap to the crowd.

Yawkey was distraught over his team's inability to produce a pennant contender and was prepared to use his financial wherewithal to rectify the situation. He approached the Indians during the spring of 1957 about purchasing twenty-three-year-old pitcher Herb Score for the record sum of $1 million. Score had pitched two seasons for the Indians, leading the AL in strikeouts with 245 and 263, respectively. Cleveland turned down the offer. Score, as it turned out, was injured early in the '57 season and only won another nineteen games in the majors.

While the Red Sox floundered, Yawkey was haunted by the reputation of being too kind to his players. The Red Sox were mockingly dubbed a country-club franchise; the word was that Yawkey would always take care of his players, even if they floundered to a second-division finish. This lack of strict discipline carried over to Yawkey's lieutenants. Manager Billy Jurges became the laughingstock of the team during spring training 1960 when he took it easy on two players who broke the team's midnight curfew. They pleaded innocence, and Jurges didn't implement any punishment. But the rest of the squad knew that the two players in question had stayed out well beyond midnight. In fact, the two players had been involved in a traffic accident, with the police report listing the time of the accident as 1:35 A.M.

Yawkey's players-first policies reached new heights that summer, when he allowed his players to determine whether Jurges should stay on as manager. They voted to bring back Mike Higgins, who managed some decent Boston teams in the late fifties. If only those Red Sox could play as well as they picked a manager; Higgins delivered three losing teams yet was rewarded by being kicked upstairs in the organization.

This was the legacy of losing that the Red Sox carried with them on that plane back from Cleveland on July 23, 1967. This is what the '67 Red Sox so wanted to divest themselves of as they cautiously made their way through the adoring mob at Logan Airport.

RIOTS RIP DETROIT

There were mobs crowding the streets of Detroit that night, too, after the Tigers split a doubleheader with the Yankees. But these mobs had nothing to do with celebrating winning streaks or talk of pennants. They were evidence of the harsh reality that there were many people living in inner-city Detroit who didn't really care whether the Tigers were winning or losing. These crowds were the beginning of the Detroit riots.

At 3:50 A.M. on July 23, Detroit police had raided a dingy, second-floor apartment at 9215 Twelfth Street, in the heart of the city's high-crime area, and arrested more than eighty people occupying what they had determined over the preceding six weeks to be an after-hours liquor operation. As squad cars and paddy wagons paraded to and from Twelfth Street for the next hour, a crowd gathered outside the apartment. At first the crowd's involvement consisted of nothing more than an occasional verbal taunt of an officer or a wisecrack made toward an acquaintance who was being hauled off to jail.

But that drastically changed when an empty bottle was heaved out of the crowd and through the back window of a patrol car. The crowd cheered initially, then began to disperse in both directions down Twelfth Street. It wasn't long before more bottles were thrown, these smashing through storefront windows. It was 5:10 A.M. when the Detroit Police Department's 10th Precinct received its first call from the Twelfth Street neighborhood asking why so many burglar alarms were going off. Patrolmen arrived within a few minutes to discover the neighborhood looking like a war zone. Most of the storefront windows were broken, and looters were scurrying in all directions.

The violence spread across the city like a slow, rolling wave throughout Sunday. As the Tigers and Yankees split a doubleheader that afternoon, the smoke could be seen rising high in the sky even by the fans in Tiger Stadium. Most of the Tigers lived out in the suburbs, and many of them were genuinely worried for their safety when word filtered into the clubhouse of what was going on only a few blocks from the ballpark. Willie Horton, who had been reared in the streets of inner-city Detroit, told many of his white teammates that he would do whatever he could to make sure they all returned to their homes safely. Denny McLain decided he would carry a gun daily while making the twenty-five-minute trip from his home.

On a lighter note, Ernie Harwell, one of the Tigers' radio announcers, returned to his home that evening in suburban Gross Pointe to hear his wife excitedly announce she had gotten a new TV that day. This was a time when it was rare to find a department store open on a Sunday, and Harwell feared for an instant that his wife had joined the looters. She explained the TV had been won at a raffle.

The violence went on into the night. As one looter calmly assessed: "You take all you can get and get it while you can." The looting was followed by fires. By midnight, Detroit hospitals reported treating more than two hundred people for injuries related to the rioting. By 1:00 A.M. on Monday, July 24, city police had made 724 arrests. Among the looters was forty-five-year-old Walter Grzanka, who stepped out of the Temple Market at the corner of Temple and Fourth streets. But Grzanka wasn't arrested. He was shot in the chest by an unidentified gunman and died soon after at Detroit General Hospital.

After the rioting had raged on for seventeen hours, Michigan governor George Romney declared a state of emergency, just short of ordering martial law. He did order more than seven hundred National Guardsmen to restore peace to the area. A curfew of 9:00 P.M. to 5:00 A.M. would go into effect on Tuesday, July 25 in the area in which most of the violence had occurred. The disturbances didn't yet affect the Tigers because they were off Monday, with the Orioles scheduled to come into town for a three-game series Tuesday through Thursday.

The rioting escalated Monday, with President Lyndon Johnson sending in almost forty-seven hundred Army paratroopers. Much of Detroit's normal Monday business activity was canceled as looting, shooting, and fires spread out from the original beseiged area. Rumors spread that the rioters were going to take their violence out to the suburbs to get even. The Tigers' front office decided there wasn't much sense in taking chances with the volatile situation by asking fans to risk their safety in coming downtown to the ballpark. They declared their Tuesday-night game against the Orioles postponed and rescheduled for later in the season. As for the Wednesday and Thursday games, the Tigers received league permission to play those games in Baltimore on Tuesday and Thursday and shift back to Detroit two games that were regularly scheduled for play in Baltimore later in the season. By 11:30 P.M. Monday, the tolls from violence in downtown Detroit had risen to fourteen dead (all from gunfire), eight hundred injured (including thirty-two policemen and fifteen firemen), and 1,663 arrested. Federal officials were at a loss to explain the motivation for such violence. They were convinced that Detroit, of all places, had benefited from the most extensive of antipoverty programs.

The Tigers were about to board a bus Monday afternoon at Tiger Stadium to take them to the airport for their flight to Baltimore when Mickey Lolich was told he had a phone call waiting for him inside the stadium. Lolich was a member of the Michigan Air National Guard, and he had just been activated to help keep the peace in Detroit; he was ordered to report to command post at Metro Airport within three hours. Even with a pitcher who had lost seven consecutive decisions, this news was not graciously received by Tigers general manager Jim Campbell, who routinely accompanied the team on its ride to the airport to begin out-of-town trips. Likewise, Lolich's wife was equally confused when her husband walked through the front door shortly thereafter. *Honey, I'm home; get my helmet and army boots, please.* With rifle in hand, Lolich soon found himself guarding the city's utilities on eight-hour shifts over the next few days.

City officials decided at noon Tuesday to encourage a special telecast of the Tigers' game that night in Baltimore. They hoped any diversion might keep people off the streets. In keeping with the city's recent fortunes, the Tigers-Orioles game was rained out in the second inning with no score. But for all the gloom, there was one reason for Tigers fans to beam. Al Kaline, who had not played since late June, took batting practice for the first time since breaking his hand and reported no pain. He also pitched batting practice for ten minutes and subsequently declared his throwing arm fit.

Rain not only washed out the Tigers' game in Baltimore but also threatened the Twins' game that night in New York. It wasn't raining, just extremely humid and overcast, at Yankee Stadium when the game began. With Jim Kaat pitching against Al Downing, Minnesota grabbed a 1–0 lead in the first inning when Harmon Killebrew blasted a home run. Kaat carried the shutout into the bottom of the ninth with the wind picking up and bringing rain closer to the stadium. With two out, Mickey Mantle worked the count to 3 and 1. At this point in Mantle's injury-fraught career, Kaat preferred to pitch to Mantle than face the on-deck batter, Elston Howard, who represented the go-ahead run. So Kaat grooved a fastball, and Mantle launched it into the bleachers in left-center, more than 450 feet from home plate to tie the score at 1–1. Kaat did get Howard out to send the game into the tenth inning. But just then the persistent winds intervened and delivered a torrential rain. The Twins, one out away from victory, were stuck with a suspended game, which was later rescheduled to be played in its entirety on August 18.

The emotion that had gripped Boston was evidenced on the night of July 27, when the Red Sox met California at Fenway Park in the finale of a three-game series. The Angels opened the series by ending Boston's winning streak at ten games, and the Red Sox answered with a victory the next night. It appeared the Angels would leave town having won the series when they took a 5–2 lead going into the bottom of the ninth inning of the third game, but Boston rallied for three runs to send the game into extra innings. Red Sox rookie reliever Sparky Lyle, called up from Toronto in early July, held California scoreless in the top of the tenth despite allowing three hits.

In the bottom half of the inning, Reggie Smith led off with a triple off Bill Kelso. The din at Fenway Park grew as Angels reliever Minnie Rojas came on and retired Russ Gibson for the first out without allowing Smith to score. And another commotion was building to the northeast of the ballpark. A cab driver stopped in traffic just before entering the Callahan Tunnel, which links downtown Boston with Logan Airport beneath the Charles River, because he feared his car radio would lose the signal from the Red Sox's broadcast. Jerry Adair became the hero of the night—sending the Fenway crowd home happy and restoring a normal traffic flow to the Callahan Tunnel—by singling past third baseman Paul Schaal into left field to score Smith.

That same Thursday night, the Tigers managed to get in an official game for the first time since the riots had broken out in Detroit the previous Sunday. Denny McLain limited Baltimore to seven hits and no walks to shut out the Orioles, 4–0. This was McLain's second shutout of the season, his first on the road, and it lowered his earned run average to 3.56, his best mark of the season. While McLain's won-lost record was a mediocre 12–11, his ERA actually was the best among Detroit's "big four" starting staff of McLain, Earl Wilson (12–8, 3.75), Joe Sparma (10–3, 3.95), and Mickey Lolich (5–12, 4.42). What hurt McLain the most was his penchant for giving up home runs. He led the AL in gopher balls in 1966 with 42 and was well on his way to repeating as the league "champion." True to McLain's personality, though, he bore this indignity with a sense of humor. McLain said he would open a restaurant some day and call it "The Upper Deck."

THE GAMBLER

McLain's cavalier attitude masked a fierce desire to succeed, a desire that was amply fed by a talented right arm. When McLain had won twenty games in 1966 at the age of twenty-two, he was the youngest twenty-game winner in Detroit since "Schoolboy" Rowe in 1934. A native of the Chicago area, McLain had realized a dream when he signed with the White Sox for a $17,000 bonus after his senior year of high school in 1962. He received $10,000 of the bonus in cash up front and promptly went out and bought two Pontiac LeManses—a convertible for himself and a hardtop for his widowed mother.

McLain's father died when he was fifteen, leaving McLain susceptible to wayward influences. It wasn't long before the man who ran the neighborhood barbershop in his hometown of Markham, Illinois, offered young Denny a chance to earn some extra money aside from his part-time grocery job. The man, called "Poppa," gave McLain five dollars to deliver a package across town to a truck stop. The service was repeated almost daily, and it didn't take the streetwise McLain long to realize he was the delivery boy for the neighborhood numbers racket. This peripheral involvement in gambling didn't bother him. In fact, his rationale for giving up the routine almost a year later was more pragmatic than moralistic; the deliveries were interfering with his ballplaying.

The White Sox assigned him to their rookie team in Harlan, Kentucky, where McLain threw a no-hitter and was impressive enough to earn an invitation to the White Sox's major league spring camp in 1963. Chicago had two other young bonus pitchers on its roster and had room to keep only two. Commissioner Ford Frick ruled that the White Sox had to protect a left-hander who also had starred as a basketball player at the University of Detroit—Dave DeBusschere—because he had received a sizable signing bonus. That meant the remaining two youngsters, McLain and Bruce Howard, were left to duel for one roster position. Manager Al Lopez matched McLain against Howard in an intrasquad game to determine the survivor; Howard's team beat McLain's team, 1–0, and McLain was placed on waivers.

McLain was quickly claimed by the Tigers for the waiver price of $8,000. Detroit made the move on the recommendation of chief scout Ed Katalinas. He had seen McLain pitching in the Chicago farm system a few years earlier and noted that the Tigers should snap up McLain if he ever became available. McLain, though, didn't share Katalinas's enthusiasm for this transaction. He was upset at being dropped by the White Sox, his first pro team, his favorite team growing up. He boldly told his girl friend and future wife, Sharyn Boudreau, daughter of former major league player and manager Lou Boudreau, that he was quitting baseball. Sharyn spouted back that there was no room in her life for quitters. That prospect helped convince McLain that life with the Tigers might not be so bad.

He wasted little time impressing the Detroit organization. He finished 13–2 at Duluth-Superior of the Northern League, added a 5–4 record with Knoxville of the Southern League, and closed the year with a three-game stint with the Tigers that included notching 22 strikeouts in 21 innings. He began the '64 season with Syracuse of the International League but was recalled to Detroit after winning three of four decisions. Back with the Tigers, he pitched 100 innings and finished 4–5. But McLain truly began to lay the foundation for his future success by pitching that winter in Puerto Rico, where he went 12–4 with a 1.92 ERA. The following spring back with the Tigers, McLain was taught the overhand curve by veteran

Frank Lary. The immediate payoff was a 1965 record of 16–6, a 2.62 ERA, and 192 strikeouts in 264 innings. McLain's ability to dominate was displayed one day when he tied a major league record by striking out seven consecutive batters. Then came the '66 season, during which McLain made the All-Star team and won twenty games.

In Detroit, McLain almost became better known for his apparently insatiable craving for Pepsi than for his ballplaying. Ed Schober, a Pepsi vice president for marketing in Detroit, got wind of McLain's situation and signed him in 1967 to a serendipitous $15,000 contract that required McLain to merely keep doing what he already was doing—drinking Pepsi. And make a couple of public appearances on behalf of the product. But basically, the Pepsi people were perfectly willing to drive over truckload after truckload of soda to the McLains free of charge.

McLain and Schober had something else in common other than the connection with Pepsi—gambling. Football. Basketball. The horses. It was part of McLain's obsession with competition. He was often in the center of clubhouse card games, though his lack of skill led his teammates to nickname him "Dolphin" because they viewed him as being a fish out of water at the card table. Outside the stadium, McLain and Schober began betting together through Clyde Roberts, who operated about fifty miles northwest of Detroit in Flint, Michigan, out of the Shorthorn Steak House, where McLain had been booked to play the organ. One day Roberts suggested that instead of making bets, the three of them start taking bets. McLain and Schober initially rejected the idea, then decided to give bookmaking a try.

To get started, McLain got a loan of $4,500 from a friend who was a banker—and a gambler. The novice businessmen began by taking bets for a nearby race track. But business got off to a terrible start, and soon McLain was back asking for another loan. In the first two months of operation, McLain and Schober didn't have a winning week. There was a good reason for this; they were getting hustled by Roberts and his partner, Jiggs Gazell.

6

AUGUST

HOWARD'S YANKEE DAYS END

While Denny McLain was getting hustled, one of the most respected players in the major leagues—and one of the last pillars from the Yankees' glory days—was about to receive a shock as great as that McLain felt when he found out what Roberts was up to. The telephone rang at Elston Howard's home in Tenafly, New Jersey, at 9:30 A.M. on Thursday, August 3, the morning after Howard pinch hit in the Yanks' 5–4 loss at home to California. The voice on the other end belonged to general manager Ralph Houk, the longtime Yankees employee who managed the team to three consecutive pennants in 1961–63. "Ellie, I don't want to shock you," Houk said. Then he proceeded to do exactly that. Howard, the 1963 American League MVP and five-time AL All-Star, was being sent to Boston after wearing the Yankee pinstripes for thirteen seasons.

Howard's contribution to the Yankees went well beyond the MVP award and the All-Star seasons. In the years following Jackie Robinson's debut with Brooklyn in 1947, the Yankees had slowly and cautiously gone about the process of deciding who would be the Yankees' version of Robinson—the first black to play for American sport's most famous franchise. The efficiency of this talent hunt can be debated, considering the Yankees dismissed Willie Mays as a candidate. General manager George Weiss signed five black prospects to minor league contracts in the early fifties. Howard—quiet, well-mannered, the product of a solid home—was the only one of the five remaining in the organization by the spring of 1954. He became the club's first black player in 1955, though he was prohibited from staying with the rest of the team during spring training at St. Petersburg, Florida, and was told to sit out an exhibition game in Birmingham, Alabama, so the Yankees could comply with local laws that prohibited blacks and whites from playing in the same game.

Howard had expressed a desire to remain a Yankee for the rest of his playing career and beyond. Shortly after Whitey Ford left the team in early June, Howard said, "No one will have to tell me when it's time to quit, but I don't think that time has arrived yet. I just hope the Yankees find a spot for me in the organization when I have to stop playing." But he discovered on the morning of August 3 that while the Yankees wanted Howard to be part of the organization after his playing days ended, they no longer wanted him to play for the Yankees. Houk told Howard that team president Lee MacPhail, who withstood heavy criticism during the previous off-season for trading the likes of Roger Maris and Clete Boyer, had unloaded Howard for cash and a player to be named later. Boston manager Dick Williams, eager to land a veteran catcher who could guide his inexperienced pitching staff through the final stages of a pennant race, apparently had got one.

Howard, though, considered retiring from baseball. It was only at the urging of former Yankee infielder Phil Rizzuto, one of the team's broadcasters, that Howard begrudgingly accepted the move to Boston. The Yankees hastily called a news conference for that afternoon at Yankee Stadium—their game against the Angels that night was postponed by rain—and made the dramatic announcement, the latest in the purge of veterans. Houk announced that Howard was welcome to return to the organization in an unspecified capacity once his playing days were over, an announcement that came off shallow. Howard was detained by reporters for almost three hours. He pointed out that others who had served less time with the Yankees than he had been unable to fight off tears when they were banished from the team, and he vowed not to cry as he left Yankee Stadium for the last time as a Yankee. Five days later, the Yankees received pitcher Ron Klimkowski as compensation from Boston and assigned him to Syracuse.

On the day they acquired Howard, the second-place Red Sox rallied from a 3–0 deficit in the first inning to beat Kansas City, 5–3, at Fenway Park to pull within two games of the White Sox. But more significant events took place hours after the game—though no one realized it at the time—when the Athletics were flying home on TWA Flight 85, a commercial flight with stops in Baltimore and St. Louis.

Most of the Kansas City players piled into the back of the plane, where they and their fellow passengers were in for a long wait because the takeoff was delayed. The stewardesses were convinced by the players that they should go ahead and distribute the meals to the passengers, though they weren't keen on the idea. This put the stewardesses in something of a hostile mood for the remainder of the flight. Some of the players offered to help hand out the meals, which the stewardesses took as an insult.

Several of the players, including Lew Krausse and Ken Harrelson, were acquainted with the flight attendants. They played peacemakers to the point of convincing the stewardesses that leaving the drink cart with the players in the back of the plane would be more convenient for them. A's manager Alvin Dark, seated near the front of the plane, was told that there was some commotion going on with the players in the back of the plane. Dark walked back, checked out what was going on, and returned to his seat apparently satisfied there was nothing out of the ordinary worth dealing with. But the impact of Flight 85 was yet to be felt.

Another behind-the-scenes drama began to unfold on Friday, August 4, in Michigan, involving Tigers pitcher Denny McLain and his ill-fated bookmaking ventures. While McLain had eased himself out of the bookmaking business, a man named Ed Voshen plunked down $8,000 with McLain's former bookmaking partner, Ed Schober, on a horse called Williamston Kid running in the eighth race that day at Detroit Race Course. The horse won—paying $21 to win, $9 to place, and $6.20 to show—to earn Voshen a tidy $46,000. Schober claimed he did not approve the bet but was led to believe by his old pals, Clyde Roberts and Jiggs Gazell, that Voshen had so-called "friends" who would take matters into their own hands if Schober didn't pay off Voshen. Schober asked McLain for a loan, which he received, but it wasn't enough to pay off the entire bet. Schober then began receiving threatening letters and phone calls. Like Flight 85, Williamston Kid's win in the eighth race at Detroit would be worth remembering.

The Red Sox also flew out of Boston on August 3, though the details of their flight were much less provocative than those of Flight 85. What lay ahead of them was an important three-game series in Minnesota. The Red Sox were alone in second place, two games behind Chicago. The third-place Tigers were only a game behind with Minnesota and California trailing Boston by three games. The Red Sox had struggled against the Twins during the season to date, going 5–8 overall and losing four of six games at Metropolitan Stadium. The upcoming three-game set would close the Red Sox's schedule at Minnesota. The only other games between the teams were scheduled for September 30 and October 1—the final series of the season for the two teams—at Boston.

Twins fans apparently read some significance into the series. A crowd of 31,645 filled the Met for the series opener on Friday night, August 4, as Minnesota left-hander Jim Merritt improved his record to 8–3 by shutting out Boston on five hits, 3–0. The Red Sox's hitting problems continued the following afternoon when they managed only three hits off righty Dave Boswell, who pitched another complete game for a 2–1 Twins win. Having lost six of eight games at Minnesota, the Red Sox's chances of salvaging one more victory in Bloomington rested on their ability to win in the Sunday afternoon matchup of the two staff pitching aces—Boston's Jim Lonborg (15–4) and Minnesota's Dean Chance (13–8). The game was scoreless—and the Red Sox didn't have a hit—as the Twins prepared to bat in the bottom of the fourth inning. But rain then became heavy enough that Jim Odom, head of the umpiring crew, ordered the tarp placed on the field, and the game was halted for twenty-five minutes. After the delay, Lonborg continued to pitch for Boston, and Cesar Tovar gave Minnesota an immediate base runner by walking on four pitches. He stole second base, but Tony Oliva failed to advance him farther when he struck out. Harmon Killebrew followed with a single to left field, but Tovar—remember, this was the same Cesar Tovar who negated a home run hit by Oliva in April when he held up at first base—thought Boston left fielder Carl Yastrzemski might catch the ball and held up at second base. This was particularly grating to Minnesota manager Cal Ermer because the poor weather made it imperative for either team to push across a go-ahead run as soon as possible. As home team, the Twins could log a victory if they led and the Red Sox got to bat through their half of the fifth. For visiting Boston to win, the game would have to last at least a full five innings. Bob Allison provided the Twins with the necessary heroics on the next at-bat, doubling over Yaz's head to score Tovar and send Killebrew to third base. With the Red Sox forced to play their infield in, trailing by a run with only one out, Rich Rollins singled to left to score Killebrew for a 2–0 lead.

Chance set down the Red Sox in order in the top of the fifth, giving him 15 consecutive batters retired on 49 pitches. With one out and Zoilo Versalles up in the bottom of the fifth, the wind-blown rains picked up again, and Odom again called for the field to be covered. The umpires waited an hour before calling the game, which became an official victory for Minnesota and a perfect game with an asterisk for Chance. This was no big deal for a man who had pitched eighteen no-hitters in high school, including four complete games. "It was a cheapie," he admitted to reporters after the game. But he still was eager to throw a real major league no-hitter. The closest he had come was a one-hitter he threw as a rookie in 1962 with the Angels against the Twins.

Chance's abbreviated perfect game also left Boston and Minnesota virtually tied in second place. They were 2½ games behind Chicago, which was rained out Friday and Saturday at Baltimore, before losing a Sunday doubleheader to the Orioles. Detroit, which split a four-game series at Cleveland, stood fourth, three games out. California blew a great opportunity to make up some ground over the weekend when it lost two of three games at home to Washington to stand 4½ games out in fifth place.

The kind of excitement that a pennant race can produce was further revealed two days later, when the Tigers and White Sox met in a twi-night doubleheader in Detroit. A crowd of 44,295 arrived at Tiger Stadium on Tuesday afternoon, August 8, to see whether the Tigers could sweep their way to within a game of the White Sox. Chicago continued to seek more firepower even after making the trade for Ken Boyer. On July 29, the White Sox had picked up thirty-three-year-old outfielder Rocky Colavito from the Indians for outfielder Jim King and a player to be named later. Colavito's home run résumé was more impressive than Boyer's—seven seasons of 33 or more homers, including a career-high 45 in 1961 with the Tigers. But, like Boyer's, this record was more past than present. He had hit only five in sixty-three games to date with the Indians. This turn of events was crushing for King, a journeyman who labored for undistinguished teams for ten years and was finally hoping to play for a pennant winner when he left Washington for Chicago in mid-June. Informed of the trade after that day's game against the Tigers—in which his ninth-inning throwing error nearly cost Chicago the victory—he wept upon learning he was being dispatched to the also-ran Indians.

What the big Tiger Stadium crowd got for its money was twenty innings of pulsating baseball that, as critics of the doubleheader concept would be quick to point out, left both teams exactly where they stood more than six hours earlier. Denny McLain pitched one of his strongest games in the opener, limiting Chicago to four hits through ten innings. The teams headed to the tenth tied, 1–1, thanks to solo home runs by Chicago's Pete Ward in the second inning and Detroit's Al Kaline in the sixth. McLain was allowed to bat in the bottom of the tenth and responded with a single off White Sox reliever Hoyt Wilhelm, who had replaced starter Gary Peters in the eighth inning. In an odd twist of strategy, the Tigers sacrificed their pitcher over to second base—Don Wert performing the honors—to put the winning run in scoring position with one out. Dick McAuliffe walked, and Kaline singled for what appeared to be the winning hit. But McLain was thrown out at the plate, leaving McAuliffe at third and Kaline at first with two out. Willie Horton came to the plate, and Wilhelm's first pitch got away from catcher J.C. Martin for a passed ball that scored McAuliffe to win the game. The second game also went ten innings, with a fielding miscue again leading to the winning run. Chicago broke a 4–4 tie in the top of the tenth when a grounder hit by Boyer bounced off the glove of McAuliffe, who had been moved over to shortstop in the nightcap. That brought home Don Buford from second base in what became a 6–4 Chicago win.

After the White Sox and Tigers divided the four-game series, there still were only four games separating the top five teams in the league going into the weekend of August 11–13. Chicago had been in first place for more than two months. But after playing four games in Chicago, the White Sox faced a critical three-game series in Minnesota against the Twins, only 2½ games back, before returning home. In other games that weekend involving the contending teams, the Tigers (three games out) were home to play four games against the Orioles while the Red Sox (two out) and Angels (four out) were scheduled to square off in three games at Anaheim Stadium.

The weekend began poorly for Detroit when it dropped the opener of the Friday twi-nighter to Baltimore, 5–1. The prospect of earning a split appeared bleak considering the Tigers' scheduled starter, Mickey Lolich, had not recorded a victory since May. He had gone from a 5–2 record with an earned run average of 3.74 on May 19 to a 5–12 record with a 4.42 ERA going into the second game against the Orioles on August 11. Lolich's ERA over the eleven starts that produced the ten-game losing streak was an unsightly 5.09. But Lolich had plenty of "help" in going two months without a victory. For instance, the Tigers only scored 16 runs in the ten losses, only 10 of those runs coming while Lolich was still in the game. He missed almost two weeks while serving with the Michigan Air National Guard. The extent of his pitching activity while on military duty was to throw with the chaplain whenever he could.

The loss in the opener didn't cost Detroit in its chase to catch first-place Chicago because the White Sox had been beaten by Minnesota and Dean Chance, 3–2. But with the Twins, Red Sox, and Angels all establishing themselves as legitimate contenders, the Tigers could ill afford not to get some productive pitching out of Lolich. After the Tigers fell behind 1–0 in the second inning, Lolich's luck finally began to turn. The Tigers struck for three runs in the fourth inning and added another

New manager Dick Williams arrived
at spring training having proclaimed
the Red Sox, coming off a 72-90
finish, would finish above .500.
(*Boston Red Sox*)

Rookie Reggie Smith (*center*) was added to the already potent outfield of Carl Yastrzemski (*left*) and Tony
Conigliaro. (*New England Sports Museum*)

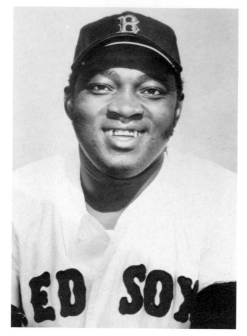

Slugging first baseman George Scott often had
problems with his weight, claiming he could add
pounds simply by looking at fattening foods.
(*Red Sox*)

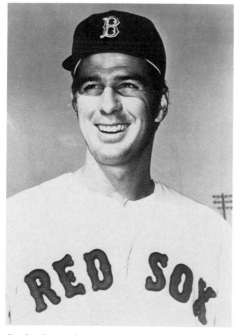

Jim Lonborg left Stanford with an eye on a medical
career only to become the Red Sox's pitching
mainstay. (*Red Sox*)

Bill Rohr had the Yankees no-hit in his major
league debut until Elston Howard's two-out single
in the ninth. (*Red Sox*)

Rico Petrocelli learned to control his often moody
behavior to become one of baseball's best
shortstops. (*Red Sox*)

Despite being a rookie, second baseman Mike
Andrews developed into one of the Red Sox's team
leaders. (*Red Sox*)

No one may have been prouder to wear a Red Sox
uniform than Russ Gibson, a New Englander who
played 10 years in the minors before reaching
Boston. (*Red Sox*)

Longtime Yankees star Elston Howard had to be
talked into reporting to the Red Sox in early
August. (*Red Sox*)

At age 22, Tony Conigliaro had become the youngest player in major league history to hit 100 career home runs. (*NESM*)

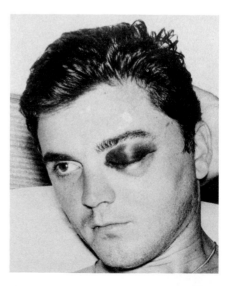

The morning after Tony Conigliaro was hit by a fastball thrown by California's Jack Hamilton. (*NESM*)

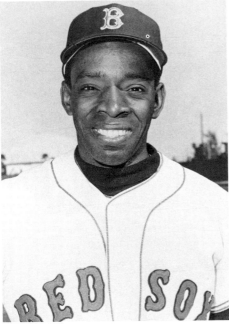

Outfielder Jose Tartabull saved a game against the White Sox in late August when he threw out Ken Berry at the plate in the ninth inning. (*Red Sox*)

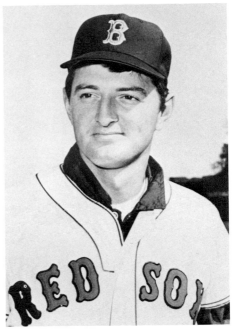

Soon after Conigliaro's injury, the Red Sox won the bidding for free-agent outfielder Ken (Hawk) Harrelson. (*Red Sox*)

When Jose Santiago got ready to pitch against the Twins on the season's final weekend, his wife provided the scouting report. (*Red Sox*)

Mayo Smith was a surprise choice to become Tigers manager, charged with taking a talented, veteran team to the top. (*Detroit Tigers*)

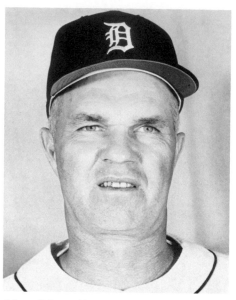

Johnny Sain was hired as Tigers pitching coach after his surprising dismissal from Minnesota after the '66 season. (*Tigers*)

An All-Star tandem poses at Fenway: Detroit's Al Kaline and Boston's Carl Yastrzemski. (*NESM*)

The biggest news from the Tigers' spring camp was the shift of All-Star shortstop Dick McAuliffe to second base. (*Tigers*)

Power-hitting Tigers outfielder Willie Horton began the season sidelined by an ankle injury. (*Tigers*)

Horton's replacement was Gates Brown, who worked his way to the majors after signing a Tigers contract while in prison. (*Tigers*)

Jovial first baseman Norm Cash had a difficult time satisfying Tigers fans after hitting .361 in 1961. (*Tigers*)

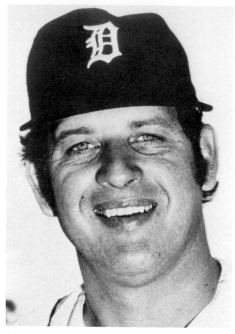

Mickey Lolich's portly build belied one of the most durable pitching arms in the majors. (*Tigers*)

Bill Freehan not only owned a potent bat but complete command of the Tigers' pitching staff. (*Tigers*)

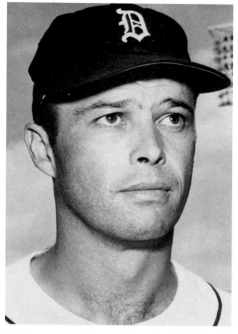

Seeking more sock down the stretch, the Tigers acquired veteran infielder Eddie Mathews in late July for a player to be named later. (*Tigers*)

Fred Gladding, baseball's most effective reliever in April, feared he would be the player to be named later—and was right. (*Tigers*)

Pitcher Denny McLain was of little use to the Tigers in September after suffering a mysterious foot injury. (*National Baseball Library*)

Eddie Stanky was confident his White Sox could contend for the pennant on pitching and defense. (*NBL*)

In April, 43-year-old Hoyt Wilhelm became the first major leaguer to record 100 career relief victories. (*NBL*)

Three reasons why the White Sox built a 5½-game lead in late June: starting pitchers (*from left*) Tommy John, Gary Peters, and Joe Horlen. (*NBL*)

Gary Peters was a better hitter than many of the White Sox's position players. (*NBL*)

Young Tommy John opened at 8-5 but only won two of his last 12 starts. (*NBL*)

Joe Horlen calmed his nerves by chewing tissue—and calmed Detroit's bats with a September no-hitter. (*NBL*)

Jim Kaat, a talented left-hander, was outspoken in his criticism of the firing of pitching coach Johnny Sain. (*Minnesota Twins*)

Winter trades allowed the Twins to anchor Harmon Killebrew, one of baseball's best power hitters, at first base. (*Twins*)

Reliever Ron Kline's disdain for Minnesota owner Calvin Griffith was so great he nearly refused to report to the Twins. (*Twins*)

Rod Carew moved all the way up from Class A ball to become Minnesota's starting second baseman. (*Twins*)

Third-base coach Billy Martin was one of Carew's biggest boosters as well as the top confidant of manager Sam Mele. (*Twins*)

Bob Allison was Killebrew's home-run hitting cohort from their days in the minors and in Washington. (*Twins*)

Al Worthington provided right-handed relief and a team conscience. (*Twins*)

Cesar Tovar could play the outfield and infield but could be a hazard on the basepaths. (*Twins*)

On June 10, Twins owner Calvin Griffith (*left*) named Cal Ermer (*right*) to replace Sam Mele as manager. (*Minnesota Historical Society*)

Jim Merritt earned a spot in the Twins' starting rotation in late May and became one of Minnesota's most dependable pitchers. (*Twins*)

Shortstop Zoilo Versalles had a difficult time recapturing his 1965 MVP form. (*Twins*)

Twins pitcher Dean Chance retired all 15
Red Sox he faced in a rain-shortened game
on August 6 to earn a tainted perfect game.
(*MHS*)

Red Sox left fielder Carl Yastrzemski plays Bob Allison's RBI double off the fence during the Twins' 2-0 win
on August 6. (*MHS*)

The Angels' Bobby Knoop avoids the slide of Minnesota's Cesar Tovar in a 9-2 California victory on September 25. (*MHS*)

Carl Yastrzemski and Red Sox owner Tom Yawkey celebrate the Tigers' 8-5 loss to California that gave Boston its first pennant in 21 years. (*The Sporting News*)

pair in the seventh; only five times in Lolich's previous eleven starts had Detroit scored as many as five runs. Lolich allowed another run but went the distance to win the five-hitter, striking out eight and walking three.

THE TWINS MOVE ON TOP

Chance's win over the White Sox that night improved his record to 15–8 and further established that Tony Oliva would have a great say in whether the AL pennant returned to Minnesota. In the Twins' victory, Oliva contributed a pair of run-scoring singles. He didn't have the home run power of a Harmon Killebrew, and his batting average was only .266, but he was the most feared hitter on the Minnesota team. A regular in the Twins' lineup beginning with the 1964 season, Oliva's career batting average in the majors stood at .310.

He had been one of twenty-one Cuban players signed by scout Joe Cambria and brought to the small Florida town of Fernandina Beach, located just north of Jacksonville, in 1961 for tryouts. Oliva's first name was Pedro, but he became known as Tony because he used his brother Tony's passport to get into the United States. He was released by the Twins after his initial tryout. But while awaiting his return to Cuba, Oliva stopped off at the Twins' affiliate at Charlotte of the Southern League and impressed manager Phil Howser enough to earn a contract. He spent the year at Wytheville of the Class A Appalachian League and hit .410 with 81 RBIs in sixty-four games.

That winter Oliva was sent to the Twins' Instructional League camp, where the law was laid down for manager Del Wilber: work on Oliva's fielding, work on Oliva's English, but don't do a thing to Oliva's swing. Oliva, now slightly more polished at fielding and ordering from a restaurant menu, continued to impress at the plate by hitting .350 for Charlotte in 1962. Once that league's season was completed, Oliva was brought up to the Twins for a quick glimpse at the end of the '62 AL season and responded with four hits in nine September at-bats. Minnesota resisted the temptation to jump Oliva over Class AAA ball straight to the majors and assigned him to Dallas–Fort Worth of the American Association in 1963. There, Oliva hit .304 and tacked onto that another successful cameo appearance with the Twins, going 3 for 7.

Minnesota was certain Oliva was ready in 1964. All Oliva did as a twenty-four-year-old rookie was lead the league in hitting at .323, runs scored at 109, and doubles with 43. He successfully defended his batting title in '65, helping Minnesota win the pennant by hitting .321, and finished second to the Orioles' Frank Robinson in hitting in 1966 at .307.

No other major leaguer had ever led the league in hitting each of his first two seasons.

Oliva was only one facet of a Minnesota attack that led the AL in hitting with a .253 average. It appeared the gamble in trading hitting for pitching had paid off. With the addition of rookie Rod Carew to Oliva, the Twins boasted two of the best pure contact hitters in baseball. Killebrew and Bob Allison provided power, and Cesar Tovar, while often an adventure in the field and on the bases, gave the Twins another valuable bat. The hitting of Carew and Tovar made up for what was proving to be a disappointing season for shortstop Zoilo Versalles. While winning the MVP award in 1965, Versalles collected 76 extra-base hits, drove home 77 runs, and hit .273. As the Twins took over first place on August 13, 1967, Versalles owned a .218 average with 20 extra-base hits. And Versalles wasn't one of those shortstops who could make up for shortcomings at the plate with stellar fielding. He led the league in errors in 1965, led the majors in '66, and was on a pace to repeat that dubious distinction again in '67.

On the mound, manager Cal Ermer and pitching coach Early Wynn had decided on a five-man starting rotation anchored by Chance, who was challenging for the league lead in victories at 15–8. Jim Kaat held his spot in the rotation despite the 1–7 start. Right-hander Dave Boswell probably was the hardest thrower on the starting staff, striking out ten or more batters five times between late May and early July in compiling a 9–8 record. Filling out the rotation were Jim Merritt, a twenty-three-year-old left-hander who began his stint in the rotation in late May by striking out 21 batters in his first two starts, and veteran Jim Perry, a thirty-year-old right-hander who had a knack for bailing out the Twins since coming over from Cleveland in May 1963.

The casualty from the four-man rotation that started the season was Mudcat Grant, a twenty-one-game winner when Minnesota won the pennant in 1965. He slipped to 13–13 in 1966 and began the '67 season by losing his first three starts. By late July his record had improved to 5–6, but his ERA still was an unacceptable 4.31. With Merritt pitching well, there was no way Grant could remain the No. 4 starter. The Twins also tried rookie Jim Ollom, a twenty-game winner at Denver in 1966. But Ollom allowed six earned runs in 6 1/3 innings of starts against Washington and Kansas City, convincing management he wasn't ready.

Minnesota had begun the year basing its bullpen hopes on a pair of veteran right-handers, thirty-eight-year-old Al Worthington and thirty-five-year-old Ron Kline. By August 13 Worthington had compiled an unusually high number of decisions for a short-relief specialist (7–7 with nine saves), but his ERA also was relatively high at 3.54. It would remain to be seen how Worthington, who had not pitched more than three innings in any game during the season, would be affected by having gone 8²/₃ innings in a twenty-inning loss to the Senators on August 9. Kline stood at a perfect 4–0 but had only three saves. He wasn't regularly asked to come in and close out a ballgame.

While Worthington and Kline did appear in the bulk of the Twins' games, it was evident Ermer was becoming less dependent on them. He was more inclined to allow his starting pitcher to go the distance; as Minnesota moved into first place, six of its last seven games were complete games, including the last four. And while it was rare for Mele, and then Ermer, to go to the bullpen in a game and not select either Worthington or Kline, those occurrences had increased in late July and the first half of August. With the Twins facing four legitimate challengers over the final six weeks, one question that begged to be answered was whether Minnesota's veteran relief tandem would wear out.

Another key question was how manager Eddie Stanky could breathe some life into the Chicago offense. In losing eight of ten games and surrenduring first place, the White Sox averaged two runs per game and only once scored more than two runs. Their .230 team batting average was the worst among the five contenders. Their attack was tailored around speed, but the latest acquisitions—veteran sluggers Boyer and Colavito—only helped to negate that advantage. Stanky was stuck in the position of trying to find ways to get Boyer and Colavito into the lineup.

THE MOLDING OF THE RED SOX

As for the Red Sox, 2¹/₂ games out following the sweep at Anaheim, Dick Williams's primary task was to prevent any sort of satisfaction with the progress to date to set in. In spring training no one had expected Boston to be anywhere near first place with six weeks to play. Doubters of Williams and the Red Sox were poised to use the words from his introductory news conference—"We'll win more games than we'll lose"—against him. To achieve Boston's first winning finish since 1958, the team needed only to go 22–27.

Williams's baseball upbringing prepared him well for facing his final forty-nine games. Like many major league managers, Williams wasn't a star player. But he had put his idle time during games to use, studying the sport constantly and soaking in baseball knowledge from all who would put up with him. Born in St. Louis in 1929, Williams became a baseball fan as soon as his father and older brother could explain the game to him. It was customary for him to race straight from school to Sportsman's Park to watch the St. Louis Browns. When his family moved to Southern California in 1942, Williams was most upset by the prospect of being separated from major league baseball by about one thousand miles. At Pasadena High School he starred in baseball and football along with another future big leaguer, Bob Lillis. Ironically, Williams lost his position as a starting halfback when he twisted an ankle while being tackled during a practice by Lillis, who then became the new starting halfback.

Tom Downing, a scout with the Brooklyn Dodgers, signed Williams immediately following his graduation ceremony at the Rose Bowl. After four seasons progressing through the minors, Williams made it to Brooklyn in 1951, hitting .200 in twenty-three games. But his primary role was to serve as manager Charlie Dressen's bench jockey, screaming whatever was necessary to distract the opposition. One of his primary rivals in this category was New York Giants second baseman Eddie Stanky, a former Dodger. Dressen, it turned out, provided the ultimate bench-jockey gaffe when he pronounced the Giants officially "dead" when Brooklyn built a 13½-game lead over New York. The Giants, of course, were far from dead, forcing a three-game playoff with the Dodgers that was won on Bobby Thomson's home run.

Williams was hitting .309 through thirty-six games in 1952, shuttling between the outfield, first base, and third base, when he broke a shoulder in St. Louis while diving for a pop fly. Typical of Williams, he completed the play by throwing the ball to the infield following the injury. He had to be helped from the field; Dressen offered only disgust that the whole procedure would slow down the game. One of those who helped carry Williams off the field was St. Louis's first-year player-manager, Eddie Stanky. Williams knew of Stanky's contempt for the Dodgers and respected the fact that he was willing to help an adversary. Williams was relegated to the disabled list for the rest of the season, watching from the press box as the Dodgers lost the World Series to the Yankees.

The shoulder healed, but Williams was never the same. The balance of his stay with the Dodgers consisted of short stints in Brooklyn and trips back to the minors. He was dealt to Baltimore in 1956 and spent the next nine years bouncing from club to club—the Orioles, the Indians, back to the Orioles, the Athletics, back to the Orioles again—before landing in Boston in December 1962. He closed his career watching many of the upcoming '67 Red Sox get their feet wet, kids like Yastrzemski and Conigliaro and Lonborg. Farm director Neil Mahoney was impressed enough with Williams's knowledge of the game and feisty personality to offer him a chance to remain in the organization as a player-coach with the Red Sox's Class AAA Seattle affiliate. Williams was told there was a good chance he would manage the club, since the franchise might be moved to Toronto, and Seattle manager Edo Vani indicated he wouldn't relocate with the club. The team did move, and Williams was named the manager of the Toronto Maple Leafs.

For all the talk of Williams being cut from the drill-sergeant mold, he also could show sensitivity when least expected. One such occurrence was when the Maple Leafs were playing in Jacksonville in 1966. Journeyman pitcher Galen Cisco had been released by the Jacksonville Suns only sixty days short of qualifying for his major league pension. Williams, familiar with Cisco from their days together playing for the Red Sox in the early sixties, called through the fence when he saw Cisco leaving the ballpark and asked what he was doing. "Looking for a job," Cisco said, then detailed his plight. "Can you pitch?" Williams asked. "No," Cisco replied, "but give me a week." Three days later, Boston signed Cisco and assigned him to Toronto. When Williams got the Red Sox job in 1967, he kept Cisco on the big-league roster but had to return him to the minors ten days short of qualifying for the pension. Williams assured Cisco he would bring him back—which he did, nine days later.

Williams also showed compassion in his handling of shortstop Rico Petrocelli, an emotional player whose responsibilities were further extended when his wife gave birth to twins during the season. Petrocelli could often be moody, but Williams didn't let that affect his handling of the talented shortstop.

Petrocelli had grown up in Brooklyn, a Yankee fan, the youngest of six boys and a girl. His father was fifty and his mother forty when he was born, meaning that he was reared more by his siblings than by his parents. He played on a sandlot team called the Cadets, which a few years earlier had boasted Frank and Joe Torre and Joe Pepitone. His brothers would take him fishing along the Jersey shore to catch flounder and bass. They also helped teach him baseball, though they usually were too busy working to help support the family to get very involved in the sport themselves. When the Petrocelli brothers went to Yankee Stadium, the team they wanted to see the Yankees face was the Red Sox. That was the team with Ted Williams, the great hitter, and Frank Malzone, the superb infielder. And it was the Red Sox who first took an interest in Rico Petrocelli, as a pitcher-outfielder. Boston scout Tom Harper summoned Bots Nekola, who had signed Carl Yastrzemski, to look at Rico. Nekola recommended the Red Sox sign Petrocelli, and they did. He was moved to third base and eventually to shortstop.

In the majors, Petrocelli often found himself drained by the energy it took to play his best. He sought outlets at home to restore his peace of mind. He turned again to fishing and also liked to play the drums, excusing himself to the basement for hours at a time to bang away. As a minor leaguer, Petrocelli established a good relationship with Eddie Popowski. It helped Petrocelli when Popowski joined the Red Sox in '67 as a coach.

While the Red Sox made a sound move by making an infielder out of Rico Petrocelli, they made an equally successful move by making an outfielder out of Reggie Smith, a castoff from the Twins. Smith had been signed as a shortstop by Minnesota in 1963. He hit .267 at Class A but committed 41 errors in 66 games. The Twins apparently found him to be too much of a defensive liability and left him unprotected for the winter draft. Boston picked him up for the $8,000 fee, decided his arm was going to waste in the infield and moved him to center field. Playing for Williams at Toronto in 1966, Smith led the International League with a .320 batting average to go with 18 home runs and 80 RBIs. While Petrocelli was described as moody, Smith could be downright hostile. In the vernacular of the day, some of his teammates considered him a militant black and tried to avoid him when possible. The fact was Smith was an intense player who preferred not to let anything—including clubhouse politics—interfere with his performance.

THE MID-MONTH SHAKEDOWN

For Boston's August 11–13 weekend near Disneyland, manager Dick Williams gave first baseman George Scott what he believed was a deserved vacation. Williams was tired of constantly fighting with Scott over his weight. So Williams decided that Scott would sit against the Angels if he weighed more than 215 pounds. He had Scott get up on the scales and trainer Buddy LeRoux performed the official weigh-in: the count came to 221 pounds. Williams started veteran Norm Siebern, a midseason acquisition, at first base. The Angels became aware of Scott's problem during batting practice and joked about taking up a collection to buy Scott a pizza. California's Jim Fregosi questioned whether the Red Sox were being run by a manager or a dietician.

Hitting was almost absent that night when the Red Sox opened the three-game series, though Scott's absence played only a small part. Jim McGlothlin limited Boston to three singles and a walk. Jimmie Hall's run in the fourth inning that scored on a wild pitch by Boston loser Lee Stange held up. The night's events left Chicago with a lead of 1 1/2 games over Minnesota, two games over Boston, 2 1/2 over Detroit, and three over California.

The five teams crowded to within two games of each other on Saturday, August 12. The Twins moved to within a half game of first place by breaking a 2–2 tie in the bottom of the eighth and striking for four runs off Gary Peters and Hoyt Wilhelm, the big blow being Bob Allison's three-run home run. The Tigers crept to 1 1/2 games out with Denny McLain winning his third consecutive game for the first time all season. The 5–4 win was McLain's fifth in his last six starts, improving his record to 15–12. With Lolich awakening from his ten-loss nightmare and McLain pitching his most consistent ball of the season, there was reason for Detroit fans to believe their Tigers stood an excellent chance to push past Chicago and Minnesota. But there were also the Red Sox and Angels to be considered, and California pitching shut down the Boston bats again with a 2–1 victory by Jack Hamilton. Boston was only percentage points ahead of California, with each team trailing Chicago by two games.

Sunday, August 13, saw the White Sox's sixty-three-day occupation of first place come to an end. Minnesota left-hander Jim Merritt stopped Chicago on seven hits for a 3–2 victory before a Metropolitan Stadium crowd of 42,418. The Twins, at 62–50, had moved into first place for the first time all season. Minnesota owner Calvin Griffith rewarded manager Cal Ermer for the achievement by extending Ermer's contract through the 1968 season. Ermer was trying to make the Twins the first team to win a pennant after changing managers during the season. And California scored its third consecutive one-run win over the Red Sox, this time by 3–2. Jim Lonborg was the loser, giving up what proved to be the winning run on a wild pitch—the second time during the season he had been beaten by the Angels by that play.

The Twins then headed to Anaheim, where the Angels were prepared for a three-game series they hoped could slingshot them all the way from fourth place to first. California's incredible three-game sweep of the Red Sox pulled the Angels within 1 1/2 games of first place. In winning seven of ten games and four straight, California rode steady pitching from starters and relievers with a couple of hot hitters. The team earned run average over the ten games was 2.60. Relief ace Minnie Rojas picked up a victory and two saves during the stretch, improving his record to 8–7 with eighteen saves. During the past five games, of which California's only loss was by 1–0 to New York, Angels pitchers had allowed four earned runs over 36 innings.

Angels fans had good reason to believe their team could continue its winning ways against the Twins. Though California was 5–7 to date against Minnesota, the Angels had won the teams' last four meetings, including three straight about a month earlier at the Big A. The pitching matchups indicated a well-fought series. In the opener, Minnesota would send Dave Boswell, 9–8 but 3–1 against California, against George Brunet, 11–13 but a winner in eight of his last ten decisions, including two over the Twins. In the second game, Minnesota would pitch Jim Perry, 4–5, who had thrown complete games in each of his last two starts, against Curt Simmons, a recent pickup from the Cubs who had shut out the Yankees on 10 hits a few days earlier in his Angels debut. The finale would be the glamour matchup, with Dean Chance, 15–8, pitching against his successor as the mainstay of the California pitching staff, Jim McGlothlin, 10–4 and 2–0 against the Twins.

More than eighty thousand fans came to Anaheim Stadium during the series. But instead of watching the Angels continue to bully their way toward the top of the AL, they saw the Twins push the Angels back toward the middle of the pack and further establish themselves as the team to beat. Minnesota swept the three games, holding their hosts to two runs over the entire series. In the opener, the Angels were betrayed by veteran shortstop Jim Fregosi. His eighth-inning error allowed the Twins to score twice after California had broken through to take a 1–0 lead in the seventh. Boswell needed ninth-inning relief help from Jim Kaat and Al Worthington to secure the 2–1 victory. The next night, Jim Perry made it three complete games in as many starts, limiting the Angels to six hits while striking out 10 in a 4–0 win. Perry survived a critical first-inning test, striking out two batters with the bases loaded. In the third and final game of the series, the Twins battered McGlothlin for five runs in the first inning as Chance coasted to a 5–1 victory.

While the Twins were building their winning streak to seven games at the expense of the Angels, Boston won two of three games at home over Detroit, and the White Sox took two of three games from last-place Kansas City. This left Minnesota with a 1½-game lead over Chicago following the games played August 17. Detroit was third, three games out; Boston trailed by 3½ and California by 4½. There was slightly more breathing room in this sardine can of a pennant race.

Boston fans followed the plight of George Scott and his expanded waistline while the Red Sox were in California. When big George stepped out on the field for the Tuesday night opener, one fan yelled, "C'mon, Twiggy!" Scott, trimmed down to 213 and in the starting lineup, answered his critics as best he could with a first-inning home run off Joe Sparma.

The Tigers salvaged the last of their three games at Boston by scoring three runs in the tenth inning. But regular third baseman Don Wert was lost for two weeks with a groin pull. Detroit general manager Jim Campbell wasted little time filling the void. A few hours after the game, he acquired thirty-five-year-old infielder Eddie Mathews, seventh on the career home runs list, from Houston for a player to be named later. To make room for Mathews on the roster, the Tigers released veteran outfielder Jim

Landis. Landis had only come to Detroit in June to help fill the void left when Al Kaline was disabled with a broken hand.

Mathews became the oldest player on the Tigers, by three months over Hank Aguirre. He had been one of the National League's most feared power hitters while playing third base during the fifties and early sixties, one of the mainstays along with Hank Aaron of the great Milwaukee Braves teams of the late fifties. This trade was no simple knee-jerk reaction to Wert's injury. Campbell had been speaking with Houston for months about obtaining Mathews. Dumped by the Braves eight months earlier, Mathews was shifted to first base by the Astros to cut down on his body's wear and tear and had hit only 10 home runs in 101 games. But Campbell figured Mathews would give the Tigers a much-needed additional right-handed bat and could play first base or third base. Even as a pinch hitter, Mathews could be valuable. Before Jerry Lumpe blooped a pinch single in that day's game against the Red Sox, Detroit pinch hitters had gone 0 for 21. And the Tigers needed all the healthy bodies they could get, facing three doubleheaders in the next four days.

At first base, Mathews could take the place of left-handed-hitting Norm Cash, who was mired in a batting slump that had Tiger Stadium crowds unleashing their annual venom on him. Over the past nineteen games, Cash was hitting .200 with only six runs batted in, three coming on home runs. With an overall average of .243, Cash was again providing baseball fans in Detroit with proof that his 1961 accomplishments— a .361 batting average, 41 home runs, and 132 runs batted in—were flukes. Since then Cash had never again hit 40 homers, never again knocked in 100 runs, and never again hit even .300. Many Tigers fans viewed this comedown as intolerable and succeeded in turn in making life intolerable for the usually light-hearted Cash. The worse a slump got, the more Cash became consumed by it, making every decision at the plate a chore. This latest struggle was compounded by the arrival of Mathews.

Cash wasn't the only Tiger infielder virtually handcuffed at the plate. Dick McAuliffe was immersed in the worst batting slump of his career (0 for 18) to drop his average to .247, Lumpe was weakened by a virus, and top reserve Dick Tracewski was hitting only .226. Despite Mathews's advanced age, the deal seemed to have no drawbacks, getting a proven hitter for nothing.

Nothing, that is, unless you were the player to be named later—later being defined as after the season. On the flight from Boston back to Detroit, Al Kaline, in the know, told some teammates that they would likely be surprised when they learned whom they had given up to get Mathews. But reliever Fred Gladding was convinced he was the player who would be leaving for Houston after the 1967 season. To have made that assumption a few months earlier would have been preposterous. Gladding had been the most effective reliever in the league and arguably one of the hottest pitchers in all of baseball. He pitched for two months before even giving up his first earned run. At the All-Star break, his earned run average still was under 2.00.

But even Gladding wasn't immune to landing in manager Mayo Smith's doghouse, that roomy structure that often contained a special wing for relief pitchers. It was Smith's contention that a manager must go with his hot hand in the bullpen, which was how Gladding got the opportunity to put together such impressive numbers early in the season. It was that same approach that knocked Gladding to the end of the bullpen line by mid-August. Ironically, Gladding that afternoon had earned the victory at Boston. That marked his first victory or save since early July. His position as the Tigers' relief stopper had been usurped by Mike Marshall, then Fred Lasher. Gladding spent much of that flight back from Boston believing he would be trying to win a pennant for a team he would be leaving that winter for Houston.

Mathews arrived in Detroit on Friday, August 18, in time to start at third base and bat sixth that night against Cleveland. He singled and knocked home a run in his first AL at-bat as Detroit scored four times in the second inning to earn a 4–0 rain-shortened victory.

THE AFTERMATH OF FLIGHT 85

That same day, a twisted drama that on the surface appeared to have no bearing on who would win the pennant began to take shape in Washington. The Athletics were there to play a three-game weekend series with the Senators in a meeting of AL also-rans. The A's came to Washington having spent the past ten days as sole residents of the AL cellar, a particularly difficult address to accept for club owner Charley Finley, who began the year fully expecting his A's to develop into a respectable ballclub.

But life with the A's meant more than losing. It was more like being trapped in a carnival fun house, unable to keep your balance as the whole world around you swayed and tumbled and spun. For A's manager Alvin Dark, August 18 began in his room at the Shoreham Hotel with his head spinning thanks to a "wake-up call" shortly before 8:00 A.M. Eastern time. It was Finley, back in his office in Chicago, and he wanted to know just what had happened on the team flight from Boston to Kansas City on August 3. Finley said he had received reports of foul language used by players, pitcher Lew Krausse in particular, and heard by the regular passengers. Dark, struggling to collect his own thoughts, told Finley he was unaware of such problems on that flight. Finley wasn't satisfied but hung up nonetheless. There apparently was no real need for Finley to go to the trouble of bothering Dark about Krausse; a few minutes later, he called Krausse directly and interrogated him about the infamous TWA Flight 85.

Things were going poorly enough for Krausse before this startling reveille. His record had dropped to 5–11, and he had been dispatched to the bullpen. He was as disoriented as Dark at the early hour, couldn't even remember the alleged incident, and denied any involvement. "You're full of shit," he yelled through the phone. "I didn't do anything on that airplane, and I'm not going to apologize to anybody." Finley then told Krausse he was fined $500 for his behavior on the flight. Krausse responded as best he knew how, by slamming down the receiver. Finley called right back and told Krausse he was suspended indefinitely from the ballclub.

Krausse then called Dark, who suggested he could straighten things out with Finley. Since receiving Finley's first inquisition about the flight, Dark had had time to question why Finley would be interested in Flight 85 and how he could possibly know what happened on it. The answer to the latter question came to Dark much easier than to the former. One of the A's radio broadcasters, Monte Moore, had turned his allegiance toward Finley and away from Dark and the players. This alignment had begun years earlier when Moore was working with a raw broadcasting partner named Lynn Ferris. Ferris admitted that his baseball knowledge was limited, certainly much less than that of an experienced announcer like Moore. But Ferris remained confident and open, asked the players for their help, and grew to become close friends with many of the A's. Even Dark did his part, disclosing the third-base coach's signs to Ferris so he could sit in the broadcast booth and know what the A's were going to do at bat. There were occasions when Ferris told listeners to expect something to happen and Moore would downplay Ferris's comments—only to see the exact circumstance Ferris described occur. Moore eventually guessed that there was something of an in-house conspiracy against him and decided to align with Finley. Dark figured it was Moore who told Finley what happened on the plane. Dark told Krausse to return to Kansas City anyway, as per Finley's directive. But not only could Dark not improve Krausse's plight, he also began to worsen his own by refusing Finley's order to implement the suspension immediately. In a huff, Finley proceeded to fly to Washington to deal with Dark himself.

That afternoon in the visitors' clubhouse before Kansas City's game with Washington, the Kansas City players learned of Krausse's suspension. Many believed it to be linked to that June night when he unknowingly shot into the Phillips Petroleum building. Jack Aker, the team's player representative, also learned that a memo from Finley was going to be posted. The message would announce not only Krausse's transgressions and subsequent penalties but that the players no longer would be allowed to drink alcohol on team flights. More bothersome to Aker was the fact that this memo would be circulated among the media, a rare airing of a club's dirty laundry that wasn't often seen in baseball. Aker called Finley and asked him not to release the memo to the reporters, telling him that the players would accept the new restrictions—though they didn't agree with them—under the condition that Finley not circulate the memo among the media. Too late, Finley told him. He already had sent a copy to the major wire services.

Finley required Dark to read a copy of the statement to the players that night before the game, a real morale booster:

> Effective immediately and for the balance of the season all alcoholic drinks no longer will be served on commercial airlines to members of the Kansas City Athletics. The Kansas City Athletics no longer will tolerate the "shenanigans" of a very few individuals who obviously do not appreciate the privilege of playing in the major leagues and being treated as gentlemen. The attitude, actions, and words of some of you have been deplorable. As a member of organized baseball, you have certain responsibilities and obligations to yourself, your family, your club, and most important of all—the fans.

These words had an absurd ring to them, as if lifted from some Lewis Carroll fantasy. The same Charles O. Finley who once rebuilt his right-field wall to a distance of 296 feet simply to mock the irregular dimensions of Yankee Stadium was berating his players for not upholding the integrity of baseball. The same man who had concentrated many of his efforts on trying to evacuate Kansas City was chastising his players for not thinking of the fans:

> To the vast majority of you who have always conducted yourselves as gentlemen on and off the playing field, I sincerely regret the necessity of this action.

Krausse told reporters before leaving for Kansas City: "I think it is an unfair ban because it was too strict for such a minute incident. The noise didn't last long, and I didn't think there was any rowdyism. He [Finley] put the blame on me because the team is not going good and I'm not having a good year." The battle had just begun. The players then decided to meet Saturday to draft a statement of their own for the media, condemning Finley's actions and defending Krausse. Such problems as the misinterpretation of what happended on Flight 85, the players said, wouldn't occur if Finley would properly delegate authority.

That night the Twins and Yankees were scheduled to replay the 1–1 suspended game from July 25 in which Mickey Mantle had tied the score with a two-out home run in the bottom of the ninth inning. Jim Kaat, who had pitched the original game for the Twins, started the makeup against Steve Barber. Singles in the bottom of the first by Horace Clarke, Tom Tresh, and Joe Pepitone gave New York a 1–0 lead. In a game that was strikingly similar to its predecessor, Barber blanked Minnesota, 1–0. For the two games, Kaat had pitched 17 innings against the Yankees, given up two runs, and earned only a loss.

THE FALL OF TONY C

The Angels had come to Boston thinking not about their three-game sweep of the Red Sox at home a week earlier but of their more recent three-game collapse against the Twins. Coming into the four-game set beginning August 18, California had won only once in five games at Fenway Park. The series would begin an eleven-game roadtrip for the Angels, continuing through Cleveland and Baltimore.

The Angels' starter in the opening game was right-hander Jack Hamilton, who had proved to be a valuable addition. Acquired from the Mets in mid-June when California was fighting to stay out of the cellar, Hamilton had compiled a 6–2 record with a 2.34 ERA. His achievements weren't without incident; most managers of opposing AL teams insisted Hamilton's best pitch was the spitball.

Spitball or not, Hamilton cruised through the first three innings that night at Fenway without allowing a run. Likewise, Red Sox right-hander Gary Bell kept California scoreless through four innings. Before Hamilton was able to open the bottom of the fourth inning against Tony Conigliaro, the game was held up for about ten minutes when a fan tossed a smoke bomb into left field. Conigliaro waited at the plate, wondering if the delay might cause Hamilton's pitching arm to stiffen. An aggressive hitter, Conigliaro had told his brother Billy before the game that he planned to inch even closer to the plate than usual in an attempt to break out of a batting slump. He entered the game with only one hit in his last 20 at-bats since August 8, dropping his average from .299 to .286. Even with the slump, Conigliaro ranked eighth in the league batting, fifth in home runs with 20, and fifth in RBIs with 67.

Of course, it was an accepted part of pitching at Fenway to keep the ball inside to a right-handed batter, not allowing him to extend his arms to launch the ball over the Green Monster and into the inviting screen that guarded Lansdowne Street. The inside pitch likely would be pulled foul harmlessly and could then set up a pitch low and outside.

Conigliaro had singled in the first inning off a curveball. When Tony C stepped to the plate in the fourth, Angels catcher Buck Rodgers called for a fastball inside. Not a knock-down pitch. Not a purpose pitch. Certainly not a spitter. A fastball, high and tight. As soon as the ball left Hamilton's hand, California second baseman Bobby Knoop thought it would strike Conigliaro. Rodgers watched the pitch come in, maybe an inch or two off the inside of the plate. But Conigliaro was practically standing on the plate and didn't have time to get out of the way. He tried at the last second to avoid the ball, tossing his hands into the air.

The pitch struck Conigliaro flush on the left side of the face. In a ballpark filled with thirty-one thousand people, the sound of the ball striking Conigliaro's head could be heard by Rick Reichardt in left field. Rodgers thought the impact sounded like a bat striking a pumpkin. He was surprised that Conigliaro had not gotten out of the way. Dozens of times Conigliaro had faced pitches thrown farther inside, Rodgers thought, yet always managed to jerk his head out of the way in time. The impact was so great that Conigliaro thought for a split second the ball might just go right through his head. He fell to the ground, never losing consciousness, rolling and grabbing his head in an attempt to ease the excruciating pain.

Manager Dick Williams was the first person to reach Conigliaro, followed shortly by Rico Petrocelli, who raced from Boston's on-deck circle. The first thing that Thomas Tierney, the Red Sox's team doctor, noticed when he arrived at the plate was a hissing sound coming from Conigliaro's head. Rodgers could see Conigliaro bleeding from his left eye and his mouth. Hamilton, who had hit only one other batter all season, made his way slowly toward the plate, but Rodgers sent him back to the mound. "Get away," Rodgers told him. "You don't want to see that." Petrocelli tried to console Conigliaro, assuring him that everything was going to be all right. Actually, Conigliaro was afraid he was going to die, that the swelling that was beginning in his mouth would cut off his breathing. The next voice Conigliaro heard was that of Red Sox trainer Buddy LeRoux, telling him to lie still until he could be carried off the field on a stretcher. LeRoux, Fred Fredrico, catcher Mike Ryan, and pitcher Jim Lonborg carried Conigliaro down through the dugout into the Boston clubhouse, where they were rejoined by Dr. Tierney. Conigliaro became more anxious when Tierney didn't have anything to say immediately. It took a few innings before Conigliaro was taken to Sancta Maria Hospital in nearby Cambridge, and various Boston players and coaches ducked back into the clubhouse to check on Conigliaro.

Even in his state of intense pain and incredible concern, it wasn't lost on Conigliaro that conspicuously absent from this parade of well-wishers was Dick Williams.

A few minutes later the immediate Conigliaro family—his mother, Teresa, father, Sal, and brothers Billy and Richie—arrived in the club-house. As big a hero as Tony Conigliaro had become across New England, he was an even larger figure to his younger brothers. Richie couldn't control his emotions and soon ran off to a remote corner of the clubhouse to cry so that Tony wouldn't hear him.

The ambulance ride to Sancta Maria took fifteen minutes. With every turn, Conigliaro's pain grew worse. By the time he reached the hospital, word of the beaning had filtered across the city. Barbara Belkin and Lorraine DiLuzio, out for their Friday-night bowling, were among the Conigliaro fans who dropped what they were doing and drove to Sancta Maria. Conigliaro arrived, and the pain soon grew even more intense—which hadn't seemed possible a few minutes earlier—when his head had to be turned constantly for X rays. Soon after, he was moved upstairs to a private room, where the family eventually left Conigliaro alone as he tried to drift off to sleep. As his family left the room, Conigliaro did not feel certain that he would live to see them again.

Games go on even after such a disquieting turn of events. José Tartabull went in to run for Conigliaro and was tripled home by Petrocelli. The Red Sox scored again in the inning and went on to win, 3–2, to hand the Angels their fourth consecutive loss. Hamilton was lifted after five innings and took the loss. After the game, he tried to calmly explain to reporters that he'd hit Conigliaro in the head unintentionally. "I certainly wasn't throwing at him," he said. "I was just trying to get the ball over. Tony stands right on top of the plate." Angels manager Bill Rigney phoned Williams from his office to express his concern.

On Saturday morning, August 19, sleep for Tony Conigliaro came in short bursts, interrupted by intense pain or a doting nurse. As Conigliaro awoke fully for the first time that morning, someone was holding his hand. It was Tom Yawkey. Some could criticize Yawkey for being "soft" toward his players, but it meant something to Conigliaro to awaken and find the team owner next to his hospital bed. Mike Ryan visited that day, and so did George Scott and Rico Petrocelli and team photographer Jerry Buckley. Jack Hamilton also went to Sancta Maria but was not allowed to visit Conigliaro.

The Red Sox went through the technicality of placing Conigliaro on the disabled list, and opinions varied on whether Tony C would be able to play again during the season. Boston signed Jim Landis, the veteran who was let go by Detroit in July after Al Kaline returned from the disabled list, to fill Conigliaro's spot on the roster. Dick Williams used José Tartabull as his new starting right fielder and leadoff hitter. That afternoon, Tartabull went 0 for 4, but the Red Sox didn't need his bat. With 17 hits, including a 4-for-5 day from Carl Yastrzemski, Boston survived a four-run ninth inning from the Angels to win, 12–11. The Twins shut out the Yankees, 3–0, on a three-hitter by Dave Boswell, while the Tigers were blanked by John O'Donoghue and the Indians, 5–0. With the White Sox getting rained out at home against the Orioles, the day's play left Minnesota with a two-game lead over Chicago, three games over Boston, 3½ over Detroit, and six over sagging California, which had lost five straight.

FINLEY FIRES DARK

The Athletics' 5–1 victory over the Senators that afternoon was only the warmup act to the Kansas City players' response to Finley's drastic actions of the previous day. They met for ten minutes after the game, a meeting that excluded manager Alvin Dark and his coaches. Afterward, Jack Aker released a statement to the press and declined to elaborate. The statement accused Finley of blowing out of proportion the August 3 flight. It also referred specifically to "go-betweens" that undermined the team's morale, stating that Finley should leave the running of the A's to "his fine coaching staff and excellent manager."

At about 7:00 P.M. Finley, still enraged and embarrassed over Dark's refusal to suspend Krausse but unaware of the players' response, summoned Dark to his hotel room and told him he would be fired for insubordination. Dark didn't put up a fight, though he genuinely wanted to remain with the players, and instead accepted his fate and calmly pointed out to Finley what a good ballclub the A's would have within a few years. Dark and Finley discussed prospects like Reggie Jackson and Sal Bando—who might help make the A's a pennant contender. This musing not only led Finley to rescind his own firing order but to offer Dark a two-year contract extention through the 1969 season.

Only in the carnival that was the Kansas City Athletics could a man sit out his own firing long enough to come away with a contract extension. And only in this atmosphere could that contract extension be blown away within a matter of hours. The catalyst of this reversal was a Kansas City sportswriter named Paul O'Boynick, who arrived at Finley's room that night with a copy of the players' statement. That was the first time either Finley or Dark was aware of such a statement, though Dark knew of the players' general intentions. Finley told O'Boynick he had been prepared to sign Dark for another two years. "But now I'm compelled to withhold the announcement until further consideration," Finley added. Dark, realizing another tempest was about to blow, told O'Boynick he wished the writer had shown him the statement back at the clubhouse.

With Saturday having turned into Sunday, Finley held another summit at 2:30 A.M. The roll call for this session included Dark, coaches Bob Hofman and Wes Stock, administrative assistant Eddie Lopat, road secretary Ed Hurley, broadcaster Monte Moore, and Jack Aker. But when word was left for Aker, he was gone, having left to spend the evening with a friend in Baltimore. Aker arrived back at the Shoreham about 3:30 A.M., received the message, and called Finley to discover the meeting still going. Aker dutifully reported—as dutifully as a ballplayer could, having missed curfew by a couple of hours. The summit broke up at 4:30. An hour later Finley called Dark to tell him he was fired for the second time in a matter of hours. For the A's, baseball history always acquired a touch of the bizarre.

Luke Appling was spending the early-morning hours on Sunday, August 20, in a more routine fashion. An A's scout, Appling was driving along a dusty North Carolina road. He had no idea he had just been selected as the seventh man to manage Charlie Finley's team in seven seasons. The players learned of Dark's dismissal as they arrived back at rainy D.C. Stadium that afternoon for their scheduled game against the Senators. Dark arrived at the ballpark and said goodbye tearfully: "I'm not upset at being fired. That's part of baseball. I hate to leave you kids." Dark was unable to continue, tears running down his face.

Upon his arrival, Appling only made a bad situation worse by trying to make an immediate impression on the emotionally wrought players. He came across as a hard-liner, the antithesis of Dark's style. This was the last thing most of the players, knocked off balance by this latest bolt of turmoil, wanted. Some of them were so disgusted they got up and left during Appling's introductory speech. Afterward, the players drafted yet another statement, this one accepting full responsibility for Dark's firing. Rain forced the postponement of Sunday's game, and the players were left to lament Dark's dismissal with the assembled sportswriters before catching a bus for Baltimore. Pitcher Jim Nash: "Dark was more than a manager. He was our leader." First baseman–outfielder Mike Hershberger: "I didn't want to see Dark get fired. I feel that Finley was wrong." Second baseman Dick Green: "There cannot be a better manager in the game." First baseman–outfielder Ken Harrelson: "I think it's a shame. Finley made a big mistake. He's bad for baseball."

Road roommates Harrelson and Hershberger, too tired to eat out that night after the team reached Baltimore, had a couple of sandwiches sent up to their room as they watched TV. One of the local sportscasters, referring to a wire-service report on the A's reaction to Dark's firing, quoted Harrelson as calling Finley a "menace" to baseball. Hershberger guffawed at the report, but Harrelson was genuinely disturbed. He realized that what he had said about Finley that afternoon was hardly flattering, but he insisted he hadn't specifically used the word *menace* to describe Finley. Harrelson went to sleep that night wondering how Finley would react to what he technically considered a misquote.

That afternoon at Yankee Stadium, New York pitcher Mel Stottlemyre made a couple of mistakes throwing to Minnesota's Tony Oliva. But even a pair of home runs by Oliva wasn't enough to prevent the Yankees from knocking around five Minnesota pitchers for 12 hits in a 7–3 victory. What made things even worse for the front-running Twins was that their three closest pursuers not only won Sunday, but they each won twice. The White Sox swept the Orioles with, as usual, a minimum of hitting, 4–2 and 2–1. In the nightcap, Chicago left-hander Tommy John was staked to a two-run lead in the first inning while making his first start since coming off the disabled list. But John had to leave one out short of qualifying for the victory, and Don McMahon held Baltimore to one hit over the final 4 1/3 innings to earn the victory. There were similar pitching heroics in the second game of Detroit's sweep of Cleveland. Rookie John Hiller was making his first start following eleven relief appearances and limited the Indians to four hits to win, 4–0.

But for all the second-game splendor provided by the White Sox and the Tigers, the Red Sox weren't outdone. Their opening victory over California was, for practical purposes, settled in the first inning. Boston racked Angels starter George Brunet for five runs and went on to win, 12–2. California responded in the second game by knocking out Red Sox starter Dave Morehead with a six-run second inning and built an 8–0 lead going to the bottom of the fourth inning. The Red Sox began to chip away, with a solo homer by Reggie Smith in the fourth, a three-run homer by Carl Yastrzemski in the fifth, and a four-run seventh to tie the score, 8–8. In the eighth inning Jerry Adair, acquired in the name of defense and versatility, connected off Minnie Rojas for only his second home run of the season to give the Red Sox an incredible 9–8 triumph. Adair's dramatic home run capped a seven-homer, 21–run day for the Red Sox.

With six weeks to play, Minnesota led Chicago by a half game, Boston by 1 1/2, and Detroit by two. The race realistically was reduced to four teams. The Angels had run aground with a record of 62–60 thanks to a seven-game losing streak. While California's breakdown was caused by many phases of the game, the fingerprints of the pitching staff could be found all over the losing streak. Angels pitchers had allowed 47 runs on 72 hits.

There was no disgrace for the Angels in falling out of the race. Of the four major league expansion teams formed in the early sixties, only the Angels had produced a winning season. The Senators, Astros, and Mets would have been ecstatic to be on the far side of .500 this late into a season. Much of the credit for California's accomplishment was tied to the front office's decision to stick with Bill Rigney as manager since the Angels first took the field in Los Angeles in 1961.

Rigney had signed on with the original Angels after being let go by the San Francisco Giants. He had managed the Giants during the difficult transition period when the club moved from New York to California after the 1957 season. While the Dodgers enjoyed almost immediate success in Los Angeles, Rigney and the Giants could do no better than third-place finishes in '58 and '59. The Giants were showing improvement in 1960—33–25—when Rigney was fired.

Ironically, Rigney's next managerial assignment brought him across town from the team that had forced him out of San Francisco—the Dodgers. But he wasn't expected to produce a winner overnight in Los Angeles with an expansion team. When Rigney's '62 Angels finished third behind the Yankees and Twins, they almost drew more attention than the Giants did that year by winning the NL pennant under Alvin Dark.

Angels management did a superb job of matching what veteran talent was available with youngsters that they developed in their own fledgling farm system. Among the best choices made in the initial expansion draft was an eighteen-year-old shortstop out of the Red Sox's organization named Jim Fregosi. Originally headed to the Naval Academy to play halfback, Fregosi impressed baseball scouts enough while playing semipro baseball around the San Francisco Bay Area to sign a contract with Boston. He hit .267 playing with Alpine before being selected by the Angels in December 1960. Fregosi was sent to Dallas–Fort Worth of the American Association, where he met up with catcher Buck Rodgers, who was drafted out of the Tigers' organization. Three young prospects picked up in the expansion draft—Fregosi, Rodgers, and Dean Chance from Baltimore—formed the nucleus of the early Angels teams. After the 1963 season, another savvy draft pick brought in second baseman Bobby Knoop, who had labored for eight years in the Milwaukee Braves' minor league system. He was an AL All-Star within three years of joining the Angels.

But it was how Angels management responded when the team digressed—two losing finishes over the next three seasons—that helped shape the franchise's stable future. There was no calling for Rigney's head. Instead, the Angels continued to build from within, maintaining confidence in talented youngsters like Fregosi and Knoop. Through it all, Rigney remained a "player's manager." He was never hung up on swaggering through the clubhouse, proving he was the man in control. On the contrary, it often bothered Rigney to see players fail. He would try to change his managerial approach to suit a certain player. He appreciated the effort that his regulars gave him and expressed that by not berating them when they didn't produce. But in not hovering over players, he also expected them to be mature enough to prepare themselves to play.

In the case of Rodgers, Rigney stuck with a young player through a horrific time on the field. Rodgers had spent five years in Detroit's minor league system and didn't hold much hope of making it to the big club when the Tigers signed a hotshot catcher from the University of Michigan named Bill Freehan. The expansion draft gave his career new life, and Rodgers began the '62 season as the Angels' starting catcher. He began his first full season in the majors by going 0 for 25, finally breaking through with a hit, then working his way to 1 for 44. Each day, Rodgers expected to hear that he was being returned to Class AAA. But the Angels, in only their second season, were winning. And Rigney knew Rodgers was doing an excellent job handling the team's pitching staff. He told Rodgers not to worry about his hitting or, more important, his job. Rigney's approach paid off. Rodgers finished the year hitting .258 and was considered one of the top rookies in the league that year.

On the technical side, Rigney employed a strategy that would become popular in the seventies—situational pitching. But he did this more out of necessity than genius. The bullpen of the early Angels didn't feature much quality. So Rigney made do with quantity. Left-hander Jack Spring, for instance, could blow a ball past a left-handed power hitter . . . and not much else. So that's what Rigney used him for. Art Fowler, Ryne Duren, and Minnie Rojas all contributed to Rigney's bullpen-by-committee.

With a 62–60 record on August 20, California would probably have needed to win at least thirty of the remaining forty games to have any kind of chance to win the pennant. More realistic goals needed to be pursued. The Angels needed to win nineteen of their remaining forty games to show an improvement over the 1966 season. A 25–15 finish would produce the best record in team history. But it wouldn't be easy, with the Angels playing only fifteen of the forty games at home. And the Angels had completed their scheduled games against only one of the four contenders, the Red Sox. But Rigney saw the difficult schedule as a challenge, not an obstacle. If realistically eliminated from pennant contention, Rigney treasured the chance to at least have a say in who would win it.

FINLEY FIRES HARRELSON

On Monday, August 21, the Athletics awoke in Baltimore, in advance of a four-game series with the Orioles. Some of the A's awoke earlier than others. A startling telephone call arrived along with the early-morning sun in the room shared by Mike Hershberger and Ken Harrelson. Hershberger let Harrelson answer it, thereby relinquishing an active part in what was about to become baseball history. This was another reveille phone call courtesy of A's owner Charlie Finley, who had used the same forum a few days earlier to suspend pitcher Lew Krausse and throw an already frenetic team into further turmoil.

Finley was still in Washington. Earlier that morning his interest had been piqued by a newspaper quote that credited Harrelson with describing him as a "menace." That seemed as good a reason as any to call Harrelson. The subsequent twenty-minute conversation boiled down to Finley demanding an explanation for being called a menace and Harrelson denying the quote—though he did acknowledge he said Finley was "bad for baseball." The call ended with both sides having spoken their piece. Finley called back a few minutes later and calmly said, "As of this moment, you are unconditionally released from the Kansas City Athletics."

With that, free agency arrived in major league baseball. Harrelson actually had to wait four days before officially becoming a free agent. This was a drastic action taken by Finley, and not just in the fact that he had made Harrelson an unemployed ballplayer. He could have simply suspended Harrelson, made him sweat for a while before returning him to the roster. Or Finley could have traded him and gotten something in return. But in his rage, Finley just cut Harrelson loose. Fired him.

All this was enough to make Hershberger sit up in bed. Harrelson thought Finley might be bluffing and called the major league offices in New York to find out if his release was official. It was. Harrelson's first reaction was panic; he was a man without a team—more important, a man without a paycheck. Hershberger, gainfully employed, was able to view his roomie's situation with a little more vision and as a fabulous opportunity. Relax, he told Harrelson, you're a free man, free to sign with any other team. Sure enough, before Harrelson could call his wife in Kansas City to tell her the news, the phone rang. It was Ed Short, the general manager of the White Sox, wanting to know if Harrelson would sign with Chicago for $100,000, a figure earned by only a handful of players at the time. Harrelson was tempted to accept immediately but instead told Short it was far too early to decide anything. The morning wore on, and the calls kept coming. The Red Sox. The Tigers. Other teams, from both leagues. It seemed as if just about every team in baseball was interested in signing a right-handed .274 hitter with decent power.

Harrelson arranged to meet with Boston vice president Haywood Sullivan that night at the airport in Baltimore, though Harrelson wasn't scheduled to leave town until the next day. He made his way to Memorial Stadium that afternoon to clear out his gear and say goodbye to his former Kansas City teammates. The scene resembled one of those Grade B movies, when the convict finally gets out of the big house, receiving hearty slaps on the back from the prisoners he leaves behind. Most of the A's were sorry to lose Harrelson as a ballplayer but glad for him, even jealous. The posturing for Harrelson's services even continued at the ballpark. He was stopped and quizzed by Frank Skaff, a scout for the Tigers. While in the clubhouse, he received a call from Orioles general manager Harry Dalton. But except for Short, no one was ready to make a firm offer.

That night the Red Sox extended their winning streak to five games when Elston Howard ended an 0-for-9 slump, since joining Boston, with an RBI single in the bottom of the ninth inning to beat Washington, 6–5. With the White Sox edging the Yankees, 4–3, and the Tigers and the Twins taking the night off, Chicago and Minnesota were tied for the league lead with Boston a game out and Detroit two out. The other significant numbers of the evening were spoken at the dinner between Harrelson and Sullivan, at which Sullivan offered the "Hawk" a package worth about $88,000. Sullivan wanted Harrelson to verbally commit, though he couldn't yet officially sign. But Harrelson said he wanted to talk more with other teams.

On Tuesday, August 22, as Harrelson was making his way back to Kansas City, another player was on his way back to Baltimore to return to the A's. Finley had decided to reinstate Lew Krausse, though Krausse was on a golf course at the time the grand pronouncement was made. Because he got the word late, he was unable to reach Baltimore until the second game of Kansas City's doubleheader that night against the Orioles. Harrelson returned home to discover messages waiting for him from the Yankees' Lee MacPhail and the Atlanta Braves' Paul Richards. Harrelson found the latter message more intriguing. The Harrelsons were from Georgia, and Richards was a longtime friend. Harrelson was unable to reach Richards that night but decided he probably would sign with the Braves as long the offer was competitive. On the field that day, Boston extended its winning streak to seven games with a sweep of the Senators. The highlight of the doubleheader came when George Scott scored on a sacrifice fly but then was called out for leaving third base too soon. As upsetting as this was to Scott, manager Dick Williams, and the rest of the Boston team, it apparently was more than Red Sox fan Duncan MacKenzie could stand. MacKenzie, from Dorchester, Massachusetts, raced out of the Fenway Park stands and onto the field to argue the call. This display of loyalty earned him a future date in Roxbury

District Court after his wife, Bonnie, handed over seven dollars to bail him out of jail.

At Tiger Stadium, a crowd of more than forty thousand watched the Tigers take two from Minnesota, winning the nightcap, 2–1, in eleven innings on a wild pitch by Al Worthington. The win was the first in the majors for sidearming reliever Fred Lasher, whom the Tigers had brought up from Toledo on August 10. At age twenty-six, Lasher was succeeding in resurrecting a baseball career he had feared had been buried in his early days in the Minnesota organization. He had signed with the Twins in 1960 and was sent from the lower minors straight to the big club for a look toward the end of the '63 season. Lasher pitched 11 innings in eleven games without earning a decision. He began the '64 season with Class AAA Atlanta and got off to a rocky start. He was clobbered for 11 earned runs in seven innings over six games. The Minnesota organization wasted little time dropping him to Charlotte and all the way to Bismarck-Mandan of the Class A Northwest League before the season was out. He pitched at Wilson of the Class A Carolina League in '65 and '66, going 5–5 and 6–10 with earned run averages of 1.94 and 2.15 as the team's main reliever. But Lasher was denied promotion, informed by the Minnesota organization that he wasn't ready to go beyond Class A. He was drafted that winter by the Tigers, a move that moved his wife, Judy, to tears of joy. Starting out 1967 at Montgomery of the Southern League, Lasher went 8–1 with an 0.68 ERA in 53 innings. The Tigers couldn't get him in—and out—of Toledo fast enough. At Toledo he struck out 17 batters in 17 innings, going 2–1 with an 0.53 ERA in nine games before he was summoned to Detroit. Here it was, almost four years since Fred Lasher had made his major league debut with Minnesota, and he'd finally earned his first big-league victory, beating the Twins.

With the White Sox splitting a pair at home against the Yankees, the AL race had reached a milestone—four teams within one game of the top:

TEAM	W-L	PCT.	GB
Chicago	68 53	.562	—
Boston	69–54	.561	—
Minnesota	67–54	.554	1
Detroit	68–55	.553	1

On Wednesday, August 23, Red Sox team physician Thomas Tierney said he believed Tony Conigliaro would be back playing before the end of the season. That same day, Paul Richards made Ken Harrelson an official offer—$112,000—and Harrelson told him he would get back to him. He phoned Sullivan in Boston to break the news that he planned to sign with another club, which Harrelson didn't identify. Sullivan was prepared to top the offer, but Harrelson insisted he wasn't out to pit one club against another. When Sullivan got Harrelson to at least admit the team was in the National League, and no threat to the Red Sox, he accepted Harrelson's decision. Harrelson then called Richards back and accepted the Atlanta offer.

That night Harrelson and his wife were getting ready to go out to watch the Kansas City Chiefs play the Chicago Bears in an exhibition football game when the phone rang. It was Red Sox general manager Dick O'Connell, and he wasn't prepared to accept Harrelson's refusal. O'Connell asked Harrelson what it would take for him to come to Boston. Harrelson didn't believe that anyone would pay him more than the $112,000 offered by Atlanta and almost flippantly put out the figure $150,000. "You got it," O'Connell replied. Harrelson accepted and decided he would consider no further offers. He then faced the awkward task of calling Richards again to tell him he planned to sign with Boston for $150,000. Richards could offer no more. The Braves were in fifth place in the National League, 12½ games behind first-place St. Louis, and certainly not in a position to make a hasty decision. Harrelson took a plane to Boston on Thursday, August 24, the same day Conigliaro was released from Sancta Maria, and was introduced as a member of the Red Sox the following day. The team announced that Harrelson would not be placed on the active roster until the following week, when the Red Sox were in New York. On the day Harrelson headed to Boston, the Twins and Tigers were ending a crucial five-game series at Detroit. The Tigers swept the first three games, only to have the Twins avoid disaster by winning the last two.

Conigliaro had tried to remain hopeful about returning to play again during the season. But that optimism quickly faded when his final eye tests at the hospital revealed that the vision in his left eye, tested at 20/15 before the accident, was 20/80. Tony C returned to his parents' home in suburban Swampscott, Massachusetts, for two weeks of relaxation. But he encountered further frustration when he was forced to quit games of catch or pepper with his brothers because he couldn't see the ball adequately. Further testing of the damaged eye by Dr. Charlie Regan from an eye-specialist group called Retina Association concluded that Conigliaro had developed a blind spot in the eye because of a cyst that had formed in the middle of the retina. Dr. Regan said he couldn't yet determine if this would affect Conigliaro's long-term baseball future.

WHO'S IN FIRST?

With the conclusion of the Detroit-Minnesota series, the focus of the pennant race shifted to Chicago and a five-game series played over three days between the first-place White Sox and the second-place Red Sox. Boston came to town trailing the White Sox by only percentage points. Pitching matchups appeared to favor the Red Sox coming away with at least three victories. Chicago lefty Tommy John, 8–8 with an ERA that had been under 2.50 since early June, was dropped from the rotation. White Sox manager Eddie Stanky elected to start lefty Gary Peters (14–6) twice during the five games, in the series opener against Boston ace Jim Lonborg (16–6) and in the finale against José Santiago (7–4). In the second game of the opening doubleheader on Friday, August 25, Stanky would provide twenty-six-year-old Francisco Carlos with his major league debut. And the White Sox would rely on another relatively unproven commodity in the first game on Sunday, August 27, in Fred Klagas (2–2).

The first doubleheader was a split. Lonborg had a shutout bid spoiled in the ninth inning thanks to a home run by Pete Ward but controlled the White Sox, 7–1. Carlos was the surprise hero in the nightcap, blanking the Red Sox on four hits through 6⅓ innings. He left the game with a 1–0 lead but lost his chance at a victory when Boston pushed across a run in the top of the eighth off reliever Bob Locker. Ken Berry, whose fifth-inning homer had given Carlos the one-run lead, singled home Sandy Alomar in the bottom of the ninth to give Chicago a 2–1 win. Eddie Stanky further endeared himself to Red Sox fans after the doubleheader by saying that only Dick Williams's "stupidity" had prevented Boston from earning a sweep. Stanky also defended pulling the rookie Carlos in the seventh inning of a scoreless game: "I'd yank my own son in that spot." The split knocked both teams down a notch, since the Twins swept Cleveland to grab a half-game lead over the White Sox and the Red Sox. Fourth-place Detroit kept pace with John Hiller, the young reliever-turned-starter, throwing his second shutout in three starts to beat Kansas City, 3–0. The Tigers remained 1½ games out.

On Saturday, August 26, victories by Boston over Chicago, 6–2, and Cleveland over Minnesota, 5–2, put the Red Sox into first place, the latest point in the season that they had occupied the top spot since the fateful 1949 campaign. In the process, the Red Sox handed Chicago ace Joe Horlen his earliest exit of the season. Horlen was sent to the showers after giving up five runs on 10 hits in only 4⅓ innings. The Tigers again beat the A's, also 5–2. This meant the Red Sox led the Twins by a half game and the White Sox and Tigers by a game. Only Boston and Chicago were scheduled to close the weekend with a doubleheader.

A disappointing crowd of 22,352—about twelve thousand fewer than had showed the previous Friday for a twi-night doubleheader—was treated to a pair of taut, tension-filled games. Carl Yastrzemski hit two home runs, giving him 34 for the season, to lead Boston to a 4–3 victory in the opener as Gary Bell beat Klagas. The game ended when Berry tried to score from third base on a sacrifice fly to right field. He was thrown out at the plate by right fielder José Tartabull. But to say Tartabull threw Berry out at the plate wouldn't be telling the full story. For one thing, Berry wasn't at full speed. He was playing with a sore ankle that he had injured the previous morning while golfing with some other players. Also, credit for the out at the plate belonged more to catcher Elston Howard. As Berry was charging toward the plate, Howard realized Tartabull's throw was going to arrive slightly up the third-baseline and Berry might be past him by the time the ball reached him. So Howard planted his size 12B left shoe firmly in the baseline. That forced Berry to decide to either knock over Howard or go around him and come back into the baseline to reach the plate. Berry tried to reach out for the plate with his left hand and never made it to the base. Howard strained to keep his left foot on the ground and still stretch his arms high above his head to catch the throw. He pulled down the ball and made the tag on Berry, with home-plate umpire Marty Springsted emphatically making the out call. That marked the first time all season that Tartabull had thrown out a runner at the plate.

In the second game, Santiago and Peters traded goose eggs into extra innings. Dick Williams pulled Santiago with two out in the bottom of the tenth as Darrell Brandon recorded the final out to keep Boston in the game. But in the bottom of the eleventh, the White Sox earned a split by scoring without a base hit. Duane Josephson walked, then was sacrificed to second by Ron Hansen. Smokey Burgess, pinch hitting for Gary Peters—who allowed only four hits through eleven innings—was intentionally walked to set up a possible inning-ending double play. Horlen was sent in as a pinch runner for the slow-footed Burgess. Pinch hitter Ken Boyer was retired for the second out. But Brandon threw a wild pitch to advance Josephson and Horlen to third and second. Williams had Brandon intentionally walk Wayne Causey to load the bases and set up a force at any base. The strategy backfired when Rocky Colavito, pinch hitting for Tommie Agee, walked to bring home the winning run. During this game, a perturbed White Sox fan ran onto the field and doused ump Springsted, who was at third base during the nightcap, for the call he had made to end the opener. The first person to come to Springsted's rescue was none other than Stanky. With the Twins beating Cleveland, 6–3, and Kansas City's Roberto Rodriguez beating the Tigers in his major league debut, 2–1, Minnesota moved back into first place by a mere percentage point over Boston. Chicago was third, a game out, and Detroit fourth, 1½ games out.

When the Red Sox hit New York, it didn't look like they were the visiting team. The first game was designated "Yaz Night," with Boston's star from Long Island honored before the game and even presented with a new Chrysler with a Massachusetts license plate reading YAZ-8. So many Red Sox fans made the trip from New England that traffic was snarled across Connecticut before each game. With the addition of Harrelson, the Red Sox released Jim Landis, who had been brought aboard only six days earlier following the Conigliaro incident. Harrelson made his debut for Boston in the third of the Red Sox's four games in New York, the second half of a twi-night doubleheader on Tuesday, August 29, after Boston had won the series' first two games. His first hit for the Red Sox was a home run, which salvaged an otherwise nondescript 1-for-4 night and helped the Red Sox take the Yankees into extra innings at 2–2. The teams traded runs in the eleventh inning, and the Yankees finally pushed across the winning run in the twentieth inning to end the six-hour nine-minute marathon. The interest in the Red Sox was such that Boston Edison Company reported its electric output increased by 40 percent that night as the game continued until 1:57 A.M. For the Red Sox, the most significant hitting news of the doubleheader came from the 0 for 10 logged by Yastrzemski. That extended Yaz's hitless streak to 17 at-bats, in which his batting average dropped from .321 to .310. That left him 22 points behind league leader Frank Robinson in the batting race.

The Red Sox and the Yankees were scheduled to close their series the following afternoon—now only a matter of hours away. Dick Williams suggested to Yaz that he take Wednesday's game off, and Yastrzemski agreed. He arrived at Yankee Stadium about an hour before the first pitch, relaxed in the clubhouse for a couple of hours, dressed out and reported to the dugout in the seventh inning with Red Sox rookie pitcher Jerry Stephenson and veteran Yankees left-hander Al Downing locked in a 1–1 duel. Yaz's replacement in left field, George Thomas, was scheduled to bat in the top of the ninth, and Williams sent in Yastrzemski to replace Thomas in the bottom of the eighth. Coming up to bat in the ninth, Yaz popped an 0-and-2 slider into right field for his 18th consecutive at-bat without a hit.

The score remained 1–1 going into extra innings, with Stephenson replaced by Johnny Wyatt. Downing was still pitching, having thrown 11 strikeouts, when Yaz, who remained in the game, returned to the plate in the eleventh inning. Yastrzemski remembered that Downing had started him off with two fastballs in the eighth inning and was sure he would use the same approach. Yaz guessed right and dispatched the pitch into the bleachers in right center for his 35th home run and a 2–1 lead that held up for the victory. The Red Sox had won three of four games from the pesky Yankees, the combined score of the games giving Boston only a 10–6 advantage. In the meantime, the Twins had lost two of three to Baltimore, Detroit had taken three of four from California, and the White Sox had lost two of three to Washington. With one day remaining in August, the Red Sox had built a lead of 1½ games over Minnesota and Detroit and 2½ games over Chicago. The Twins still had one more game remaining in their series with the Orioles. But the upcoming weekend would then be reserved for the contenders. The White Sox and the Red Sox would play four games in Boston, the Twins and the Tigers three games in Minnesota. The right set of circumstances might reduce the pennant race to only two legitimate contenders.

The Tigers, while not scheduled to play on August 31, spent a busy day in the front office. They bought thirty-two-year-old outfielder Don Demeter from Cleveland for a reported $40,000. It was Demeter whom the Tigers had traded to Boston in 1966 to get Earl Wilson in a deal that was incredibly one-sided for Detroit. Demeter had begun the '67 season with the Red Sox and was sent to the Indians in the Gary Bell–Tony Horton deal. His overall batting averge with the Red Sox and Indians was .227. The Tigers also activated outfielder Gates Brown and pitcher Johnny Podres and brought up infielder Tom Matchick and catcher Bill Heath from Toledo.

The Twins and Orioles closed their series at the Met on the afternoon of August 31, finishing up just before the White Sox and the Red Sox took the field in Boston. Minnesota entrusted an 8–6 lead to Ron Kline going into the ninth inning only to have Kline give up consecutive doubles to Boog Powell and Dave Johnson and a home run to Curt Blefary for a 9–8 Baltimore lead. Moe Drabowsky was brought in to pitch for Baltimore in the bottom of the ninth. With one out, Cesar Tovar singled and pinch hitter Rich Reese delivered a homer. The dramatic 10–9 victory pushed Minnesota within a game of the Red Sox, pending Boston's game that night against Chicago.

Red Sox fans had not forgotten that Chicago manager Eddie Stanky had referred to Carl Yastrzemski as an All-Star from the neck down. One Red Sox fan brought a banner to the series opener proclaiming: STANKY A GREAT MANAGER FROM ANKLES DOWN. The White Sox opened the series with rookie pitcher Francisco Carlos, who held the Red Sox scoreless through 6⅓ innings six days earlier in his major league debut. Chicago gave him a run to work with this time when Don Buford hit a one-out triple off Gary Bell and scored on an infield out by Ken Boyer. Carlos left with one out in the seventh, having given up a walk to Yastrzemski and a single to George Scott. Hoyt Wilhelm came on and allowed Yaz to score the tying run on a groundout by Ken Harrelson. Rico Petrocelli then doubled to score Scott to give Boston a 2–1 lead. In the Chicago eighth, the White Sox scored three runs to retake the lead when Bell gave up home runs to Tommie Agee and Pete Ward, silencing the better part of a Fenway Park crowd of 35,158. Don McMahon, the former Boston reliever who was sent to Chicago in June for Jerry Adair, held off the Red Sox over the final two innings. The White Sox were within 1 1/2 games.

Even without a win, Francisco Carlos had become an immediate celebrity with his two superb outings against the Red Sox. It had been a long wait for Carlos, a twenty-six-year-old rookie mired in the minors since 1961 who had come close to quitting baseball in 1966. As a youngster growing up in Monrovia, California, Carlos had found it difficult to play as much baseball as he liked because his father wanted him to help out at his grocery store whenever possible. When he signed in March '61, Carlos was already 6 feet 3 and 200 pounds. It took him five years just to reach Class AA. With Lynchburg of the Southern League, Carlos finished with an ERA of 4.35 in '64, then led the league in losses in '65. Just when Carlos was prepared to seek another livelihood, he finished 15–8 with Evansville in the Southern League to turn around his career. With Indianapolis in '67, he was 11–8 before being called up to the White Sox.

7

SEPTEMBER:
The First Two Weeks

Friday night, September 1, saw Chicago's Gary Peters (15–7) matched against Boston's José Santiago (7–4) and Detroit's Joe Sparma (13–7) against Minnesota's Jim Kaat (9–13). In Boston the Red Sox wasted little time getting to Peters, who had beaten them twice in three previous starts. Peters was knocked out after two innings, allowing seven runs on eight hits in his worst outing of the season. Boston went on to win, 10–2, with Harrelson knocking in four runs with a double, a triple, and a home run. In Minnesota the Twins likewise got off to a quick start against Sparma thanks in part to Detroit's spotty defense. Tigers third baseman Eddie Mathews committed two errors in the first inning to help Minnesota take a 2–0 lead. The Twins added another run in the second with Kaat scoring on a double, infield out, and wild pitch. The Tigers fought back with two runs in the top of the third, only to have Minnesota build its lead back to two runs with the assistance of another Detroit error. Kaat went all the way and held on for a 5–4 victory for his first win since August 12 and only his second since the All-Star break.

Some of the Minnesota players groused about their front office not swinging the same kind of deals that their competitors had in recent weeks. The Red Sox added Harrelson and Elston Howard, the Tigers got Mathews, and the White Sox landed Ken Boyer and Rocky Colavito. And the Twins? Nothing. Snapped one of the Minnesota regulars, "We've got a

$35,000 bench." It even took pitcher Dave Boswell to provide the hitting heroics on Saturday, September 2, while he shut out Detroit on six singles. Boswell had the only extra-base hit of the game, a double. With the Chicago-Boston game televised nationally that day by NBC, the Twins cut short their postgame congratulations on the field and raced into the clubhouse to tune in. The pitching matchup at Fenway was the glamour confrontation of the series—Chicago's Joe Horlen (14–6) against Boston's Jim Lonborg (18–6). Horlen's ERA of 2.55 was among the best in the league, but he was on a three-game losing streak that included a start against the Red Sox in Chicago in which he'd been blasted for 10 hits in 4⅓ innings. Lonborg, conversely, had allowed a total of only two runs in back-to-back complete-game victories over the White Sox and Yankees. So it shocked the Fenway crowd when Chicago knocked Lonborg around for three runs in the first inning. Horlen allowed only one run on six hits as the White Sox assured themselves of no worse than a split of the four-game series with a 4–1 win. Lonborg suffered his first loss at Fenway since late July. The Twins, having won three straight games, were back in first place. The Red Sox were a half game back, with the White Sox in third at two out and the Tigers in fourth, 2½ back.

On Sunday, September 3, White Sox left-hander Tommy John made his first start of the season at Fenway, the supposed graveyard for southpaw pitchers. Before John's start that day, Red Sox opponents had come away with only four victories in the fourteen games in which they started lefties at Boston. Only once had an opposing lefty thrown a complete game at Fenway—Baltimore's Dave McNally, who made it a shutout. In six of the fourteen games, the opposing lefty failed to last through the third inning. So much for tendencies: John blanked Boston on five singles for his sixth shutout of the year. John at one point retired 12 consecutive batters. He had four strikeouts, four fly outs, and 23 outs on ground balls. This was just the kind of game Eddie Stanky liked. So much so that he promised his pitchers a new suit if they got at least 20 groundouts, win or lose. The hitting hero of the series for Chicago was Tommie Agee, who went 8 for 17 with a double and a home run. On a team that yearned for hitting, Agee was the most versatile threat despite having a disappointing season. His 12 home runs trailed only Pete Ward's 17 for the club lead. Likewise, his 46 runs batted in trailed only Ward's 53. With 25 stolen bases, Agee was behind only club leader Don Buford. His most glaring weakness was a .242 batting average. With about a month to play, it was obvious Agee wouldn't be able to match his 1966 figures of 22 homers, 86 RBIs, 44 stolen bases, and a .273 average.

Carl Yastrzemski was not the hitting hero for Boston, news in itself. In going 3 for 13, his batting average dropped to .308, 22 points behind Frank

Robinson. As the rest of the Red Sox boarded a bus for the airport and a flight to Washington, Yaz remained back at Fenway. The batting cage was pulled back out, and Yastrzemski worked on his swing, watched by Tom Yawkey and batting coach Bobby Doerr. At Minnesota, the largest crowd to watch a Twins regular-season home game (43,444) was hoping that, with the Red Sox loss, Dean Chance could pitch the Twins to a lead of 1½ games. But the Tigers stung Chance for three runs on four consecutive hits in the second inning, and Earl Wilson outpitched Chance to break a tie with Lonborg for the league lead in victories with his nineteenth for a 5–0 win. Wilson left the game with one out in the sixth inning, the bases loaded, and the Tigers leading, 3–0. Enter sidearming reliever Fred Lasher. The first Twins batter he faced was Cesar Tovar, who sent a wicked liner sailing to the left side of the diamond. What looked like a sure hit that would at least pull Minnesota within a run was snagged spectacularly by Dick McAuliffe, who was playing shortstop. With two away, Lasher needed only three pitches to strike out Russ Nixon to end the inning. Lasher pitched 3⅔ scoreless innings, his longest stint in the majors, to give him a win and four saves to show for seven appearances.

Chicago and Boston had finished their play against each other during the season (assuming they wouldn't meet in a postseason playoff) with the White Sox winning ten of the eighteen games. Likewise with Detroit and Minnesota, the Twins winning ten. With four weeks left in the season, the four contenders stood thusly:

				HOME	ROAD
Minnesota	76–59	.563	—	12	15
Boston	77–61	.558	½	13	11
Chicago	75–60	.555	1	16	11
Detroit	75–61	.551	1½	15	11

In five Labor Day doubleheaders scheduled for Monday, September 4, none of the four contenders was matched against another. And all four split their twin bills, leaving the standings unchanged from when the day began. The Red Sox fell behind at Washington, 3–0, before breaking an 18-inning scoreless streak in a 5–2 loss to the Senators. Washington appeared headed for a sweep when it grabbed a 4–2 lead off the Red Sox's Jerry Stephenson through five innings of the nightcap, but Boston rallied for four runs in the sixth inning for a 6–4 win. Red Sox manager Dick Williams benched first baseman George Scott after the first game, explaining that Scott was trying too hard to hit a home run in each at-bat. Scott displayed some power in his reaction, heaving some ice and a bat bag. Scott did pinch hit in the second game and doubled.

After the doubleheader, Williams told Carl Yastrzemski he might profit from taking a day off and having George Thomas play left field. Ken Harrelson started both games, going 0 for 7 against the team that he began the season with. Some of his former teammates predicted Harrelson wouldn't get a hit during the series. The Yankees and the White Sox traded 3–2 victories in their meeting at Yankee Stadium, with New York winning the opener scoring all unearned runs. At Minnesota, the Twins nearly took two from Cleveland but lost to the Indians in ten innings in the second game. Al Worthington was pitching his third inning of relief for Minnesota when Cleveland put runners at second and third with two out, with the help of a passed ball by reserve catcher Enrique Izquierdo. Fred Whitfield then hit a bad-hop grounder to first base. Harmon Killebrew managed to control the ball, then tried to beat Whitfield to the bag in a running battle of big men that would be mislabeled if called a race. Whitfield got there first, allowing Chuck Hinton to score the go-ahead run, and Cleveland reliever George Culver shut down Minnesota in the bottom of the tenth to preserve the win.

The Tigers split at home against Kansas City with Mickey Lolich continuing his dramatic turnaround with a fourth consecutive victory. The same team that had scored a total of 16 runs for him during his ten-game losing streak had scored 18 in his last two starts. In the second game, John Hiller suffered his first loss in five decisions. Hiller had allowed only one run in 26 innings during his previous three starts. California, still hanging on to slim hopes of getting back in the race, salvaged a split against Baltimore by winning the nightcap in twelve innings to remain six games out in fifth place. The Orioles' Frank Robinson had begun the day with a comfortable 22-point lead over Carl Yastrzemski in the batting race. But Robinson went 1 for 10 in the doubleheader against the Angels. Combined with Yaz's 3 for 9 against Washington, Robinson's lead had dropped to 15 points, .324 to .309.

The top four teams all won again on Tuesday, September 5, meaning that the only thing close to movement in the race was California's sweep of Baltimore to move the fifth-place Angels within 5½ games. Rich Rollins's bases-loaded triple capped a four-run first inning for the first-place Twins in their 9–2 win over Cleveland. Having a 5–0 lead after two innings allowed Minnesota manager Cal Ermer to rest his bullpen as starter Jim Kaat went all the way for his second consecutive victory despite allowing 13 hits. The Red Sox won at Washington, 8–2, as Yastrzemski broke out of his batting slump by going 3 for 4 with two home runs (for a league-leading 38) and four runs batted in. Yaz came out of the game late, replaced by Thomas. Ken Harrelson got a hit against

Washington, three of them in fact. The catalyst of the White Sox's 5–3 win over the Yankees was pinch hitter Smokey Burgess. When Eddie Stanky brought Burgess up to bat in the top of the third inning in a 3–3 game, it meant he would be calling on his third pitcher in as many innings. Burgess was mired in an 0-for-18 hitting slump but didn't fail Stanky, in this case using his ability to draw a pinch-walk with two out and the bases loaded. Armed with the lead again, Stanky used Steve Jones and Fred Klagas to hold on for a 5–3 victory. Detroit's Joe Sparma began the game against Kansas City with four strikeouts and finished with his fifth shutout of the year, a two-hitter, to beat the A's.

The Tigers received bad news, though: outfielder Don Demeter, who had yet to join the team, would not be coming to Detroit. His doctor back home in Oklahoma City had told him a day after the deal was made to stay home until he fully recovered from a muscle strain on the left side of his chest. The doctor's latest diagnosis was that the problem was more than a simple strain; it was a disturbance of Demeter's heart. The doctor told Demeter not to take part in any strenuous physical activity for six to eight weeks, ruling out his playing any more baseball in 1967.

The following day, Wednesday, September 6, Indians pitcher Luis Tiant possessed Cleveland's most dangerous bat in the series finale at Minnesota. Tiant singled in two of Cleveland's three runs in the fourth inning as he beat the Twins and Dave Boswell, 3–2. No one was hitting that night in Chicago, at least not until extra innings. The White Sox's Joe Horlen shut out the Angels through eight innings. But the White Sox couldn't break through against Angels starter George Brunet. The game remained scoreless going into the eleventh inning, when California scored twice on Don McMahon. But in the bottom of the eleventh, the White Sox answered with two runs. The first was scored on doubles by Tommie Agee and pinch hitter Burgess. Bill Voss went in to run for Burgess, advanced to third when the bases were loaded on two walks, and scored on a passed ball by Buck Rodgers. In the thirteenth inning Ken Berry doubled home Duane Josephson to give Chicago a 3–2 win. Meanwhile, the Tigers swept a twi-night doubleheader from the Athletics to give them four wins in five games against Kansas City. In the opener, Detroit rallied from a 4–2 deficit in the seventh inning with four runs. In the second game, the Tigers' Earl Wilson became the major leagues' first twenty-game winner and contributed his fourth home run of the season. When Wilson retired his final batter to end the doubleheader, the virtual four-way tie for first place was created. Chicago and Minnesota each stood at 78–61 for a winning percentage of .561. Boston and Detroit were 79–62, one percentage point behind at .560. Fittingly, this was the same day that baseball commissioner William D. Eckert told all four teams to go ahead and print World Series tickets.

The Red Sox and Twins were the only contenders scheduled to play on Thursday, September 7. Boston opened a four-game series at home against the Yankees, who had proved so difficult for the Red Sox the previous week at Yankee Stadium. Minnesota faced five games at Baltimore. After having the day off, the Tigers and White Sox would meet in a four-game series at Comiskey Park, capped by a Sunday doubleheader.

In Boston, Jim Lonborg equaled his combined victory total for the previous two seasons by improving to 19–7 with a 3–1 win over the Yankees. Lonborg also had two hits and added his first career stolen base. A few minutes after the Red Sox's game ended, Dean Chance pitched the Twins back into first place by one percentage point with his eighteenth victory, 4–2 over the Orioles. Chance also singled, giving him three hits for the season. With three hits in 80 at-bats, Chance's batting average had climbed to a lofty .037. And with only a few weeks to play, it was a lock that Chance couldn't plunge to the .026 figure he had earned in 1966 by going 2 for 76.

The fans at Fenway cheered Bill Monboquette on Friday night, September 8, just like the old days, though "Monbo" was wearing a grey uniform featuring NEW YORK across the front. The former Boston pitcher beat the Red Sox with relief help from Joe Verbanic, who retired the last eight Red Sox in order. Tom Tresh had three hits in the Yankees' 5–2 win, including a liner to right field that prompted some fans to boo Ken Harrelson for a perceived lack of effort.

THE WHITE SOX DROP THE BALL

In Chicago, friction between the Tigers and the White Sox surfaced even before their games began. The AL sent former umpire Charlie Berry to Comiskey Park on the eve of this important series to inspect the condition of the infield. Two nights earlier, Angels manager Bill Rigney had called the area around the plate a swamp. As could be expected, White Sox manager Eddie Stanky wasn't exactly thrilled at this version of being frisked, though Tigers officials insisted they didn't initiate any protest. Berry determined the field's condition was unsatisfactory. He told Gene Bossard, head of the grounds crew, to roll the plate area to make it firmer. Minutes before a series that figured to be critical to the outcome of the pennant race, a Comiskey Park grounds crew member was steering a one-ton roller around home plate.

It was Mickey Lolich who rolled once the game began, to his fifth consecutive victory. He improved to 10–12 as the Tigers opened their four-game series at Chicago with a 4–1 win. Two of Detroit's runs were unearned, one scoring as a result of Pete Ward's first error in 134 games as a White Sox outfielder. Afterward, Stanky's remarks were predictably aimed at the pregame antics. "We have now entered Russia," Stanky told reporters, "when they come in here and dictate to you about the conditions of your infield. Just like Russia."

In Baltimore, Harmon Killebrew hit his 37th home run to help Jim Merritt go to 12–4 in a 7–2 victory over the Orioles. But in the nightcap, Minnesota right-hander Jim Perry gave up four runs in the Baltimore second, and the Orioles went on to win, 5–3. Tony Oliva did more than his part in trying to gain the sweep, going 8 for 9 in the doubleheader with five consecutive hits in the second game. The split left Minnesota in a flatfooted tie for first place with Detroit at 80–62, with Boston a half game back and Chicago one game back.

The second game of the Tigers–White Sox series at Comiskey matched Detroit's young John Hiller against veteran Chicago left-hander Gary Peters. The White Sox scored a run in the fourth and two more in the sixth to build a 3–0 lead. Peters had pitched well against the Tigers previously during the season, winning three of four decisions against Detroit, and it looked like he had found the club against which to break his own two-game losing streak. He was working on a three-hit shutout going to the ninth inning.

Al Kaline began the Tigers' last shot at Peters with a lined single to left field. Up to the plate stepped Willie Horton, 0 for 3 in the game and hitless in three games. Horton smacked a fly ball deep to left field that appeared headed for the stands until it got caught in a stiff wind. The ball hung up long enough for White Sox left fielder Walt Williams to make the catch, while backed up against the fence, for the first out of the inning, sending Kaline back to first base. Horton trotted back to the dugout, distraught that he had just missed a home run that would have pulled Detroit within a run. What made him even more upset was spotting Chicago's Ken Berry mocking him from the top step of the dugout by waving a towel. Horton yelled at Berry and gave him the thumbs-down sign.

Bill Freehan followed Horton with a single off the glove of Chicago shortstop Ron Hansen, and Eddie Mathews walked to load the bases. Stanky then strolled out to the mound and lifted Peters, opting for right-hander Bob Locker to get the final two outs. Don Wert immediately greeted Locker by smacking his first pitch to right field to score Kaline and reload the bases. With relief pitcher Pat Dobson due up next in the order hitting eighth, Tigers manager Mayo Smith sent up Jim Northrup as a pinch hitter. Northrup hit the first pitch to left field for a hit. Freehan scored from third base, and Mathews lumbered his way in from second base to tie the score at 3–3. Two pitches by Locker, two hits, two runs. By this time, the Detroit dugout had gone berserk while the Chicago dugout had lost much of its life. There were no towels being waved.

Stanky continued to try to punch the right buttons to get the White Sox out of the inning still tied. He summoned Wilbur Wood, the left-handed knuckleball pitcher. The Tigers' scheduled batter was right-handed-hitting Dick Tracewski, but Smith instead sent up Norm Cash, another lefty but one with dangerous power. Wood worked the count to 1 and 2. The next pitch was a knuckler, and Cash belted it to right field to score Wert with the go-ahead run, 4–3. Stanky had seen all he wanted of Wood and made him the second consecutive Chicago pitcher to leave the game without retiring a batter. He brought in righty Don McMahon, who promptly walked Mickey Stanley to reload the bases. That brought up left-handed-hitting Dick McAuliffe, but Stanky elected to stay with McMahon. The ninth Tiger to bat in the inning, McAuliffe fouled out to third baseman Ken Boyer for the second out. Then Kaline walked to force in Northrup and increase the Tigers' lead to 5–3. Horton came back up, still remembering the near-miss home run and Berry's wave. Horton lined a shot over second base to score Cash and Stanley.

Stanky returned to the mound again, his team now having given up seven runs in the ninth inning, and replaced McMahon with rookie Roger Nelson. Freehan, who made a habit of hanging over the plate in his normal batting stance, was plunked in the left arm—breaking a team record by being hit for the eighteenth time during the season—to reload the bases. Nelson avoided further disaster by getting out Mathews to end the inning. Fred Lasher pitched the bottom of the ninth for the Tigers, struck out two and didn't allow a base runner. Detroit had transformed what looked like a three-hit shutout for Gary Peters into a remarkable 7–3 win.

The celebration in the visitors clubhouse at Comiskey Park was worthy of a pennant clinching, minus the champagne. Horton happily answered reporters' questions despite the standard pain he felt in his injured left heel. "When we win the World Series," Horton boasted, "I'll soak it in champagne." A newspaper photographer asked to take a shot of Northrup and some other Tigers heroes. Northrup screamed across the room, "Get over here, Willie! We gotta integrate this picture!"

The scene, zany as it was, spoke volumes for the Tigers in general and Horton in particular. This was the same summer that blacks had rioted in downtown Detroit only a few blocks from Tiger Stadium. This was the same summer that Horton had, without hesitation, accepted the unofficial role of spokesman for the Tigers' black players with the white players.

Horton was a quiet man with a knack for getting along with people. He had to, coming from a family with ten brothers and ten sisters. His father, Thomas (Clint) Horton, had played for the old Birmingham Black Barons before moving to Virginia to work in a coal mine. When the mine shut down, the Hortons joined other relatives in Detroit. Willie's first baseball experience came from throwing a ball against a wall in the housing projects about two blocks from Tiger Stadium in a game called "strikeout." He never lifted weights, but he became a thickly built, muscular youngster. Horton was a Golden Gloves boxer at age thirteen and continued to box until he was seventeen. He became a clubhouse boy at Tiger Stadium, his chores regularly including getting hot dogs for Al Kaline and Rocky Colavito. Soon Horton was a star baseball player at Northwest High School, playing against future teammates Mickey Stanley and Jim Northrup in high-school and summer ball. He was already coveted by the Tigers after his junior season. Horton's father by then had gone on disability, and Willie was eager to sign a baseball contract to help the family. When he signed with the Tigers after his senior year, Willie handed over to his parents the entire $65,000, as well as a new house, and continued to live at home.

Horton hit .295 in his first minor league season at Duluth-Superior and immediately headed south to play winter ball. On his first trip home during a break, Horton's father asked him what he planned to do after the winter season. Horton was somewhat surprised by the question and proceeded to explain how many weeks it would be before he left for spring training. The elder Horton politely interrupted: "What are you going to do before then?" Now Willie was really confused: "What do you mean, Dad?" "Well," Mr. Horton explained, "you've got to get a job." And almost before Willie knew it, his father had set him up with a job with a company called S&S Contractors.

That episode taught Willie Horton a lesson, that time was never to be taken for granted, should never be wasted. It was a lesson he painfully learned to appreciate on New Year's Eve 1965. He was playing ball in Puerto Rico in anticipation of becoming a regular in the Tigers' outfield, when he learned that both his parents had been killed in an automobile accident back home. Horton had never imagined losing both his parents at once, nor so soon. Suddenly there was no one to call, no one to turn to. The Tigers became Horton's surrogate family, and he became very close with general manager Jim Campbell. Manager Charlie Dressen took a plane from his off-season home in California to Detroit and offered Horton the chance to take an entire year off to get over the trauma. Horton declined, though he never forgot the kindness Dressen showed him. Horton dedicated the 1965 season to his parents and became an All-Star, hitting .273 with 29 home runs and 104 RBIs. It also helped that Dressen convinced Horton to stop swinging a thirty-two-ounce bat and switch to a much heavier model. This cut down on his swing and made him use the entire field instead of pulling everything to left.

Horton generally wasn't one to gloat in victory, but he couldn't resist the opportunity following the miracle victory over the White Sox. "They asked for it," he told reporters, "and we gave it to them." Norm Cash called his own ninth-inning pinch-hit "the biggest hit I ever got for the Tigers." On the previous home stand, Cash had gone 0 for 11 and incurred the wrath of the Detroit fans. He had merely increased the pressure by smashing a bat, kicking the resin bag, and further inciting the crowd by retaliating with a mock bow. Cash often was the life of the Tigers' party, but while his teammates reveled, he treasured the satisfaction of his big hit without breaking into a smile.

The Tigers' Jerry Lumpe noted that the White Sox had blown a chance to gain a virtual tie for the lead and now trailed the Tigers by two games. "That looks like a backbreaker for the White Sox," Lumpe said. Indeed, that was just the sentiment Chicago manager Eddie Stanky was trying to avoid overwhelming his team in the other clubhouse. In such situations, Stanky often would attract attention to himself, as if creating a diversion to spare his players from the critical press. That's exactly what he did in this case. "We still got a long way to go," Stanky growled, "and I ain't gonna resign if that's what you're thinking about." The clubhouse emptied quickly and quietly. Pitcher Joe Horlen, scheduled to start the first game of the next day's doubleheader, went out to dinner in downtown Chicago with Ken Boyer, who had moved in with him since coming to the White Sox, and WBBM sportscaster Bruce Roberts and bemoaned the White Sox's fate that day.

The Twins didn't wait until the ninth inning to win at Baltimore to remain tied for first place with the Tigers. Jim Kaat went the distance, allowing five hits for his third consecutive complete-game victory, 3–2. Harmon Killebrew homered for the Twins, tying Carl Yastrzemski for the league lead at 38, and Tony Oliva went 2 for 3, making him 10 for 12 in the series. Killebrew's position tied atop the home-run race was short-lived. That night in Boston, Yaz clubbed No. 39 as Dave Morehead and Sparky Lyle combined on a four-hitter to beat the Yankees, 7–1. Morehead was a last-minute pitching replacement for scheduled starter Jerry Stephenson, who was sidelined with a virus just before gametime. Lyle came on in the eighth to protect a 6–1 lead when New York loaded the bases with no one out. He struck out Jake Gibbs and got Tom Tresh to hit into a double play. The win enabled Boston to stay one-half game behind the Tigers and Twins.

Yastrzemski's home run not only pushed him back into the league lead but also helped establish a curious superstition that lasted throughout the pennant race. Yaz's wife, Carol, happened to have left her seat to go buy a hot dog when her husband hit his home run. Therefore, she decided that she would abandon her seat in the fourth inning of every remaining home game and wait out the balance of the game down by the concession stands, perchance bringing good luck to the Red Sox.

For the fourth time in their five-game series, the Twins didn't need to go to the bullpen against Baltimore on Sunday, September 10. This time it was right-hander Dave Boswell beating the Orioles, 4–2, on a five-hitter. The Birds bunched three of their hits along with a walk in the fourth inning to take a 2–1 lead. But Oliva continued his one-man assault on Baltimore pitching. After knocking in Minnesota's first run in the first inning, he tripled in the fifth to score Killebrew with the tying run. The Twins scored the go-ahead run in the seventh inning thanks in part to a rare error committed by Orioles Gold Glove third baseman Brooks Robinson. Oliva finished the game 3 for 5, making him 13 for 17 in the series.

In Boston, Mike Ryan tripled with the bases loaded to break open the Red Sox's 9–1 rout of the Yankees. Ken Harrelson hit his third home run as a Red Sox player, his first since September 1. In his eleven games with Boston, the "Hawk" was hitting .240 with three homers and nine RBIs. He had hit three homers in the twenty-six games he played with Washington and six in sixty-one games with Kansas City. So far, with the Red Sox still a half game out, the signing of Harrelson looked like a great move.

HORLEN SENDS MESSAGE TO TIGERS

The final chapter of the pennant race that day was played out at Comiskey Park in the doubleheader between the Tigers and the White Sox. The pitching matchups were Joe Sparma (14–8) against Joe Horlen (15–6) in the opener and Denny McLain (17–15) against rookie Francisco Carlos (0–0) in the nightcap. Sparma was rated a good overall athlete, considering he played quarterback at Ohio State. But he proved in the first inning that his fielding was a detriment when he dropped an easy toss at first base from Norm Cash to help the White Sox to a five-run inning. Sparma faced just six batters, retiring only Don Buford on a strikeout. Not only did the game remain scoreless from that point until Chicago broke through for another run in the eighth, but also the Tigers remained hitless throughout. Nor did Horlen walk a batter. The only Detroit base runners came when Horlen hit Bill Freehan in the right arm in the third inning and Eddie Mathews reached on an error made by Ken Boyer in the fifth inning.

This was the second consecutive day that Freehan had been hit by a pitch. It was obvious to Horlen when he next came to the plate that

Freehan was none too pleased about this latest shot. "Bill, you all right?" Horlen asked the catcher rather innocently in his Texas drawl. The closest thing to a response from Freehan was a kind of snarling grunt. It got across the message: be prepared for a little retaliation. The first pitch from Detroit reliever Dave Wickersham zinged past Horlen's chin. The second came across his ribs. The third came straight for Horlen, and he was unable to get out of the way. The ball struck him in the inside of his left knee, causing a bad bruise. From that point on, Horlen didn't sit down in the dugout when it was Chicago's turn to bat. While some fans would have guessed that Horlen was nervous about pitching a no-hitter, the actual reason was he was afraid his knee would stiffen. Some no-hit superstitions were observed in the Chicago dugout. The only person to talk to Horlen was pitching coach Marv Grissom, who told him early he wasn't throwing straight overhand.

In the top of the ninth, Horlen was scheduled to face Nos. 8, 9, and 1 in the Tigers' batting order—Jerry Lumpe, Bill Heath, and Dick McAuliffe. To aid Horlen's quest, Eddie Stanky made two defensive replacements— Buddy Bradford in left field for Pete Ward and rookie Cotton Nash, the former All-American basketball player at Kentucky, at first base for Boyer, a converted third baseman. Lumpe fouled off the first pitch, then took a ball inside. On 1 and 1, he grounded the pitch back up the middle. Chicago second baseman Wayne Causey ranged behind the bag, made a backhanded stop, and followed with an off-balance throw in midair to Nash for the out. Mayo Smith raced out of the Detroit dugout and, along with Lumpe, disputed the call made by John Stevens, the league's senior umpire, to no avail. Next up was Heath. He worked the count to 3 and 1 before hitting a grounder that third baseman Don Buford made a running pickup on near shortstop to throw out Heath for out No. 2. McAuliffe was the Tigers' last hope of avoiding the second no-hitter of the season—and this time, the Tigers would even lose. McAuliffe looked at ball one, then strike one. The next pitch was fouled off near the plate. Then there was another foul tip. Then ball two, and ball three, just outside. With the count full—only the fifth time in the game Horlen had gone to a three-ball count—McAuliffe tapped a grounder to shortstop Ron Hansen, who made the throw to Nash to end the game. As Nash squeezed the ball, Horlen heaved his glove high over the mound to begin the celebration of his 5–0 no-hitter. It proved to be a welcome salve for the wounds inflicted upon the White Sox by their devastating loss the previous day.

This marked the second game in which Horlen had a no-hitter with one out to go in the major leagues. He had one in 1963 against Washington, only to have Chuck Hinton single. Horlen didn't even win that game, giving up a home run to the next batter, Don Lock. No such reversal this time. Horlen retired the last fourteen batters after Boyer's error in the fifth inning. "This time, I was determined to make them hit it on the ground," Horlen told reporters afterward. "I wasn't coming over the plate with nothing, no matter what." General manager Ed Short rewarded Horlen with a new contract after the game.

Horlen appeared to be a calm individual in complete control of his emotions, a slow-talking Texan whom the White Sox signed in 1959 after he helped pitch Oklahoma State to the NCAA championship. But Horlen's sedate manner belied the volcano that churned within him. He usually worked himself up so much for each start that he was lucky to sleep three or four hours the following night. He spent most road trips simply window-shopping to walk off nervous tension. Some teammates suggested to him that chewing tobacco would relieve much of his tension, but Horlen only discovered it made him sick. Nor did he like chewing gum. Nerves aside, he had developed quickly into a major leaguer, finishing his third pro season with a five-game stint with Chicago in 1961. Except for a four-game cameo at Class AAA in 1963, Horlen had made the big leagues for good. And Horlen eventually discovered a suitable outlet for his nerves. He began chewing tissues. This somehow appealed to him more than gum and didn't have him throwing up like tobacco did. When news of this odd habit became known, the Kimberly-Clark Company provided Horlen with an unlimited supply of Kleenex. Thus began one of the strangest commercial relationships in the majors.

Horlen also may have been the only major league pitcher with his own bat contract. The unlikely set of circumstances began one day early in his career. He innocently asked Frank Ryan, a representative of Louisville Slugger, if he could get a souvenir bat featuring his signature to display at his home. Ryan laughed and told Horlen he could have a such a bat—if he got a hit that day. Horlen promptly went out and got two hits and the only two RBIs of the day in a 2–1 victory over Detroit. After the game, Ryan returned to the clubhouse and routinely asked Horlen to sign a bat contract. Horlen was confused; all he wanted was one bat. But Ryan insisted that giving out even one bat required a signed contract—and a fee. Horlen continued to plead his case but eventually gave in, signing the "contract" and accepting $1 from Ryan. From then on, all of Horlen's bats came from Louisville Slugger as signature models.

In the second game, the White Sox struck quickly again. Detroit starter Denny McLain lasted only one pitch into the second inning, leaving with a muscle strain in his back—and a 2–0 deficit. With one out in the home half of the first, Buford singled off third baseman Eddie Mathews' glove. Bill Voss singled between first and second to send Buford to third base. Voss then stole second and advanced to third on a wild pitch that scored Buford. Pete Ward added a sacrifice fly for a 2–0 lead. White Sox starter Francisco Carlos finally had some runs to work with. He had no won-lost record to show for following his first three starts in which he compiled an earned run average of 1.56. Still holding a 2–0 lead in the top of the seventh inning, Carlos was pulled after allowing a lead-off single to Jim Northrup. Hoyt Wilhelm and Bob Locker finished up as Chicago completed a doubleheader shutout sweep of the Tigers, 2–0.

A day earlier the White Sox had been all but left for dead after giving up seven runs in the ninth inning to lose, and the Tigers were on top of the heap. But on the evening of September 10, the White Sox were far from dead, and the Tigers had taken a huge one-day plunge from first to fourth. Their starting pitchers, Sparma and McLain, had lasted a combined 1 1/3 innings. Except for the seven-run outburst on Saturday, Chicago's pitching had handcuffed the Tigers in the series: Dick McAuliffe went 1 for 17, Al Kaline 1 for 13, Willie Horton 1 for 14, Eddie Mathews 2 for 13, Norm Cash 1 for 9. McLain, lifted with the back injury, was scheduled to be examined the next day for an injury that trainer Bill Behm feared might sideline him for the balance of the season. And Freehan, too, was smarting, having been hit twice in the past two days. He sat out the second game, and Mayo Smith listed him as doubtful for Detroit's next game against Baltimore in two days.

Eddie Stanky couldn't resist taking a shot at the local newspapers, which had all but eulogized the White Sox after Saturday's stunning defeat. "It looks like a Detroit runaway, quote, unquote," Stanky repeated after the doubleheader. "It looks like a clean sweep for Detroit, quote, unquote. Well, the walking dead are walking again."

With three weeks remaining, the Twins led by a half game over the Red Sox and 1 1/2 games over the White Sox and Tigers. The Twins would stay on the road for another week, playing three games at Washington before closing the trip with three games at Chicago. That would complete Minnesota's play against Chicago for the season. With the season's series with Detroit already finished, that would leave only two more games for the Twins against contenders—the last two days of the season at Boston.

Minnesota and Chicago were the only contenders scheduled to play on Monday, September 11. The first-place Twins were counting on Dean Chance, going in with a record of 18–11, to get them off to a winning start in their three-game series against the Senators. But even staked to a 2–0 lead in the first inning, Chance lasted only three innings. His undoing was a five-run Washington first in which Chance, Harmon Killebrew, and

Zoilo Versalles all committed costly errors. But the Twins roared back for a 13–5 victory by scoring seven runs in the fourth inning and four more in the fifth. Tony Oliva continued his torrid hitting with a double in two at-bats before being rested. Through the six games of the Minnesota roadtrip, Oliva was 15 for 21 (an incredible .714 average), with five doubles and a triple. Another encouraging sign for the Twins was the pitching of Jim Perry. He followed Chance by shutting out Washington on four hits in six innings. Perry had served the Twins admirably as the fifth starter since late July but now figured to be used out of the bullpen the rest of the way.

The Twins' victory officially eliminated the world-champion Orioles from the pennant race, though it had been obvious since late May that this Baltimore team wouldn't pose much of a threat. The Birds swung through Chicago to make up a rained-out game from August 19. Even with the White Sox coming off the Sunday sweep of the Tigers, including Joe Horlen's no-hitter, only 4,048 fans showed up that night at Comiskey Park for the makeup game. The rest of the White Sox fans didn't miss much. Baltimore rookie right-hander Jim Hardin limited Chicago to four hits to beat Fred Klagas and the White Sox, 4–1. Monday's play left Minnesota with a one-game lead over Boston, two games over Detroit, and 2½ games over Chicago.

The matter of White Sox fan support—or lack thereof—had become a ticklish subject in Chicago. Total attendance stood at 849,509, an average of 16,028 every time the White Sox opened the gates. It seemed plausible that the White Sox could break the million mark; all it would require was a slight boost in average attendance—to 16,721—over the final nine home dates. But the fact was that the other AL contenders were enjoying record years at the turnstiles, too, thanks to the tight pennant race. Talk of a White Sox move to Milwaukee had run rampant around baseball since the White Sox and Twins played an exhibition game at Milwaukee County Stadium in late May. Al Hirshberg of the *Boston Traveler American* reported in August that such a move was being negotiated. The most significant detriment to the White Sox's drawing fans was the team's stadium—fifty-seven-year-old Comiskey Park—and location—Chicago's crime-ridden South Side. Team owner Arthur Allyn was hoping the city would put together a new sports complex tentatively planned for construction in 1969. But regardless of the city's action, Allyn said he was confident his White Sox would be playing in a new stadium in Chicago by 1972.

Other league matters were going on in Chicago, also in relative obscurity. A's owner Charlie Finley, operating out of his Chicago office, invited former Minnesota manager Sam Mele to discuss taking over as A's manager in 1968. Just where that specifically would be still had not been decided; Finley told Mele he expected the A's to play in either Oakland or Seattle. No matter the locale, Mele wasn't interested. While being paid by Minnesota for the balance of the season, he planned to sign on as a Red Sox scout after the season.

After playing in Chicago the previous night, the Orioles had to play at Detroit on the afternoon of Tuesday, September 12. It turned out the Tigers probably went through a rougher Monday than the Orioles, though they didn't play. Eddie Mathews was forced out of the lineup because of injuries suffered when he fell down twelve stairs at his off-season home in Milwaukee. Mathews had been given permission to stop in Milwaukee after the Tigers finished their weekend series in Chicago. He caught a foot in a rug and fell down the stairs. He suffered a bruised hip and forehead along with a torn ligament in his right thumb. Mathews had hit .233 for the Tigers with five home runs—but had as many strikeouts as hits (17). After he was examined by team doctors in Detroit, the Tigers were hoping Mathews could come back by the following Friday, missing only the two-game series against the Orioles. The good news was that the fears that Detroit catcher Bill Freehan would be sidelined with an injured left elbow were unfounded. Freehan was in the starting lineup to face the Orioles, though he did play with the elbow heavily wrapped. Nor would starting pitcher Denny McLain lose any time. The muscle strain that forced him out of the game against the White Sox was diagnosed as nothing serious, and he was penciled in for his next start that Saturday against Washington.

Baltimore built a 4–2 lead through 4½ innings and knocked out Detroit starter Earl Wilson in the second inning—the third straight game in which the Tigers' starting pitcher couldn't make it into the third inning. But Detroit tied the score in the fifth when Norm Cash drove in two runs with a bases-loaded single. In the sixth, Al Kaline tagged reliever Eddie Watt for a two-run home run that proved to be the difference in Detroit's 6–4 victory. It was Kaline's first home run since August 20, a span of twenty-two games, and helped erase the memory of Kaline's 1-for-13 series in Chicago. Fred Gladding got the win in relief but had to leave the game with a strained hip after his warmup pitches before the eighth inning. Fred Lasher, who had replaced Gladding as the Tigers' stopper out of the bullpen, shut down Baltimore over the final two innings to earn a save. That gave Lasher seven saves and a win in eleven appearances since joining the Tigers in mid-August.

The Red Sox opened a two-game series at home against Kansas City and collected only five hits while Catfish Hunter tied an A's record with 12 strikeouts. That didn't stop Boston from beating Kansas City, 3–1, as Jim

Lonborg became the AL's second twenty-game winner, following Earl Wilson. Lonborg himself drove in what proved to be the winning run when he swung away in a sacrifice situation in the eighth inning and tripled.

The White Sox were playing host to the Indians in a twi-night double-header at Comiskey. What was originally scheduled as a two-game series had become a four-game set thanks to back-to-back rainouts on the Indians' last visit to Chicago in late July. No rolling of the plate area was required beforehand, but the White Sox probably wished afterward that something had been done differently. Indians pitching held the White Sox to 10 hits overall in the doubleheader and swept Chicago, 4–3 and 7–1. The Indians had come to Chicago having lost eight of eleven previous games with the White Sox during the season. The White Sox had the tying and go-ahead runs on base with one out in the bottom of the eighth inning of the opener. Cleveland manager Joe Adcock brought in pitcher Bob Allen, who promptly struck out Tom McCraw and Wayne Causey to end the inning. Luis Tiant limited Chicago to one run and four hits in the second game, sending the White Sox to their third consecutive defeat since the doubleheader sweep of Detroit.

The Twins needed another victory at Washington to remain a game ahead of the Red Sox, but Senators pitcher Frank Bertaina held Minnesota in check and also drove home two runs with a bases-loaded single. Minnesota collected 12 hits off three Washington pitchers but still lost, 5–4, to fall into a first-place tie with Boston. The Tigers were a game out and Chicago three games out. The White Sox, who led the AL by 5½ games on July 1, had reached their largest deficit of the season—with sixteen games to play.

The race remained unchanged when all four contenders won single games on Wednesday, September 13. The Red Sox trailed the Athletics, 2–1, going to the bottom of the eighth inning before rallying for three runs off reliever Jack Aker. With the Red Sox winning that afternoon, Twins manager Cal Ermer showed that night just how important it was to him for Minnesota to stay tied with Boston. Jim Kaat faltered in the ninth inning at Washington, allowing the Senators to pull within 3–1 and leaving the game with runners at second and third and no one out. Ermer elected to bring in right-handed starter Dean Chance to preserve the win. Rich Coggins hit a sacrifice fly to cut the Twins' lead to 3–2. But with Fred Valentine at second base, Chance struck out Mike Epstein and Cap Peterson to end the game.

In Detroit, the Tigers' Mickey Lolich extended his personal winning streak to six games by beating the Orioles, 6–1. Dick Tracewski started at second base for Detroit in place of Dick McAuliffe and responded with his first home run of the season and only his fourth in five big-league seasons. Al Kaline, who only the night before hit his first homer since late August, followed Tracewski's blast with his second in as many games, giving him 24 for the season.

The prototypical White Sox game took place that night as Chicago and Cleveland played scoreless baseball for four hours and thirty-two minutes before Rocky Colavito singled home pinch runner Buddy Bradford for a 1–0 victory. Starters Sonny Siebert of Cleveland and Gary Peters of Chicago each pitched the first eleven innings. Siebert allowed four hits and walked none, while Peters allowed only one hit—a triple by Joe Azcue—but was lucky to hold the Indians scoreless in spite of 10 walks. In the bottom of the seventeenth, Ken Boyer singled off Bob Tiefenaur, the third Cleveland pitcher. Bradford ran for Boyer and advanced to second on a passed ball charged to Cleveland rookie catcher Ray Fosse. Tom McCraw was walked intentionally to set up a double-play possibility that would end the inning. Then Colavito followed with the game-winning single.

The tightness of the pennant race forced Major League Baseball to come up with an ingenious design for a postgame playoff that could accommodate from two and four teams. If any two teams tied for first place, a best-of-three series would be played October 2–4 with no days off and the team earning the home-field advantage playing host to Games Two and Three. In each head-to-head comparison, the Tigers had earned that advantage over each of the other three teams. Chicago earned the advantage over Boston and Minnesota. The advantage in a Boston-Minnesota playoff would go to the Twins.

A three-way tie would lead to a round-robin, double-elimination playoff staged over three or four days, October 2–5 or October 2–6. If all four teams tied, the playoff would take the form of best-of-three semifinals followed by a best-of-three finals. The Twins and Red Sox would be paired (following their regular-season finale at Fenway), playing Game One in Boston on October 2, Game Two in Bloomington on October 3, and Game Three if necessary back in Boston on October 4. The Tigers–White Sox semifinal would be played the same days, opening in Detroit and returning from Chicago if a third game was needed. The survivors would advance to the finals, October 5–7, with the same format featuring alternating sites. The Twins would earn the extra home game whether they played the Tigers or White Sox. Conversely, the Red Sox would travel for a third game against either Chicago or Detroit.

All plans called for expediency, making travel days a luxury that could not be afforded. The World Series was scheduled to start Wednesday, October 4, in the pennant-winning AL city, with the competing teams ordinarily receiving two days off between the regular season and the Series. It would still be possible to open the Series on time if there were a two-team tie and the playoff were decided in a two-game sweep. That would send the AL winner into the World Series with no days off between the regular season and the Series, possibly flying back home on the morning of the Series opener. It would be possible, in the case of the four-way playoff, that the AL champion would play six consecutive play-off games directly following the regular season, take a day off, then begin a postponed Series facing an NL team (probably the Cardinals) that had had a full week's rest.

8

SEPTEMBER:

The Third Week

The White Sox and Indians played another ten innings of scoreless baseball on Thursday night, September 14, in the only AL game of the day. This time, Francisco Carlos went the full ten for Chicago, allowing five singles and no walks. Orlando Pena, the third Cleveland pitcher, retired Rocky Colavito to open the tenth before running into trouble. Ron Hansen and Duane Josephson singled to put runners at first and third. Pinch hitter Smokey Burgess was intentionally walked to load the bases. Ken Boyer pinch hit for Ken Berry and was retired for the second out. That brought up Don Buford, who ended the game with his fourth home run of the season for a 4–0 victory. That pulled Chicago within 2½ games of first place, with the Twins coming to town for three games. The rest of the schedule involving the contenders that weekend had Baltimore at Boston for three games and Washington at Detroit for three games.

While the Twins weren't scheduled to play that day, circumstances forced them, wherever they were, to think about a former teammate. Outfielder Walt Bond had spent much of spring training with Minnesota, though diagnosed as having leukemia. When questioned about the disease by reporters in Florida, Bond reacted as if he didn't believe the doctors. On September 14 he died of the disease at his home in Houston at age twenty-nine.

Baltimore pitchers Tom Phoebus and Moe Drabowsky combined to hold the Red Sox to six hits as the Orioles opened their weekend at Fenway Park with a 6–2 victory on Friday, September 15. Frank Robinson began the day with a six-point lead over Carl Yastrzemski in the batting race. But Yaz was Boston's only hot hitter that day, going 3 for 4 while Robinson was held to 1 for 3. Robinson dropped to .315, while Yastrzemski improved to .313. Yes, there was a batting race, and Yaz was in position to challenge for the Triple Crown.

In Detroit, the Senators were cruising along with a 4–1 lead going to the bottom of the eighth inning before the Tigers suddenly tied the score on a three-run home run by Bill Freehan. In the bottom of the ninth, Dick McAuliffe singled with one out. Mayo Smith let reliever Fred Lasher, who had pitched one inning, bat and try to move McAuliffe to second base, taking his chances with Al Kaline batting with two out. Lasher successfully bunted McAuliffe over, and Senators manager Gil Hodges then decided to walk Kaline and pitch to Willie Horton with runners at first and second. The strategy appeared to work perfectly when Horton hit a foul pop-up that catcher Paul Casanova lined up. But Casanova was unable to make the catch. Horton, given a second chance, singled home McAuliffe to give the Tigers a 5–4 victory.

The White Sox picked an opportune time to flex their hitting muscles, having scored on only two at-bats in the previous 27 innings against the Indians—27 innings in which they didn't allow a run. Chicago knocked out Minnesota starter Dave Boswell in the second inning of the opener of the teams' three-game weekend series at Comiskey Park. And with Joe Horlen making his first start since no-hitting the Tigers, that was about all the White Sox needed. Horlen went the distance, holding the Twins to one run until giving up an inconsequential two-run home run in the ninth inning to Tony Oliva, as Chicago won, 7–3. Horlen's chance at a second consecutive no-hitter was broken up in the second inning on a single by Rod Carew. But Horlen didn't allow another hit until the ninth and gave up only three overall. Horlen himself almost equaled that, collecting two singles and knocking in a run. Chicago's victory left Boston, Detroit, and Minnesota in a flatfooted tie for first place at 84–64 with fourteen games to play. The White Sox stood in fourth place at 83–66, only 1 1/2 games out. But time was working against their chances of passing three teams in less than three weeks. Not only would Chicago have to keep winning, but it also would have to benefit from just the right combination of wins and losses from its three competitors. But this was just the right weekend for the White Sox to get plenty of help, with the Red Sox and Tigers playing competition outside the race.

Detroit and Boston took their respective home fields with their respective ace right-handed pitchers on Saturday afternoon, September 16—Earl Wilson (20–10) for the Tigers and Jim Lonborg (20–7) for the Red Sox. The Tigers scored five runs in the fourth and fifth innings and survived a shaky ninth inning from reliever Fred Lasher to beat Washington, 5–4. Lasher allowed two runs on three singles and a walk but still managed to come away with his eighth save. The victory, Detroit's fourth consecutive, meant that the Tigers were assured of no worse than a tie for first place depending on how the Red Sox and Twins did. In Boston, Lonborg was outpitched by Orioles rookie Jim Hardin, who had easily handled Chicago a week earlier. Hardin held Boston to three hits, and Boog Powell broke a 1–1 tie in the seventh with a three-run home run off reliever Johnny Wyatt to give Baltimore the 4–1 victory. In the batting duel between Frank Robinson and Carl Yastrzemski, Robinson went 1 for 3 and Yaz 0–3. Robinson was at .315, Yastrzemski at .311.

Before the game, Tony Conigliaro had made his first return to the Red Sox clubhouse since he was struck in the head on August 18. Tony C was greeted warmly by his teammates but almost immediately began to sense a certain uneasiness. It was as if he were out of place and had no business being in the clubhouse if he wasn't going to put on his uniform and help Boston win a pennant. He didn't stay long, bolting out after giving the excuse that he had a headache. Conigliaro returned home but didn't turn on the telecast of the game.

The White Sox continued to do their part to keep the race tight that night, when they rallied from a 4–0 deficit in the seventh inning and scored four in the bottom of the ninth to stun the Twins, 5–4. Minnesota scored three runs in the fifth inning and another in the sixth to provide what looked like an insurmountable lead for Dean Chance, who was seeking his nineteenth victory. Chicago broke up the shutout with a run in the seventh, then Chance ran into serious trouble in the ninth. He gave up consecutive singles to Tom McCraw, Ron Hansen, and Rocky Colavito to cut Minnesota's lead to 4–2. White Sox manager Eddie Stanky then called for Duane Josephson to bunt Colavito into scoring position to put the tying run at second base with only one out. Josephson bunted back to the mound, and Chance was unable to make the play, leaving the bases loaded with one out. Twins manager Cal Ermer then spurned his regular relievers to reverse a move that worked out well three days earlier. He brought in left-handed starter Jim Kaat to pitch to left-handed-hitting Wayne Causey. Kaat let loose with a wild pitch that scored Buddy Bradford, running for Hansen, to pull the White Sox within 4–3 and advance the other runners to second and third. Causey then delivered the necessary sacrifice fly to score Tommie Agee, running for Colavito, with the tying run. The fly also sent Bill Voss, running for Josephson, to third base with the potential winning run. Ermer brought in Al Worthington and had him intentionally walk pinch hitter Smokey Burgess and Don Buford to load the bases and set up a force at any base. Pete Ward, hitless in his first four at-bats, singled to score Voss with the dramatic winning run. The day ended with the Tigers alone in first place, the Red Sox and Twins falling to a game out, and the White Sox holding at 1 1/2 back.

Conigliaro came back to Fenway Park again on Sunday morning, September 17, as the Red Sox prepared to finish their series against Baltimore. This time he went so far as to put on his uniform for the first time since the beaning. He knew it would be foolish to try to do any kind of batting with the vision in his left eye still so impaired. But he headed into the outfield during batting practice to shag some fly balls. There he experienced multiple vision, often seeing two or three baseballs flying off the bat through the air toward him. Even in his panic, Tony C managed to bluff his way through the ordeal, making his misplays look skillful enough to appear staged. It's doubtful anyone guessed Conigliaro could barely see the ball coming at him.

The Orioles made it three straight wins over the Red Sox on Sunday afternoon, September 17—much to the chagrin, paradoxically, of fans back in Baltimore. At Fenway Park, the Birds knocked around Boston starter Gary Bell for three runs in 2 1/3 innings and went on to hit three home runs in a 5–3 win. This was not well received back in Baltimore, where many fans had at least temporarily attached themselves to the long-shot Red Sox since their own Orioles had been eliminated from the race. That day at Memorial Stadium in Baltimore, many of the fans attending the Baltimore Colts' football game against the Atlanta Falcons booed the announcement that the Orioles had beaten the Red Sox. With Robinson going 0 for 4 and Yastrzemski 1 for 4, Robinson stood at .312 and Yaz at .310 in the batting race.

In Detroit, the Tigers' four-game winning streak was snapped by Washington's Frank Bertaina. He held Detroit to seven hits while the Senators handed John Hiller his second consecutive loss as a starter, 5–0. Hiller was knocked out after pitching 4 2/3 innings, the shortest stint of his six starts.

As for the White Sox, they closed out a sweep of the Twins with a 4–0 win behind the four-hit pitching of Gary Peters. The game was a scoreless duel between Peters and Minnesota left-hander Jim Merritt until the bottom of the fifth inning, when Duane Josephson reached on an error by third baseman Rich Rollins and scored on a triple by Tom McCraw. Chicago added two runs in the sixth and another in the seventh as Peters improved to 16–9.

In the wacky world that was the 1967 American League pennant race, the White Sox had begun the week losing three games, including a doubleheader sweep to Cleveland, then managed to win two games without scoring before the tenth inning, and finished the week with a five-game winning streak. With two weeks to play, Chicago had nudged its way into second place, trailing Detroit by a half game. Boston and Minnesota still were a game behind the Tigers but were tied for third place.

The Angels' slim hopes were helped by a three-game sweep of the Athletics in Anaheim, each win coming by one run. Kansas City was no doubt hurt by the absence of shortstop Bert Campaneris. It was more than a coincidence that of the fifteen games that Campaneris sat out in 1967, nine of them were Athletics games at California. It turned out a Los Angeles woman named Lonnie Crawford had filed a paternity suit against Campaneris on October 7, 1965. Campy's mere appearance in the state of California would leave him vulnerable to legal attack. His replacement at shortstop, Ted Kubiak, went 2 for 12 in the three games. Hence, it wasn't too much of an exaggeration to extend some of the credit for the Angels' still being alive in the AL pennant race to Lonnie Crawford.

The Red Sox left town on their final roadtrip of the season—two games in Detroit, two in Cleveland, and three in Baltimore. That would bring them home with only four games to play during the final seven days of the season, two each with Cleveland and Minnesota. There would not be much time to make up ground at Fenway if things got away from them on this trip.

Likewise, the White Sox left home for the last time during the season. Chicago faced an eight-game trip that would extend into the middle of the season's final week—three at California, a travel day, three at Cleveland, another travel day, and two at Kansas City. Chicago would finish with three at home against Washington.

The Twins were left with a peculiar schedule. Beginning with the just-concluded series at Chicago, they were scheduled to play thirteen consecutive days, then take two days off before finishing with a two-game series at Boston. This would include some odd game times during the upcoming weekend at home against the Yankees to avoid conflicting with the University of Minnesota's football game against Utah. The Twins' game against New York on Saturday, September 23, was scheduled for 10:00 A.M. And because of that early starting time, the teams couldn't be expected to play on the previous night. So the Friday date was made a day game.

The Tigers weren't exempt from weird scheduling. After playing host to Boston the next two nights, Detroit would welcome in New York for one game, then take off for a swing through Washington and New York before finishing at home with a four-game series against California.

On Monday, September 18, the Red Sox opened a crucial three-game series at Detroit. That afternoon back at Fenway Park in Boston, Tony Conigliaro faced a pitcher for the first time in exactly a month. Conigliaro took the opportunity to make Fenway his own baseball laboratory. Thirty days after being struck above the left eye by a pitch, he stood in the same batter's box. This time, it was Moe Rosenfield, a Red Sox batboy, on the mound. Tony C wanted to know if he could still hit a baseball, if the eye had improved enough for him to even begin thinking of putting on a Red Sox uniform again during the season, to be part of this unparalleled pennant race. Rosenfield pitched, and Conigliaro was able to hit the ball. He made contact on more pitches than not. But Conigliaro also recognized that he wasn't able to adequately pick up every pitch. His vision had improved but not enough for him to consider rejoining the team. He simply would wait until his next visit with Dr. Regan the following week.

The opener of the Boston-Detroit series that night matched Red Sox rookie Jerry Stephenson against the Tigers' Denny McLain. Stephenson had pitched well since being placed in the starting rotation in late August, compiling a 3–0 record in four starts. Conversely, McLain had failed to win any of his last three starts, lasting less than two innings in his last start against the White Sox. But a crowd of more than forty-two thousand that gave Tiger Stadium a World Series atmosphere was banking on McLain keeping the Tigers in first place.

It was apparent in the first inning that McLain was still groping to find his control. He gave up three runs on three hits in the first, though the Tigers put him back on equal footing by scoring three runs in the second. But McLain opened the third inning by walking Mike Andrews and giving up a single to Carl Yastrzemski. That was enough for Detroit manager Mayo Smith. McLain was out, and Fred Gladding made his earliest relief appearance of the season. McLain stormed into the clubhouse and vented his frustration by kicking a locker with his left foot. Meanwhile, Gladding held the Red Sox that inning to a sacrifice fly by Reggie Smith, putting Boston back ahead, 4–3.

Detroit tied the score at 4–4 in the sixth on Norm Cash's second home run of the game. In the eighth, the Tigers moved ahead when Al

Kaline singled, was sacrificed to second by Willie Horton, and scored on a double by Jim Northrup. All that stood between the Tigers and a two-game lead over Boston was reliever Fred Lasher, who had retired the Red Sox harmlessly in the eighth, pitching a scoreless ninth inning. That would give Lasher an incredible record of 3–0 with eight saves in fourteen games. It was consoling for Smith and the rest of the Tigers to recall that Lasher had not given up a home run all year, in the minors or majors.

Lasher struck out Andrews for the first out. That brought up Yastrzemski, already 2 for 3 with a run batted in. With the count 2 and 0, Yaz was thinking fastball and thought correctly. He blasted Lasher's next pitch into the upper deck in right field for his 40th home run to tie the score, 5–5. In the bottom of the ninth, Red Sox manager Dick Williams juggled relievers Johnny Wyatt, Sparky Lyle, and José Santiago to get out of the inning without giving up a run. Santiago came in with two on and two out and got Mickey Stanley to hit a harmless fly ball for the final out.

Dalton Jones led off the tenth inning for Boston as Smith went to his bullpen again for Mike Marshall, who had not given up an earned run in his last seven appearances covering 10 innings. Jones was a reserve infielder, filling in mostly at third base and some at second. Williams had started the left-handed hitter against McLain because Jones had a good history of hitting at Tiger Stadium. Of 17 career home runs in the majors, five had been hit at Tiger Stadium. So far, Williams's hunch had worked. Jones came up to bat in the tenth inning with three hits in four at-bats and an RBI. Jones hit Marshall's second pitch into the upper deck in right field—the sixth of 18 career homers to be hit at Detroit—to quiet the big crowd and give Boston a 6–5 lead. Santiago put down the Tigers in order in the bottom of the tenth, with Jones fittingly ending the game with a leaping catch of a line drive hit by Bill Freehan.

The Detroit clubhouse was deathly silent. McLain sat with his chin cupped in his hand. Cash, who often broke the tension in such situations, sat still and said nothing. Reporters didn't so much talk with Lasher as wander past his locker and catch bits of his own mumbling. "I'd never give him that pitch again," Lasher said, referring to Yastrzemski's game-tying homer. "Anyone could have hit it out—even myself."

For Yastrzemski, the homer had ended a six-game home-run drought. The three-hit game improved his average during September to .357. More important, he passed Baltimore's Frank Robinson to take over the batting lead, .314 to .312. Yaz also led Minnesota's Harmon Killebrew in home runs (40–39) and runs batted in (107–102). When a mob of reporters—many coming from around the country to follow this series—arrived at his locker after the game, Yaz got in the first question: "Who's pitching tomorrow?"

Boston's dramatic victory left the Red Sox and Tigers tied for first place at 85–66. They could be joined by the Twins, if Minnesota beat the A's that night in Kansas City. Aside from the pennant significance of the game, there was a secondary plot involving Minnesota pitcher Jim Kaat. Following a nightmarish 1–7 start, Kaat had steadily worked his way back to a .500 winning percentage. A victory over the Athletics, who had beaten Kaat four straight times, would give Kaat a five-game winning streak and an overall record of 14–13. For this to happen, the Twins would have to rediscover their hitting; they came into the game dragging a streak of 13 consecutive scoreless innings.

Things didn't get any better for the Minnesota hitters against Kansas City starter Catfish Hunter. Kaat and Hunter matched scoreless innings through nine, with the Twins managing only three hits. In the tenth, Bob Allison singled and advanced to second on a walk to Rod Carew. With the slow-footed Allison representing the go-ahead run at second base, Cal Ermer sent in rookie speedster Pat Kelly as a pinch runner at second base. Ted Uhlaender then followed with a single to center field to score Kelly. When A's center fielder Joe Nossek bobbled the ball, Carew came around to score a second run. Kaat blanked the A's in the bottom of the 10th, finishing with a six-hitter and 12 strikeouts, to give Minnesota the 2–0 victory. The Twins had joined the Red Sox and Tigers at 85–66, atop the league.

That is, pending the outcome of the White Sox's game at California later that night. A Chicago victory would put the White Sox a half game ahead of the other three contenders. Chicago would start the stretch-run sensation, Francisco Carlos, against Rickey Clark. Coming off a 10-inning shutout of the Indians, Carlos was 2–0 with an ERA of 0.81 in five starts since joining the White Sox in late August.

Clark was working on a one-hitter with a 2–0 lead going into the eighth inning before the Angels aided the Chicago cause. Ken Boyer opened the inning by reaching on an error by California shortstop Jim Fregosi and was replaced by pinch runner Tommie Agee. After Clark retired Tom McCraw for the first out, Ron Hansen beat out an infield hit that left runners at first and second, with Buddy Bradford running for Hansen. With Rocky Colavito up next, Chicago manager Eddie Stanky wasn't content to leave matters to the hitters. He had Agee steal third. Then Colavito delivered a single to center to score Agee and send Bradford to third base. Smokey Burgess pinch hit for Duane Josephson and, batting against reliever Curt Simmons, hit into a groundout that would have been the final out were it not for Fregosi's error. Instead, it was the second out—and allowed Bradford to score the tying run. With only three hits in the game, the White Sox had managed a 2–2 tie with the Angels to get Carlos off the hook.

But the White Sox's magic wore off in the bottom of the ninth. With one out, Don Mincher singled off Chicago reliever Bob Locker. Roger Repoz ran for Mincher and accomplished the unusual feat of advancing to second base on a long fly out by Jimmie Hall. That brought up Rick Reichardt, who delivered a two-out single to end the game and place the White Sox in fourth place, one-half game behind the three leaders. Even the fifth-place Angels were still mathematically alive, six games out. That same night, the Cardinals clinched the National League pennant by winning at Philadelphia.

Back in Detroit, an event off the field in the early morning hours of Tuesday, September 19, had what may have been a significant bearing on the pennant race. Denny McLain had, by his account, fallen asleep on his couch while watching "The Untouchables" after being knocked around by the Red Sox. He said he was awakened suddenly by a noise in his garage and hurt his left foot when he awkwardly rose off the couch to investigate. When McLain arrived at the ballpark the following afternoon he had his foot examined by the Detroit team doctors to determine the extent of the injury. His explanation of the cause of the injury wasn't readily accepted by all of his teammates; many knew McLain had a way of bending the truth.

That night another monstrous crowd of 43,004 made its way to Tiger Stadium. This time Mickey Lolich, winner of six straight after losing ten in a row, was matched against Boston's Lee Stange in the final regular-season meeting of these teams. The Red Sox took a 1–0 lead in the second inning on a single by Reggie Smith, a sacrifice, and a two-out single by Russ Gibson. But the Tigers knocked out Stange in the sixth when Al Kaline doubled and Jim Northrup homered.

Here again were the Tigers, heading into the top of the ninth inning with a one-run lead over the Red Sox. Lolich had struck out 13, given up only four singles, and allowed only two runners to advance beyond first base. Jerry Adair opened the ninth with a single to right and was replaced by pinch runner José Tartabull. Carl Yastrzemski walked on four consecutive curveballs. With right-handed-hitting George Scott coming up against lefty Lolich with the tying run in scoring position and no one out, Mayo Smith walked to the mound to talk with Lolich about pitching to Scott in this sacrifice situation. Smith did have a right-hander throwing in the bullpen. Curiously, it was a starter—twenty-one-game winner Earl Wilson.

Smith elected to stay with Lolich. Scott went up to the plate with the intention of sacrificing Yastrzemski over, to give Boston runners at second and third with one out. But Scott fouled off Lolich's first two pitches. He then singled to center to score Tartabull with the tying run. Smith returned to the mound and lifted Lolich in favor of Wilson, who was about to make his first relief appearance of the season.

It's debatable whether Smith was really strapped enough in his bullpen to necessitate using Wilson. In the previous four days, Smith had gone to the bullpen for thirteen total appearances by relievers. That included Fred Lasher pitching three times for $4^2/_3$ innings and Mike Marshall working three times for $4^1/_3$ innings. Fred Gladding's availability probably was hampered by the fact that he had pitched $4^1/_3$ innings—his second-longest relief stint of the season—the previous day when McLain left the game in the third inning. Before that, Gladding had not pitched in five days. Pat Dobson had faced one batter in three days.

Wilson gave up a fly out by Smith that advanced Yastrzemski to third base representing the go-ahead run with one out. Smith had Wilson intentionally walk pinch hitter Dalton Jones, hitting for Ken Harrelson, to load the bases and set up a force at any base and a potential inning-ending double play. That brought up left-handed pinch hitter Norm Siebern. Wilson's first pitch to Siebern sailed low and inside, bouncing past catcher Bill Freehan and allowing Yastrzemski to score the go-ahead run. Siebern was intentionally walked to set up the same situation, but Russ Gibson hit a sacrifice fly to Kaline to score Scott for a 4–2 lead. For the second consecutive game, Detroit had allowed a lead to escape in the top of the ninth inning.

The Tigers came to bat having stranded eight runners. José Santiago, who pitched a scoreless eighth inning, served up a liner to Don Wert that Yastrzemski ran down with a sliding catch for an out, then walked pinch hitter Lenny Green and Dick McAuliffe. Red Sox manager Dick Williams replaced Santiago with Bill Landis, who had not pitched since August 29. When Landis made it to the mound, Williams held up the baseball and asked him, "Do you know what this is?"

Detroit's Smith sent up Eddie Mathews as a pinch hitter. Landis, apparently familiar with the round object, struck out Mathews for the second out. Then Williams copied Smith's strategy and brought in a starter, Gary Bell, to try to get the final out against Kaline. On Bell's first pitch, Kaline smacked a liner to center that Reggie Smith squeezed in his glove for the final out. Most of the huge crowd had remained to the finish, and many fans vented their frustration with resounding boos before heading for the exits. For the second consecutive night, the Tigers had let a game—against one of their toughest competitors, no less—slip away in the final inning.

Tigers owner John Fetzer decided it was time to ignore his own rule about keeping distance between himself and his players. He came down to the clubhouse just to let his players know he was there, to let them know the owner had not given up on the team. Kaline was the first to notice Fetzer, and walked over and shook his hand. Fetzer spent about ten minutes talking with Kaline, then Mathews, before quietly leaving the clubhouse. He had made his point and was on his way without fanfare.

Yastrzemski went 0 for 3 while Frank Robinson went 1–2 against the Yankees. That put Robinson back in the league lead in hitting, .313 to .312.

In Kansas City, the Twins needed a victory in front of a Municipal Stadium "crowd" of fewer than four thousand fans to keep pace with the Red Sox. That appeared unlikely the way Minnesota starter Dave Boswell began the game. He walked five, hit one, and threw two wild pitches in four innings, somehow managing to maintain a 4–2 lead. Then Boswell settled down to retire the next 14 batters. Meanwhile, Minnesota scored another run in the fifth inning and added a four-run outburst in the seventh to beat the A's, 8–2. Boswell ended up pitching a complete game to improve his record to 14–11.

The White Sox needed a win to remain a half game behind Boston and Minnesota. Their chances were in the hands of the hottest pitcher in baseball, Joe Horlen. In four September starts, Horlen was 3–0 and had given up three earned runs in 35 innings, including the September 10 no-hitter over the Tigers. He added to his amazing run with a six-hit shutout of the Angels, 3–0. Chicago scored all of its runs in the sixth inning with an assist from its pitcher's bat. Horlen singled off Angels starter Jim McGlothlin and advanced to second base on a wild pitch. Tommie Agee singled to score Horlen. Tom McCraw later tripled home Agee and scored on a single by Ken Boyer to account for the White Sox's three runs. Horlen had pitched 12 complete games and five shutouts to highlight his 18–6 record. His latest win enabled Chicago to remain a half game out, now in third place, a half game ahead of Detroit.

On Wednesday, September 20, the Red Sox and Tigers moved on to other series, the Twins and the Athletics made a rare about-face by moving from Kansas City to Minnesota for two more games, and the White Sox finished their three-game series at California. The Red Sox faced the Indians, with ace pitcher Jim Lonborg seeking his twenty-first victory to tie Detroit's Earl Wilson for the league lead. Lonborg had already pitched three complete-game victories over Cleveland during the season. The

Indians took a 2–0 lead in the fifth on a two-run home run by Larry Brown, but Boston handed Lonborg the lead in the sixth when Carl Yastrzemski hit his 41st home run (coming off Sam McDowell; it was only his fifth of the year off a left-handed pitcher), George Scott singled, and Rico Petrocelli followed with another homer for a 3–2 lead. Boston added another run in the seventh on, what else, a home run, this time by Mike Andrews. But Lonborg couldn't hold the lead in the bottom of the seventh. Tony Horton, the former Boston first baseman, preceded Max Alvis on a string of back-to-back homers that tied the score, 4–4.

The score remained tied going to the ninth. Andrews led off with a walk against reliever George Culver, but Jerry Adair hit into a double play. Yastrzemski kept the inning alive with a single to left-center. Scott fell behind on the count 0 and 2, shortened up his swing, and worked out a walk, moving the go-ahead run into scoring position. Reggie Smith also fell behind 0 and 2, then lined a fastball into right field to score Yaz and put Boston ahead, 5–4. Red Sox reliever Johnny Wyatt, who got the final out of the eighth inning, held the Indians scoreless in the bottom of the ninth to improve his record to 10–6. Cleveland got a runner aboard, but Petrocelli turned a grounder hit by Joe Azcue into a game-ending double play. For the third consecutive game, Boston had won a road game in which they went to the ninth inning without leading. In going 4 for 5, Yastrzemski regained the league lead in hitting over Robinson, .316 to .312.

Enthusiasm in Detroit was tempered, as expected, as the Yankees hit town to play one game. After more than eighty-five thousand fans watched the Tigers play the Red Sox, the crowd for New York's Wednesday night cameo was about fourteen thousand. Maybe Tigers manager Mayo Smith was trying to take the pressure off his team when he started rookie Wayne Comer, fresh up from Toledo, in center field. Luckily for the small gathering, the Yankees' threat loomed about as large as the crowd. The Tigers battered four Yankees pitchers for an easy 10–1 victory as Joe Sparma won his fifteenth. Al Kaline had three of Detroit's 12 hits—two doubles and his 25th home run. Five of Kaline's last six hits were for extra bases, and the 3-for-4 effort pushed Kaline's September average up to .413.

Tony Oliva continued his own hot hitting as the Twins made it three consecutive wins over the Athletics, this time beating Kansas City, 6–2, at the Met for Dean Chance's nineteenth victory. Oliva had a single and a home run to give him a .378 average for the month. Not that Chance needed much help. His four-hitter was the third consecutive complete game thrown by Minnesota pitchers, all against the A's.

The White Sox scored four runs in the first inning to knock out California starter George Brunet en route to their 6–4 victory. Tommie

Agee led the Chicago attack with three hits and three runs batted in. With the White Sox's victory, all four contenders had won, leaving the pennant race unchanged by the day's events.

But there was a loser. Before the Tigers' victory over the Yankees, it was determined that Denny McLain, now limited to walking with crutches, would have to miss at least his next start because of the injury to the toes on his left foot. An exhausted bullpen had prompted manager Mayo Smith to use starter Earl Wilson in relief that week in a crucial situation against Boston, and now the Tigers were down to three starting pitchers. Team physician Russell Wright told reporters that McLain might be able to return in about a week, which would be the middle of the season's final week. The very real possibility also existed that McLain had pitched his final game of the season.

All good things must come to an end, and so it was for the Twins and their sparring partners, the Athletics, on the afternoon of Thursday, September 21. Jim Merritt gave Minnesota its fourth consecutive complete-game victory over the A's in as many days, shutting them out on two hits, 4–0. Merritt didn't walk a batter, and, with John Donaldson being picked off after hitting a single, he faced only 28 batters—one over the minimum. The Twins gave Merritt more than enough runs when they scored three times in the sixth. Cesar Tovar walked, Harmon Killebrew hit his 40th home run, and Tony Oliva followed with his 17th homer.

That night, Boston almost let a 6–1 seventh-inning lead get away but hung on for a 6–5 victory over the Indians in a game that was delayed by rain. The Red Sox closed out their brief visit to Cleveland, matching Minnesota with four straight wins. Boston starter Gary Bell recorded his third win over Cleveland since the June 3 trade that brought him over from the Indians. He helped his own cause with an RBI double in the seventh. Johnny Wyatt pitched the ninth inning for the Red Sox to notch his seventeenth save. Since the game started late because of rain, the Red Sox didn't arrive at their next stop, Baltimore, until 3:00 A.M.

With the Angels and Tigers off, the stage was set for the next-to-last weekend of the season. The Red Sox and Twins were still tied for first place. Boston would play its final road series of the season, four games in three days at Baltimore. Minnesota, after feasting on the A's, would play its last series of the season against a team with a losing record, with the Yankees coming to Metropolitan Stadium for three day games. The White Sox were in third place, only a game out of first, with three games ahead of them in Cleveland. And fourth-place Detroit, 1½ games out, faced an odd alignment of games in Washington. They would play the Senators in a

Friday doubleheader, one of the games being the makeup of a rainout, then take Saturday off before finishing the series Sunday.

On Friday, September 22, the Twins began their series against the Yankees with an 8–2 victory and, for the fifth consecutive game, respectfully declined any contribution from their bullpen. Jim Kaat, who started the complete-game string four days earlier at Kansas City, improved his record to 15–13 with a seven-hitter in which he yielded only a pair of unearned runs. Cesar Tovar hit a pair of home runs, and Zoilo Versalles added another as the Twins struck with two runs in the first inning, and broke open the game scoring four more in the fifth. But Kaat was feeling the strain of pitching so many innings and was taking cortisone shots to relieve the inflammation in his left elbow.

In Baltimore, the Red Sox knew that with the result of Minnesota's afternoon game they would have to sweep the Orioles to stay in first place. The pitching matchups for the doubleheader were rookies Jerry Stephenson of Boston and Jim Hardin of Baltimore in the opener, then José Santiago, the Red Sox's star in relief at Detroit, making his first start since September 1, against the Birds' Pete Richert. Hardin had been one of the few bright spots in Baltimore's otherwise dismal season. When he shut out the Red Sox on five singles to open the doubleheader, he improved his record to 8–2 with seven wins in his last eight decisions. With the loss, the Red Sox needed a split just to stay within a half game of the Twins. That's just what Santiago—with help from Boston's suddenly potent bats—provided in the nightcap. After the Orioles took a 2–0 lead in the third inning, Boston stormed back by scoring five in the fourth and beat Baltimore, 10–3. Santiago himself scored three runs, reaching base on an error, a single, and a double. Yastrzemski retained a four-point lead in the batting race, since he and Frank Robinson each went 2 for 7.

The Tigers' fears about being short of pitching were unfounded, at least for one day. In Washington, Detroit starters Earl Wilson and Mickey Lolich threw complete games despite having only two days' rest each to sweep the Senators, 8–3 and 4–0. For Wilson it was win No. 22, putting him two ahead of Lonborg. For Lolich, it marked seven victories in his last eight decisions. Even with Wilson's complete-game win, Mayo Smith was thinking of bringing him back on two days' rest again Monday in New York. Wilson speculated that Smith wanted to use him Monday in New York, the following Thursday night at home against California, and have him ready in the bullpen on the final day of the season against the Angels. "Well, I'll be ready," Wilson told reporters. Detroit wracked Washington pitching for 21 hits in the doubleheader, with catcher Bill Freehan being the only Tiger to get two hits in each game.

The White Sox played at Cleveland that night, having shut out the Indians over the last 27 consecutive innings when the teams met at Comiskey Park the previous week. The Tribe broke that streak in the second inning when Larry Brown doubled home Vern Fuller for a 1–0 lead. Cleveland's Luis Tiant had the White Sox shut out until the top of the ninth. Don Buford doubled, for only Chicago's fourth hit, and scored on a single by pinch hitter Smokey Burgess. The 1–1 tie continued into extra innings, until it was broken in the thirteenth inning when the Indians' Tony Horton hit the first pitch made by rookie reliever Roger Nelson into the seats for his 10th home run. A situation that troubled Chicago manager Eddie Stanky was that the White Sox had scored in only six of their last 58 innings in five games against the Indians.

A more troubling problem for the White Sox was that they stood in fourth place, two games behind the first-place Twins with only seven games to play. It was paramount that staff ace Joe Horlen and rookie sensation Francisco Carlos stop the Indians the next two games, or Chicago would be in serious trouble.

Friday, September 22, saw the race officially narrowed to four teams. The fifth-place Angels lost at Kansas City, 3–1, and were eliminated.

There was no morning glory for the Minnesota Twins as they faced the Yankees on Saturday, September 23, in the game starting at 10:00 A.M. Twins starter Dave Boswell struggled early for the second consecutive start, giving up two singles and two walks to give the Yanks a 1–0 lead. A three-run homer in the third inning by Yankees rookie Tom Shopay, his first home run in the majors, knocked out Boswell, causing Cal Ermer to go to his bullpen for the first time in seven games. By then the damage was done. New York went on to win, 6–2.

That afternoon in Cleveland, Indians right-hander Sonny Siebert took the mound against the White Sox with a string of 23 consecutive scoreless innings. That ended in the first inning, when Chicago strung together a single by Don Buford and doubles by Pete Ward and Ken Boyer to take a 2–0 lead. With Joe Horlen pitching for Chicago, the game already was over. He threw his second consecutive shutout, and the fourth in his last five starts, as the White Sox beat the Indians, 8–0. Horlen's numbers for September were astounding: six starts, five complete games, three shutouts, 53 innings, 23 hits, four earned runs, 25 strikeouts, nine walks, and an earned run average of 0.68.

The Red Sox could take over first place with a victory that night at Baltimore. The Boston starter was Lee Stange, winless in his last five starts. The Orioles made it six straight for Stange, knocking him out by taking a 4–0 lead through three innings. But the Red Sox rallied with a run in the fourth and four in the fifth—the rally including Carl Yastrzemski's 42nd home run and an error by Brooks Robinson—to take a 5–4 lead. Baltimore tied the score in the bottom of the seventh off rookie reliever Gary Waslewski. Red Sox manager Dick Williams called upon his top reliever, Johnny Wyatt, in the bottom of the eighth with the score still tied, 5–5. With one out, Frank Robinson singled to center, and Brooks Robinson homered into the left-field seats to put the Orioles ahead, 7–5. Boston failed to score against veteran reliever Stu Miller in the ninth, leaving the Red Sox a half game behind the first-place Twins. Boston had fallen into third place, just percentage points behind Detroit, which also was a half game out. The White Sox, still in fourth place, were back within a game of the top. Robinson went 3 for 4 and Yastrzemski 2 for 3, leaving Yaz with a two-point lead in the batting race.

Dalton Jones proved on Sunday afternoon, September 24 that he didn't always save his best hitting for Tiger Stadium. At Baltimore's Memorial Stadium, Jones banged out four hits—as did teammates Jerry Adair and George Scott—as the Red Sox built a seven-run lead and cruised to an 11–7 victory that allowed Boston to claim a split in the four-game series. Needing to pitch five innings to qualify for a victory, Red Sox starter Jim Lonborg worked six innings of shutout ball and was lifted to get some added rest. Williams had toyed with the idea of altering his rotation and have Lonborg pitch only one more game—Saturday against Minnesota—instead of two—Wednesday against Cleveland and the final Sunday against the Twins. Using the latter plan, José Santiago would make Lonborg's original starts against the Indians and Twins. But Lonborg's six innings were impressive enough for Williams to commit himself to having Lonborg make two more starts. The Boston-Baltimore game, the last head-to-head confrontation in the AL batting race, left Yastrzemski ahead at .317, Frank Robinson second at .314.

In Washington, the Tigers broke a 1–1 tie in the seventh inning with the help of home runs from Jerry Lumpe and Eddie Mathews to take a 4–1 lead over the Senators. With the three-run cushion, it appeared Mayo Smith might be able to stick with starter Joe Sparma the rest of the way and avoid dipping into the bullpen for the third consecutive game. But Sparma allowed the first two hitters to reach base, and Smith immediately called upon Fred Lasher. In his last two outings, Lasher had given up three earned runs in 3⅔ innings on six hits and three walks. He allowed one of the runners he inherited from Sparma to score, then carried the 4–2 lead into the ninth inning.

The Senators opened the bottom of the ninth with singles by Mike Epstein and Frank Coggins. The latter reached base on a chopper to second baseman Dick McAuliffe, who decided to try to tag Epstein on his way to second base but missed. By then it was too late to throw out Coggins. The fallacy in McAuliffe's thinking was that Epstein's run meant nothing with the Tigers leading by two. The logical play in that situation was to throw to first base.

Ken McMullen tried to bunt the runners into scoring position, but Ed Stroud, who was pinch running for Epstein, was thrown at third base by Lasher for the first out. Paul Casanova then singled to center to score Coggins and cut the Tigers' lead to 4–3.

With runners still at first and second, Smith brought in John Hiller to replace Lasher. Hiller, who had been primarily a starter since mid-August, had not pitched in a week. He got Cap Peterson to line out to left field for the second out. But pinch hitter Doug Camilli, with a batting average of .173, recovered from an 0-and-2 count and singled to right to score McMullen with the tying run. Fred Valentine also fell behind 0 and 2 on two foul balls, then singled to left just beyond the reach of Jim Northrup to bring home Casanova with the winning run. For the third time in a week, the Tigers lost a game in which they either led or were tied going into the ninth inning. Smith tried to put on a positive face in the clubhouse afterward but had a difficult time convincing his audience. "What the hell? We've been down before," he told reporters. "They have written us off before."

Actually, it's doubtful the Tigers had been written off previously in the roller-coaster race. But George Cantor, the Tigers beat writer for the *Detroit Free Press,* came close to doing it that night, in the press box at D.C. Stadium. His story for the next day's edition began: "When somebody writes the book about the Tigers' role in the 1967 pennant race, he should leave the last chapter blank. That would sum it up pretty eloquently."

In Minnesota, the Twins erupted for seven runs in the first two innings as Dean Chance coasted to his twentieth victory, a 9–4 decision over the Yankees. Though Chance gave up 12 hits, he also struck out 10. That gave him 23 strikeouts in his last two games. At the plate, Harmon Killebrew collected three hits, including home-run No. 41. With Boston already having won at Baltimore, the Twins knew this victory moved them back into first place going into the final week of the season.

And the White Sox kept their hopes alive with a 3–1 win at Cleveland, keeping Chicago a game behind Minnesota. The White Sox scored a run each in the first and second innings, each knocked in by Don Buford, and Ken Boyer homered in the third inning with no one aboard. But there was cause for concern when Chicago starting pitcher Francisco Carlos, who retired the first six Indians in order in the first two innings, left the game after giving up a single and a walk in the third. Don McMahon came on and pitched five innings to earn the victory. Chicago manager Eddie Stanky even called upon Gary Peters to retire a batter before allowing Bob Locker to finish up for his sixteenth save.

Seven days remained in the season, and here's where each of the four AL pennant contenders stood and what they faced ahead:

Minnesota	90–67	.573	—	3 at home vs. Cal.; 2 at Bos.
Boston	90–68	.570	1/2	2 at home vs. Cle.; 2 at home vs. Min.
Chicago	89–68	.567	1	2 at KC; 3 at home vs. Wash.
Detroit	88–68	.564	1 1/2	2 at NY; 4 at home vs. Cal.

The Red Sox were the only team with the luxury of playing all of their remaining games at home. The White Sox had the advantage of playing all five of their games against teams with losing records, including two against the last-place Athletics. Only the Twins had to play every game against teams with winning records. The Tigers, in addition to having the most ground to make up, were the only one of the contenders that was scheduled to play each of the final four days of the season.

The only way first-place Minnesota could clinch the pennant before going into Boston was to sweep the Angels three straight, have the Red Sox lose both games to Cleveland, have the White Sox lose both games to the A's, and have the Tigers lose two of their next three games. The odds remained high that an AL pennant race that had been so close since mid-August would be decided on the final weekend, maybe on the final day, and maybe even in the final game.

9
THE FINAL WEEK

The California Angels, having already been eliminated from the pennant race, continued their season-ending roadtrip by moving on from Kansas City to Minnesota. In the final week of the season, the Angels had a chance to play the spoiler, with three games at Minnesota and four in Detroit in consecutive days. The trip to Minnesota marked the final confrontation of the season of the prinicipals in the Chance trade.

Dean Chance had held up his part of the deal, going 20–12 for the Twins and leading them into first place. Minnesota overall had put together the second-best team earned run average in the league at 3.08, only trailing Chicago's incredible 2.46. In the closing weeks, Chance often had said he hoped the pennant race would come down to him pitching against the Red Sox on the final day of the season at Fenway, and the pitching rotation indeed had him scheduled to pitch that day. While most of Chance's teammates were glad it might come down to him—he was known affectionately as "Big Boy" since he was the club's top pitcher—others feared Chance had placed too much pressure on himself.

In the other half of that trade, Don Mincher certainly couldn't be faulted for the Angels' shortcomings in the pennant race. He led California in home runs with 21 and runs batted in with 68, and was second among the team's regulars in batting average at .273. Jimmie Hall had been in and out of the lineup, compiling some respectable numbers—16 homers, 53 RBIs, and a .249 batting average in 124 games. Pete Cimino didn't make much of an immediate contribution, appearing in 43 games and compiling a record of 3–3.

The three former Twins were returning to Minnesota with a chance to seriously damage the Twins' pennant hopes. While there was incentive to try to knock out the team that traded them away, there was no genuine animosity toward their former employers. In particular, Mincher and Hall were thankful that the Twins had provided them the opportunity to play every day with another club.

Don Mincher was a hulking ballplayer at six feet three, 205 pounds. Some of his teammates liked to call him "Mule." Back home in Huntsville, Alabama, his size was no big deal. He had been just another football player, and his nickname was simply "Donnie." Mincher excelled in base-ball and football at Butler High School. And even though Mincher wasn't enamored with football—he never learned to enjoy practice—there was no way a young man could turn down a football scholarship offer from the University of Alabama. The program was far removed from its glory days of the 1930s, with players like Don Hutson and Paul (Bear) Bryant. But still, the Tide was the Tide, and Mincher signed in 1956 with coach "Ears" Whitworth to play offensive end and defensive tackle.

But Mincher's first love remained baseball; it was even fun to prac-tice. So when the White Sox came along that summer and offered him the opportunity to become a professional athlete immediately, he gave up the chance to play football for the Crimson Tide. Donnie Mincher packed his bags and prepared to start his career with Duluth-Superior. He was told to meet the team for a road game in St. Cloud, Minnesota. Seventeen years old and feeling his way along in the world, Mincher dutifully reported to the front desk of the team hotel as instructed, picked up his room key, and set off to find his room and roommate. Mincher arrived at the room, opened the door—and could barely be-lieve what he saw.

A black man. His roommate was a black man. It had never entered the mind of young Donnie Mincher that he would be rooming with a black man. The prospect of that occurring back in Huntsville, back in Alabama, was unthinkable. While nine years had passed since Jackie Robinson had broken major league baseball's color line, no such toler-ance had found its way to Alabama. There were no blacks at Butler High School. Or at Huntsville High or Lee High, the city's other mainstream high schools. The blacks in Huntsville attended Councill High School, and that's just the way things were. And as far as most people in

Huntsville were concerned, that's the way things were going to stay. Integration was not in Hunstville's plans, not in Alabama's plans. But none of that helped Donnie Mincher, suitcase in hand, as he stared into his hotel room at Milt Bohannian, a journeyman outfielder.

Mincher had never really found himself in a social situation with a black person in his life. He wasn't sure what to do. Mincher was so shocked, he didn't even exchange much of a greeting with Bohannian. He excused himself from the room, returned to the hotel lobby, and did what the average teenager does when confronted by such a dilemma; he telephoned his father. Dad was not of much help. He was as baffled by the turn of events as Donnie was. Devoid of a clever escape plan, Mincher simply returned to his room and tried to make the best of things.

Milt Bohannian was from New York and was trying to keep alive a pro career that never had reached the majors. He remembered when he had walked into his first room as a professional ballplayer, and he knew Donnie Mincher faced a difficult transition. As the days turned into weeks and weeks into months, Milt Bohannian taught Donnie Mincher about being a professional ballplayer. Oh, he didn't teach him things like what kind of pitch to look for on 2 and 0 or when to punch the ball into left field; Milt Bohannian taught the teenager from Alabama how to act like a ballplayer off the field. He taught Mincher how to dress, what to say, when to say it, when to shut up, and other such intricacies that can't be learned in the batting cage. Statistics show that Don Mincher hit .282 playing seventy-eight games as a first baseman at Duluth-Superior in 1956. What they don't show is that Don Mincher learned how to take ribbing from most of his teammates for his Southern accent or that the closest friendship he established was with a black man, the first black man that Mincher had really gotten to know in his life.

MONDAY

With second-place Boston and third-place Chicago idle, the Twins had a chance to build a one-game lead over the Red Sox with a victory over the Angels on Monday, September 25. Minnesota had won ten of fifteen previous meetings with California. That included four of six at Metropolitan Stadium and a three-game sweep of the teams' most recent meeting, a series at Anaheim in mid-August. The Twins sent lefty Jim Merritt to the mound, coming off a two-hit shutout of Kansas City. Merritt had lost twice to California during the season and was 1–5 lifetime against the Angels. California countered with lefty George Brunet, 0–6 with four no-decisions since winning against Washington on August 4 and overall a league-high eighteen losses. In his most recent start five days earlier against Chicago, Brunet had failed to retire a single batter.

Angels manager Bill Rigney called the final week's games against the Twins and Tigers "our World Series" and prepared for the stretch by resting Mincher, second baseman Bobby Knoop, and shortstop Jim Fregosi over the weekend in Kansas City. Before the final game of the series against the A's, Rigney had gotten right in Fregosi's face and explained the purpose of the rare off day. "You're gonna get a day off here," Rigney told him, "but the last seven games, you're playing every single game, every single inning, because we're not going to let anybody back into the pennant." Rigney also set up his starting pitching rotation with Brunet, Jim McGlothlin, and Rickey Clark pitching against both Minnesota and Detroit. "We can't win the pennant," Rigney told reporters, "but we can spoil it for the Twins and Detroit."

Rigney picked the White Sox to win the pennant, because of their schedule. He in fact went into the final week with mixed emotions, having been close to many of the people connected with the contending clubs. Deep down inside, Rigney was probably hoping the Tigers would win the pennant. He and Detroit manager Mayo Smith had become close friends early in their baseball careers. And Rigney had twice come close to becoming manager of the Tigers. He was one of two finalists for the job before the 1961 season, when Bob Scheffing was hired. And he was offered the position before the '67 season before Smith was hired. But Rigney was caught up in his loyalties to the Angels and stayed with California. It was the one move in Rigney's long baseball career that he later regretted.

Rigney's intent was especially distressing to a dedicated Twins fan named Ralph Belcore, from Melrose Park, Illinois. Belcore, sixty-two, set up temporary residence at the gates to Metropolitan Stadium on that windy Monday morning to be all the more ready for the upcoming World Series. Stocky and cigar-smoking, Belcore had attended twenty-two World Series and planned to make it twenty-three at the Met. "The Twins are going to win," he told reporters. "That's why I'm here." He brought a portable heater and, looking like a hobo settling in by the railroad tracks, propped himself up atop a coffee crate.

The Angels wasted little time trying to spoil things for Belcore and the Twins. Fregosi, Rick Reichardt, and Bubba Morton pieced together one-out singles to give California a 1–0 lead in the first inning. Merritt's undoing in the second inning began with one out on an unlikely base hit by Brunet himself. Aurelio Rodriguez, a rookie third baseman called up in early September, followed Brunet with a single. With Fregosi up, Merritt threw a curve high. Fregosi jumped on it for a triple, scoring Brunet and Rodriguez and giving California a 3–0 lead. Minnesota manager Cal Ermer quickly went to his bullpen for right-hander Jim Perry, as Merritt headed to the showers after his shortest starting assignment of the season.

Reichardt then blooped a fly ball into the wind in short right field that second baseman Rod Carew was unable to grab. Fregosi broke from third base as right fielder Tony Oliva came up with the ball and fired it home. The throw was in time to get Fregosi at the plate, but catcher Jerry Zimmerman dropped the ball. Less than two innings were complete, and the Angels already led, 4–0.

California added three more runs in the fourth inning for a 7–0 lead. Despite this run support, Brunet was unable to last through the fourth inning—giving up two runs—and didn't qualify for the victory. Jack Hamilton and Curt Simmons finished up for the Angels in the 9–2 victory that pushed Minnesota back into a first-place tie with Boston. With four games to play, Cal Ermer was set to alternate lefty Jim Kaat and righty Dean Chance as starters to finish the season. With two days off between series, Ermer left the door open to using Chance on Wednesday against the Angels and again Saturday in the first of two games at Boston.

In the Twins' clubhouse after the game, shortstop Zoilo Versalles was particularly miffed at Rigney's attitude toward beating Minnesota. "He picked the White Sox, so he's trying to beat us," said Versalles, who called Rigney a hot dog. Twins owner Calvin Griffith didn't share Versalles' disdain for Rigney's strategy, which included sacrificing in the seventh inning to build on a five-run lead. "This is exactly what I'd want my manager to do," Griffith said. "I know he'll do the same in the four games at Detroit this weekend." In the Angels' clubhouse, some of the sportswriters told Rigney that Versalles called him a hot dog—and worse. Mincher overheard this and couldn't help but laugh. "I could have told Zoilo that a month ago," he said.

In New York, the fourth-place Tigers had a chance to pull within a game of the Red Sox and the Twins, which would enable them to tie the White Sox for third place. It was a good sign for the Tigers that their leader, Al Kaline, was seemingly immune to the pressure of the pennant race. The morning of the first game in New York, a day after a crushing loss at Washington, Kaline was having breakfast at the Hotel Roosevelt with Joe Falls, sports editor of the *Detroit Free Press*. "I can't understand it, but I'm not feeling any pressure at all," Kaline told Falls. "In fact, I'm getting a kick out of the whole thing. I'm not tired or anything, and I really look forward to going to the ballpark."

Kaline couldn't have been faulted for feeling confident going into Monday night's game. Detroit sent Earl Wilson, the top winner in the AL with a 22–10 record, back to the mound on only two days' rest. But Yankees starter Al Downing limited Detroit to four hits and didn't allow a runner past first base as New York won, 2–0. The Yankees scratched out both runs off Wilson in the third inning, the catalyst being a one-out walk to Downing. The Tigers were fortunate to be within striking distance the rest of the way. Wilson and reliever John Hiller, who pitched the eighth inning, worked with men in scoring position in each inning after the third.

The loss left Detroit 1 ½ games out, now having only five games with which to pass three teams. Tigers manager Mayo Smith, so buoyed by the Twins' loss that afternoon, was proportionately deflated as he prepared to face the postgame audience of reporters while pulling on a cigarette, his legs shaking. "OK, OK, let's go," he said. "Start shooting your questions." One reporter meekly asked if Smith still thought the Tigers could win it. "We still got a chance," Smith replied tersely. "Sure, why not? Who knows what's going to happen?" Another reporter mentioned a gutty performance by Wilson and earned a blunt retort from Smith. "He's a twenty-two-game winner; he's had to be a gutty pitcher to win twenty-two games," he said. Another writer noted that Yankees right-hander Mel Stottlemyre was scheduled to start the next game, and considering how Tigers right-handed hitter Willie Horton was hitting . . . "Green!" Smith snapped, referring to left-handed-hitting utility man Lenny Green. "Green will be out there and every left-handed hitter I can find."

The White Sox enjoyed a crisp workout Monday in Kansas City, many of the players wishing they could go ahead and play that night against the Athletics, who had compiled a record of 8–26 since Luke Appling took over for Alvin Dark. For Joe Horlen, Monday marked the chance to spend some time with Kansas City first baseman Mike Hershberger, a former teammate in the White Sox's minor league system and in Chicago. Hershberger drove Horlen to Wichita, Kansas, to appear on a radio show because the White Sox were thought to be closing in on the pennant. Hershberger waited outside and, on his car radio, heard Horlen say that Chicago would be in great shape with wins the next two nights in Kansas City. Horlen came outside, and Hershberger rather drolly told him: "We're gonna kick your ass." The two friends laughed, then got back in the car for the drive back to Kansas City. Jokes aside, Hershberger thought more that night about how badly he wanted to beat his old team.

TUESDAY

It was a cool Tuesday afternoon in Boston on September 26 when a crowd of only 16,652 showed up at Fenway Park to watch the Red Sox play Cleveland with a chance to move into first place. But that was enough to bring the Red Sox's season home attendance to 1,606,752, a club record. The crowd also included baseball commissioner William D. Eckert, making his first Fenway appearance of the season.

That morning's edition of the *Boston Globe* didn't pretend to approach the Red Sox's final home stand objectively. A front-page headline read: LONBORG AND BELL; AND GO LIKE HELL. And with the Red Sox having won thirteen of sixteen games in 1967 over the Indians, there was sufficient reason to believe Boston indeed would go like hell against Cleveland. Gary Bell, who had defeated his former Indians teammates a week earlier, would start for Boston against Luis Tiant. Boston manager Dick Williams went with his lefty platoon—Jerry Adair instead of Mike Andrews at second base, Dalton Jones instead of Joe Foy at third base, and José Tartabull instead of Ken Harrelson in right field. Harrelson, as it turned out, had not been the magic ingredient that would assure Boston a pennant. In his first ten games with the Red Sox, he had hit .289 with two home runs and seven runs batted in. But since that time, he had hit .190 with no homers and three RBIs and sat out five games.

The game was scoreless until Bell, 3–0 against Cleveland since coming to the Red Sox in June, ran into trouble in the top of the second inning. Cleveland took a 2–0 lead on a single by Tony Horton, an RBI double by Chico Salmon, a groundout by Richie Scheinblum, and a run-scoring groundout by Joe Azcue. In the third inning, the Indians added another run with the help of a throwing error by center fielder Reggie Smith. Tiant avoided trouble when he struck out Norm Siebern, pinch hitting for Bell, on a called third strike with the bases loaded and two out in the fourth inning. Williams called upon José Santiago, who had thrown a complete-game victory against Baltimore four days earlier, in relief in the fifth inning. But Santiago was roughed up for three runs in the sixth on home runs by Chuck Hinton and Salmon into the screen above the Green Monster in left. All that was left for the Red Sox fans to cheer was a three-run home run hit by Carl Yastrzemski up fifteen rows in center field in the seventh inning. The homer was Yaz's 43rd, tying him with Ted Williams for the most hit by a Red Sox left-handed hitter. "I just wish it had come in a winning game," Yastrzemski lamented. Indeed, it did little to prevent Boston from dropping out of a tie for first place, pending the Twins' game at home that afternoon against the Angels. For all the excitement that was bottled up at Fenway before the game, Cleveland's Azcue compared the crowd that exited that day to that of a church funeral. The bright spot for Boston in an otherwise bleak day was that Yastrzemski's 2-for-3 day at the plate, combined with Frank Robinson sitting out the Orioles' game that day against Washington, increased Yaz's batting lead from three to five points.

The Twins, like the Red Sox, set a home attendance mark that day. The afternoon gathering of 8,012 brought the year's total at the Met to 1,467,024, with one more date left. The crowd included advance scouts

Frank Malzone of the Red Sox and Rick Farrell of the Tigers. Minnesota grabbed a 1–0 lead on California starter Jim McGlothlin in the second inning when Bob Allison tripled and scored on a single by Rod Carew. But California answered in the third inning against Twins starter Jim Kaat. Bobby Knoop singled, and Buck Rodgers walked. McGlothlin bunted back to Kaat, intending to advance the runners to second and third. Kaat, a Gold Glove fielder, made the play with enough time to throw to Cesar Tovar at third base and nab the lead runner. But Tovar took his right foot off the bag when he stretched his left arm up to grab Kaat's throw, leaving all three runners safe. Aurelio Rodriguez singled right through Kaat's legs to score two runs, giving California a 2–1 lead. Jim Fregosi reached on a force play, Rick Reichardt was hit, and Bubba Morton followed with an infield single to increase the Angels' lead to 3–1. Minnesota manager Cal Ermer decided he would pull Kaat if he gave up another hit. Kaat responded by striking out Mincher and Woody Held to end the inning.

The Twins hung in against McGlothlin. In the fourth inning, they pulled within 3–2 on a solo home run by Allison. In the sixth, they knocked out McGlothlin with four runs. The first two came home on Harmon Killebrew's 42nd home run. Killebrew added No. 43 in the seventh with no one on against former Twin Pete Cimino to close the scoring in the Twins' 7–3 victory. Kaat survived the shaky third inning, finishing with a five-hit complete game and 13 strikeouts. He and the Twins had received a slight scare in the ninth inning when a line drive off Rodgers' bat struck him on the top of his left thumb. But Kaat indicated everything was fine and struck out Moose Skowron to end the game. For Kaat it marked seven consecutive wins in seven starts with six complete games. It was Kaat's first win in 1967 over the Angels, giving him a victory over each of the Twins' nine AL opponents. The 13 strikeouts gave Kaat 207 for the season. Combined with Dean Chance (217) and Dave Boswell (204), the Twins became the first team in major league history to have three pitchers strike out 200 or more batters in a season. More important, with three games left in the regular season, Minnesota had first place to itself.

The Tigers came to bat that night in New York, in their last road game, knowing they needed a victory to remain 1½ games behind the Twins. With Mayo Smith's lineup weighted heavily with left-handed hitters, one run was enough for Mickey Lolich. Yankees right-hander Mel Stottlemyre had Detroit no-hit through five innings, but the Tigers bunched two of their three hits overall in the sixth inning to produce the game's only run and back Lolich's four-hitter. Lenny Green, the left-handed-hitting replacement for Willie Horton in left field, led off the sixth by slicing a double to left field. Dick McAuliffe followed with a line single to center, and when Joe Peptione's throw home made Green stop at third, McAuliffe moved to second base. Yankees manager Ralph Houk had Al Kaline intentionally walked to load the bases, but Eddie Mathews followed with a sacrifice fly to left to provide the winning margin.

In the home sixth, the Yankees put together a two-out threat beginning with a single by Horace Clarke. With Jerry Kenney at bat, Clarke stole second base on a swinging strike. Tigers catcher Bill Freehan protested the call, claiming Kenney actually had fouled off the pitch and Clarke should be returned to first base. Freehan unwittingly threw down his mask during the argument. Home-plate umpire Hank Soar got the last word, ejecting Freehan from the game. Freehan was absolutely shocked; since coming up to Detroit in September 1961, this was the first time he had been tossed from a game. Mayo Smith raced to the plate and rebuked Soar for picking what he thought was an incredibly inopportune time to eject his starting catcher. Jim Price was sent in to replace Freehan. Lolich walked Kenney, giving the Yankees runners at first and second with two out for Mickey Mantle. With the count 0 and 1, Mantle popped a foul high behind the plate in play. But Price never saw the ball, and the foul fell to the ground to give Mantle and the Yankees another life. Lolich struck out Mantle to end the inning.

Lolich caused his own problems in the seventh with a two-base throwing error with one out. But he recovered to retire Frank Fernandez and Steve Whitaker to end the inning. The Yankees threatened again in the ninth inning with a leadoff single by Kenney. That brought up Mantle, which brought some life to those who remained from the announced Yankee Stadium crowd of 8,418. Mantle hit a hard grounder to second base that appeared to be a certain double-play ball. But as McAuliffe began to make his throw to shortstop Ray Oyler, he lost control of the ball. He still had time to turn and make the play at first base to retire Mantle, but the tying run had reached second base with one out. The situation was strikingly similar to the one that cost the Tigers a victory the previous week in Washington. In this situation, the point could be raised that McAuliffe had started the game at shortstop—manager Mayo Smith wanting to get second baseman Jerry Lumpe and his left-handed bat into the starting lineup—and had to make the late-inning adjustment in moving over to second base, his regular position throughout the season. Joe Pepitone came up next and hit a fly ball to Jim Northrup in short center that left Kenney at second with two out. The Yankees' final hope was Roy White. He hit a harmless fly to short left field that shortstop Ray Oyler drifted back to catch for the final out.

The atmosphere in Mayo Smith's postgame session was far different from that of the night before. Whereas Monday night's first question implied the Tigers definitely were out of the race, Tuesday night's version implied exactly the opposite: "Who's going to start the first game of the World Series?" Smith feigned fear and replied: "No-o-o-o-o, you're not going to get me on that one. No comment." What Smith would comment on was his starting rotation for the first three games of the four-game finale at Tiger Stadium against the Angels. He listed, in order, Joe Sparma, Earl Wilson, and Mickey Lolich. "If none of them falls off a sofa," Smith said, referring to the missing Denny McLain. Had the Tigers let another game get away, they would have faced a 2½-game deficit with four games to play. At this stage of the season, the one-game difference was huge. Now the Tigers headed home for a day off before facing the Angels, who still had one more game to play in Minnesota the following day, in single games Thursday through Sunday.

The White Sox faced a similar climb that night in Kansas City, trailing the first-place Twins by a full game following Minnesota's victory that afternoon. But a steady rain fell in Kansas City, preventing the White Sox from playing the A's that night. The game was rescheduled for the following night as part of a twi-night doubleheader. Said White Sox manager Eddie Stanky: "I detest doubleheaders." The White Sox actually had fared well in double dips, sweeping nine, splitting fifteen, and being swept only three times. Stanky said Gary Peters, Tuesday's scheduled starter, would start Wednesday's opener, with Joe Horlen going in the nightcap. Chicago's remaining schedule called for two games on Wednesday night in Kansas City, a travel day Thursday, and single games Friday through Sunday at home against Washington.

WEDNESDAY

With the weekend set against the Twins looming ahead, most Red Sox fans viewed a victory by Jim Lonborg over the Indians on the afternoon of Wednesday, September 27, at Fenway Park as essential to Boston's chances of winning the pennant. Even Tony Conigliaro returned to the team, in uniform, though he wasn't on the active roster. By this time Conigliaro's vision in the injured eye had deteriorated to 20/100. The blind spot still was there, and Dr. Regan had told Conigliaro the words he didn't want to hear: don't even consider playing any more baseball this season. He had returned to his Boston apartment, the one with the view of Fenway Park, where he in fact could see who was playing right field in his stead.

Things looked promising for Boston when Lonborg opened the game by decking Vic Davalillo. But it was Lonborg who was about to be flattened. Cleveland erupted in the second inning for four runs on six hits off Lonborg, who was pitching on only two days' rest. Boston came right back to load the bases with one out in the bottom of the second, but Elston Howard grounded into a double play, drawing boos from the Fenway fans. Indians right-hander Sonny Siebert had the Red Sox under control until the fifth inning, when Jerry Adair and Carl Yastrzemski singled and Reggie Smith walked. Cleveland manager Joe Adcock called upon Bob Allen to strike out Dalton Jones, then summoned Stan Williams to retire George Scott and Rico Petrocelli to squelch the Boston threat. Williams remained in the game, allowing the Red Sox only one hit over the final 3²/₃ innings while striking out five. The combined five-hitter gave the Indians a 6–0 victory, the second time in eight days that they failed to lose to Lonborg. Pending Minnesota's game against California that afternoon, the Red Sox were 1½ games behind the Twins with two games—both against Minnesota—to play. If the Twins won later that afternoon, Boston would have to sweep the weekend series just to earn a tie with Minnesota. That, of course, was assuming that neither Detroit nor Chicago finished with or ahead of the Red Sox.

The Boston players expected manager Dick Williams to be livid with them. The clatter of his cleats against the wooden floor dominated the silent clubhouse. Williams walked across the room to the beer cooler, picked out a bottle, yanked off the cap on the cooler opener and calmly said, "Fuck it. Forget it. We'll get 'em tomorrow." In his postgame meeting with reporters, Williams was asked his opinion of the fans booing a team that in the preseason had a 75-to-1 shot at being in the pennant race. Williams didn't bite at the opportunity to lash out in frustration: "What did you think they'd do, applaud a shutout?" With Lonborg having been knocked out early, Williams said he would consider bringing him back Saturday with two days' rest.

In the batting race, Yastrzemski held steady at .319 after going 1 for 3. The Orioles had the day off, leaving Robinson at .314. The Red Sox and Orioles had only two games each to play over the season's final four days. It would be difficult for Robinson to make up five points on Yastrzemski in two games. Winning the Triple Crown remained a very real possibility with Yastrzemski. He was tied for the league lead in home runs with Harmon Killebrew at 43 and led the league in runs batted in by four over Killebrew, 115–111.

That afternoon in Minnesota, the Twins knew they could come tantalizingly close to their second pennant in three years if Dean Chance could deliver one more victory over his former California teammates. That would send the Twins to Fenway Park with a two-game lead over both

Boston and Detroit and at least a half-game lead over Chicago depending on the White Sox's doubleheader that night at Kansas City. The pennant anticipation that had run rampant in Boston on Tuesday morning had reached a similar fever pitch in Bloomington, Minnesota, on Wednesday morning. California manager Bill Rigney was in no mood to be a spectator. He still was rankled that Twins shortstop Zoilo Versalles thought Rigney was going overboard in trying to beat Minnesota. As Versalles stepped into the cage during batting practice, Rigney yelled out at him in a girlish voice, "Hello there, Francis!" Versalles looked back with a disgusted grin and replied, "Hello, Bill." Rigney shouted back, "Go fly a kite." And Versalles said nothing back. Rigney even received a letter from an elderly Minneapolis woman who said it was the Angels' duty to lose to the Twins, that former Minnesota players Don Mincher and Jimmie Hall didn't really want to cost their former teammates a World Series trip. "No way," Rigney said. "The Twins aren't even going to beat us today."

The Angels and Twins were scoreless going to the fourth inning, but Hall came back to the California dugout in the third inning insisting that Chance wasn't throwing as hard as he was earlier in the game. Then Mincher worked the count to 2 and 2 before sending a curve ball into the right-field bullpen for his 22nd home run for a 1–0 lead. Consecutive singles by Rick Reichardt, Hall, and Roger Repoz produced another run for a 2–0 lead. Twins manager Cal Ermer, so close to pulling the hook on Jim Kaat the previous day only to have Kaat pitch a five-hit complete game, stuck with Chance. With first base open, Chance intentionally walked Buck Rodgers to load the bases. That brought up Bobby Knoop, who singled to score another run for a 3–0 lead. Ermer couldn't stay with Chance any longer and lifted him in favor of Ron Kline. The bases still were loaded with no one out when Aurelio Rodriguez greeted Kline with another single. Six consecutive California batters had reached base, giving the Angels a 4–0 lead.

Angels starter Rickey Clark worked into the seventh before giving up pinch-hit singles to Frank Kostro and Rich Reese with two outs. Rigney brought in his relief ace, Minnie Rojas, who gave up an RBI single to Cesar Tovar. Harmon Killebrew came to the plate representing the tying run. Killebrew worked the count to 3 and 0, looked down to third-base coach Billy Martin, and discovered he had the green light to swing at the next pitch. Rojas was convinced Killebrew would, against typical baseball strategy, be hitting away. So instead of simply floating up a helpless fastball just to throw a strike, Rojas delivered a slider, and Killebrew swung. The result was a lazy fly ball to center field that Repoz squeezed in his glove for the final out.

The run that Tovar brought home in the seventh was negated in the ninth, when Hall tripled and scored on a wild pitch by starter-turned-emergency reliever Jim Merritt. Rojas retired Minnesota quietly in the ninth and set a club record with his twenty-second save. The loss left Minnesota only a half game ahead of Chicago and a game ahead of Boston and Detroit.

Mincher's home run in the fourth started Chance's downfall and may have cost the team that traded him away a pennant. For some players, such an important home run might mark retaliation. But remember that Mincher welcomed the trade from Minnesota and was grateful for the chance to go somewhere else and play every day. So when reporters zeroed in on him in the clubhouse after the game, hoping they would hear a tale of realized revenge, they got something far different. He said he actually hoped the Twins would win the pennant. "I've still got a lot of friends over there," Mincher said.

Another observer at Metropolitan Stadium, a Cardinals scout, told a Minneapolis reporter, "Nobody is good enough to win the pennant in the American League this season, but several clubs are going to lose it."

With Boston and Minnesota losing, the White Sox's twi-night doubleheader at Kansas City became an incredible opportunity to return to first place for the first time since September 6. Joe Horlen, who had spoken in terms of a Chicago sweep on the radio the previous day, wasn't the only White Sox player who was thinking in such optimistic terms. Pitcher Tommy John, not scheduled to start in either of the games, stood in the outfield shagging flyballs before the twin bill and talked with Kansas City outfielder Jim Gosger about the games at hand. Gosger was incensed to hear John making reference to "when" the White Sox swept the doubleheader, not "if." If Gosger needed any extra incentive, he had received it.

Among the interested fans listening to the Chicago–Kansas City broadcast on radio that night was Boston manager Dick Williams, who had to retreat to his car to find adequate radio reception. Kansas City, with Chuck Dobson starting the opener, struck first with a run in the second inning: Mike Hershberger doubled, stole third, and came home on a fly out by Gosger. Peters was mowing down the A's but wasn't getting any support from the Chicago batting order. He was hurt further by the White Sox's defense in the sixth inning. John Donaldson reached with one out on an error by Chicago third baseman Ken Boyer. Joe Rudi got on when Donaldson was forced out at second base, then Rudi moved up on a passed ball charged to catcher J.C. Martin. Rudi scored on a single by Rick Monday to give Kansas City a 2–0 lead.

Chicago manager Eddie Stanky brought in Don McMahon to try to get the last out. But not only did McMahon walk Sal Bando, but ball four was a wild pitch that sent Monday all the way around to third base. That brought up Gosger to face Wilbur Wood. Gosger shocked the White Sox with a two-out bunt that scored Monday for a 3–0 lead, much to the delight of the 5,325 fans that rattled around Municipal Stadium. Bando and Gosger added RBI singles in the eighth inning off Hoyt Wilhelm to extend the lead to 5–0. Dobson limited Chicago to two hits going into the ninth inning. Tommie Agee led off the inning with a triple. After Don Buford was retired without scoring Agee, Tom McCraw walked. Kansas City manager Luke Appling brought in Lew Krausse, who walked Boyer to load the bases and then walked pinch hitter Smokey Burgess to force in a run. Rocky Colavito singled to score McCraw, pulling the White Sox within 5–2. Appling lifted Krausse and brought in Paul Lindblad, who got pinch hitter Wayne Causey to hit a harmless fly ball to center and Ron Hansen to hit a game-ending groundout. A Chicago team that depended so much on pitching and defense handicapped itself with two errors, a wild pitch, and a passed ball.

The first-game loss left the White Sox a game out of first, tied with the Tigers and percentage points ahead of the Red Sox. With a win in the nightcap, Chicago would be alone in second place, trailing by only a half game. But a loss would hurl the White Sox into fourth place, 1 1/2 games behind Minnesota and in a position in which Chicago could only hope to finish the regular season in a tie for first place. At least the White Sox could look to the hottest pitcher in the major leagues, Joe Horlen. He was 5–0 in six September starts with three shutouts and an 0.68 earned run average. He was matched against Catfish Hunter, who came in with a 12–16 record including eleven complete games and four shutouts. Stanky shook up his batting order, moving Ken Berry into the leadoff spot and dropping Agee to third. Horlen and Hunter hooked up in a scoreless duel until the A's broke through in the sixth inning. Hunter led off the inning with a single, his second hit of the game. Ted Kubiak followed with a single, and Donaldson singled to score Hunter—forcing Chicago catcher Duane Josephson to leave the game following their violent collision at the plate—for a 1–0 Kansas City lead. After Mike Hershberger was retired for the first out, Ramon Webster singled to score Kubiak and Donaldson for a 3–0 lead. Horlen was lifted in favor of Wilbur Wood, who had pitched 1 1/3 innings in the opener. Monday reached on an error by Don Buford. Gosger, who batted in three runs in the opener, followed with a single, but Webster was thrown out at the plate. Monday advanced to third base on the throw and scored on a passed ball. It was the second passed ball charged against Martin—who had replaced the injured

Josephson—during the doubleheader. And it allowed a run to score, to increase the Athletics' lead to 4–0. Hunter didn't let up, allowing only three hits in collecting his twelfth complete game and fifth shutout. The unlikely sweep left the White Sox 1 1/2 games out, with only a faint chance of winning the pennant.

The doubleheader loss by Chicago left Minnesota and Detroit with the fewest losses in the league at sixty-nine. If either team won all of its remaining games to finish 93–69, that would match the worst winning percentage ever to win an AL pennant—by the 1945 Tigers, Detroit's last pennant winner.

THURSDAY

The updated Las Vegas odds for winning the American League offered no surprises, considering the standings. First-place Minnesota was made the favorite at even odds. Second-place Detroit was listed at 3–1, with third-place Boston and fourth-place Chicago each at 5–1.

California-Detroit was the only game on the AL schedule on Thursday, September 28—a 7:30 P.M. start. With the Red Sox and Twins each having two days off before their Saturday-Sunday showdown at Fenway, each team took Thursday off at home. The White Sox returned home after their disastrous trip to Kansas City, needing to win Friday through Sunday against the Senators simply to have a chance of tying for the pennant.

In Kansas City, news that had no effect on the '67 pennant race— but which would have a huge impact on the structure of major league baseball—was unfolding. The Athletics' lease on Municipal Stadium had expired with the team's last home game of the season the previous night against the White Sox. So Charlie Finley wasted no time in announcing his intentions to move the franchise to Oakland. He also sent such notice in writing to Kansas City mayor Ilus Davis. Finley had made similarly bold proclamations in the past, only to be shot down by his fellow AL owners. But this time he already had been given the unofficial OK by the league to seek greener pastures. And the league anticipated possible legal action by the city of Kansas City to reclaim its team. On the same day Mayor Davis received Finley's letter, the mayor received a letter from Alexander H. Hadden, legal counsel for the American League. Hadden assured him Kansas City would receive a team in the league's next expansion. The timetable for such an expansion had not yet been set, but it appeared the AL would increase to twelve teams in 1969 or 1970. Just as the league jumped through hoops to appease Washington with an expansion team upon the shift of the Senators to Minnesota for the 1961 season, here was the league scrambling to satisfy Kansas City after its abandonment by Finley.

A steady rain was falling in Detroit, with temperatures hovering in the low forties, when Larry Napp, the umpiring crew chief, decided at 8:10 P.M. to postpone the first game of the Tigers' four-game series against California. Without playing a game, Detroit's chances of winning the pennant had decreased. Sweeping a doubleheader is tougher than winning single games in consecutive days. Now the Tigers needed to sweep the Angels in a doubleheader Friday to tie Minnesota for first place going into the final two days of the season.

While Tigers manager Mayo Smith had received an extra day's rest for his bullpen, the rainout confronted him with a new dilemma for his starting pitching rotation, which was lacking the injured Denny McLain. Smith had hoped to start Joe Sparma on Thursday and bring him back for Sunday's finale. But with the rainout, there was no way Sparma could be expected to pitch Friday and Sunday. Sparma had spent much of Thursday waiting out the rain and listening to pitching coach Johnny Sain's records about positive thinking. "And I may do it again Friday," Sparma said. "The important thing is not to get too ready. I did it once in Chicago and couldn't make it past the first."

Smith had no plans to use McLain, who had not pitched since September 18 and had not recorded a victory since August 29. Nor was Smith completely convinced by McLain's explanation of the accident that caused the injury. "How could I make up a story like that?" McLain told a reporter before making his first appearance at Tiger Stadium since the accident. "It's too crazy. It really happened." While some may have doubted McLain's story, there was no debating whether McLain wanted to return to the mound. He spent twenty-five minutes Wednesday afternoon pitching in his backyard. "All I can do is tell the man I want to pitch," McLain said, referring to Smith. "I know I can't sit around the house anymore. I'm going crazy."

Angels manager Bill Rigney set his revamped rotation for the weekend—Clyde Wright and George Brunet pitching Friday, Jim McGlothlin on Saturday, and Rickey Clark, the Detroit native drafted off the Tigers' roster the previous winter, on Sunday.

FRIDAY

The Twins worked out in Minnesota on Friday before taking a flight to Boston, though Tony Oliva sat out the practice with a heavy cold. The Red Sox had scheduled a similar session for Fenway Park, only to have it washed out. Saturday's forecast for Boston also called for rain, prompting AL president Joe Cronin to announce that the teams would play a doubleheader Sunday in event of a rainout.

Hotels and motels as far away as Quincy were filling up with Red Sox fans. Final touches were put on a special platform that was built to accommodate a band during the World Series. Showing the same confidence back in Minnesota, the traditional Series bunting was being hung around Metropolitan Stadium, where the regular season had been completed and the next visiting team was expected to be the National League champion Cardinals.

Red Sox manager Dick Williams decided against bringing back Jim Lonborg on two days' rest Saturday. Instead, Lonborg would be saved for Sunday, though a Minnesota victory Saturday would make Sunday's game meaningless. Williams's choice to start Boston's "must" game was José Santiago on Saturday.

The thought of Boston's pennant hopes resting on the right arm of Santiago would have been untenable at midseason. He had been banished to the bullpen, giving up a slot in the starting rotation in early June. At the All-Star break, Santiago was 4–4 with an earned run average of 4.58. As recently as early August, Santiago still was a middle reliever. He was given a start on August 19 but was knocked out by California in the fifth inning. Williams brought him back in relief the following day, and Santiago finished with two scoreless innings to get the victory as Boston dramatically dug itself out of an 8–0 hole to win, 9–8.

Since then, Santiago had served the Red Sox effectively both as a spot starter and as a reliever. From the 4–4 record at the break, Santiago had improved to 11–4, culminating with a shutout of the Orioles on September 22. His most recent outing was hardly comforting to Boston fans, though. Pitching in relief the previous Tuesday after Gary Bell fell behind the Indians, 3–0, Santiago had been tagged for three runs on three hits in two innings. Santiago had pitched 6$^1/_3$ innings against the Twins during the season, all in relief, allowing three runs on eight hits. With left-hander Jim Kaat starting for Minnesota, Williams would go with righty hitters Ken Harrelson in right field and Mike Andrews at second base. Williams also decided to start Jerry Adair at third base instead of Joe Foy, and Russ Gibson behind the plate instead of Elston Howard.

The Minnesota players met on the off day to discuss the distribution of World Series money, which was awarded to the top five teams in each league. The issue in question among the Twins was whether to vote a share to former manager Sam Mele, who was fired in mid-June with the Twins struggling along at .500. Some players argued that any additional money paid to Mele should come from the team and not affect the players' shares in any way. To the argument that the manager's share should be divided between Mele and current skipper Cal Ermer, other players insisted that

Ermer should deserve the full share if Minnesota won the pennant because he would be the first manager to accomplish that feat after taking over a club during the season. As rationales were exchanged, it became an increasingly awkward scene—players on the eve of the season's biggest series playing a game of verbal tug-of-war over who should receive how much money.

The first snow of the season fell gently across much of Michigan's Lower Peninsula on Friday morning. Temperatures reached the low forties by early afternoon, though, preventing any significant accumulation. In Detroit, where the Tigers and Angels were scheduled to start a twi-night doubleheader at 6:00 P.M., sleet fell much of the morning and turned into rain. By 4:30 P.M. it was obvious to the umpiring crew that forcing games that would affect a pennant race to be played in such sloppy conditions would be foolish. The games were postponed, placing the Tigers in the unenviable position of having to complete the season with back-to-back doubleheaders. Saturday's twin bill would start at 2:15 P.M., Sunday's at 1:30 P.M. Detroit had played twenty-four doubleheaders during the season, sweeping seven and being swept three times. Four of the seven sweeps had come since August 20. Tigers manager Mayo Smith again reworked his pitching plans, settling on Mickey Lolich and Earl Wilson for Saturday and Joe Sparma and either John Hiller or Denny McLain, depending on the latter's availability, for Sunday. Bill Rigney's rotation for the Angels was George Brunet and Jack Hamilton on Saturday, Clyde Wright and Rickey Clark on Sunday.

In Chicago, the White Sox opened their do-or-die series against Washington in front of only 12,665 fans, hardly a gathering indicating much faith in the home team's chances. Tommy John needed to right himself if Chicago was to have much of a chance. He had failed to last through the seventh inning of his last four starts. His opponent was Phil Ortega, who had not won since August 7. Tim Cullen opened the game by hitting a grounder to third baseman Ken Boyer. First baseman Tom McCraw dropped Boyer's throw, and Cullen was safe. Washington's second hitter, Hank Allen, hit a grounder to shortstop Ron Hansen that had all the makings of a double-play ball. Hansen threw to second baseman Don Buford to force Cullen at second, but Buford's relay to first sailed far over McCraw's head and into the Senators' dugout to allow Allen to advance to second. Frank Howard walked, putting runners at first and second with one out. Fred Valentine followed with a single to left field to score Allen for a 1–0 lead—on one hit. John avoided further damage by getting Ken McMullen to ground into a double play to end the inning.

John allowed three hits and three walks over five innings, but the White Sox couldn't make much of a mark on Ortega. John was lifted for a pinch hitter in the bottom of the fifth, and Don McMahon held Washington scoreless through the sixth and seventh. Still Ortega wouldn't give in to the White Sox. Bob Locker came out of the Chicago bullpen and shut down the Senators in the eighth and ninth. Still nothing for the White Sox. In the end, Ortega blanked Chicago on four hits, only one for extra bases. A team that won ten times by a 1–0 score, tops in the majors, lost the game it needed to stay alive, 1–0. After 160 games, the White Sox finally were eliminated.

Stanky, who often ranted and raved at his players in defeat, went off on no such tirade after Friday night's loss. He complimented the players on how far they had come, on how they had nearly achieved what so many of their critics considered impossible—winning the American League with one of the worst-hitting teams in baseball. Stanky then headed for his office and begrudgingly faced an onslaught of reporters.

"I could chase all of you newspapermen out of here and be justified," he said. "We're out of it now, and maybe Detroit and Minnesota and Boston can feel relieved. The laughingstock of the American League is no longer a contender. It's true, but for 150 games those guys [the White Sox] made a joke out of it, and I enjoyed every minute of it.

"All year long, the elephants feared the mice. Well, they can have it all to themselves with a sigh of relief. . . . There's only one thing I really wanted outside of winning it. I wanted to hang on until the final day. Make every one of them sweat until the last minute." Stanky asked if there were any further questions. When there was no reply, he left the room, tears running down his cheeks. Two days short of season's end, the race was reduced to the following:

Minnesota	91–69	.569	—	at Bos. Saturday and Sunday
Detroit	89–69	.563	1	vs. Cal. (2) Saturday, (2) Sunday
Boston	90–70	.562	1	vs. Min. Saturday and Sunday

10

DOWN TO
THE WIRE

SATURDAY

José Santiago was understandably nervous the night before the biggest game of his career. He went out to eat with some friends and his wife, Edna, trying as best he could to forget about Saturday's game. So whom should they run into at dinner but Massachusetts senator Edward Kennedy, a staunch Red Sox fan who planned to attend Saturday's game. Santiago promised Kennedy he would give him the game ball after the victory. The evening did little to calm Santiago's nerves. After returning home, he took two sleeping pills. Then his wife, his unofficial pitching coach, began to go over the Minnesota batting order with him as he paced the bedroom floor. "Oliva will give you trouble," she said. To which Santiago replied, "Honey, they all give me trouble."

The crowd began to fill Fenway Park early on Saturday morning, September 30. Skies were generally overcast but not threatening, leaving no doubt that the day's game between the Red Sox and the Twins would be played. The dedicated Red Sox fans who made the pilgrimage from throughout New England to the old ballpark on Jersey Street were joined by both of Massachusetts's U.S. senators, Ted Kennedy and Ed Brooke, as well as vice president Hubert Humphrey, the former mayor of Minneapolis. The highlight of Humphrey's baseball season to date was his being denied access to the White Sox's clubhouse by Stanky when he wanted to congratulate the Chicago skipper. Even Twins owner Calvin Griffith, who rarely watched his team play on the road, couldn't resist this final series. There were times when Griffith would have sat with the opposing owner. But the significance of this visit dictated that Griffith not sit with Tom Yawkey. He instead simply took a seat in the press box.

With Carl Yastrzemski tied with Harmon Killebrew for the AL home run lead while trying to win the Triple Crown, Santiago promised Yaz he wouldn't let Killebrew hit a home run off him. Yaz in turn promised to hit one for Santiago. Zoilo Versalles led off for Minnesota and greeted Santiago with a single. After Cesar Tovar was retired on a fly ball, Harmon Killebrew walked. Oliva lined a single to center to score Versalles and give Minnesota an almost immediate 1–0 lead. With Killebrew on second and Oliva on first, Bob Allison singled to load the bases. Santiago stood out on the mound, still confident that he had his good stuff that day as long as he started to get the ball down. He settled down to retire Rod Carew on a soft liner to Jerry Adair at third base for the second out. Ted Uhlaender then worked the count to 3 and 1 but grounded out to end the inning, leaving the bases loaded and allowing Minnesota only the one run.

With Boston still trailing, 1–0, Santiago led off the bottom of the third for the Red Sox. He struck out on a 1-and-2 pitch, Kaat's fourth strikeout already. But on the final pitch, Kaat felt an odd sensation in his pitching elbow, the kind of feeling a person gets when he is hit on the funny bone. As he took the throw back from catcher Jerry Zimmerman, Kaat shook his left arm, as if he could simply rattle the feeling out of the arm, and prepared to pitch to Mike Andrews. But it became obvious this was something more serious than a knock on the funny bone and could not be solved with a shake. Kaat's first pitch to Andrews sailed high over batter, catcher, and umpire. Kaat realized something was dreadfully wrong, but he didn't want to even glance toward the Minnesota dugout. He feared any indication that he was worried would lead manager Cal Ermer to remove him from the game immediately. Kaat had waited two years, since pitching the pennant-clinching game in 1965, to pitch in a game this big. It would have to be evident to him beyond any doubt that his arm was done before he would accept leaving the game.

Kaat didn't have to wait long. His next pitch to Andrews dove like a misguided rocket toward the ground about ten feet short of the plate. Ermer hurried to the mound along with the team trainer and got the bad news from Kaat about his elbow. Kaat was replaced by right-hander Jim Perry, who had pitched only 7 1/3 innings since being returned to the bullpen in early September. Kaat was taken to a local hospital for X rays, wondering during the trip if all the cortisone shots he had taken during the season in the name of getting in enough innings had come back to sabotage his arm.

Perry held the lead through the third inning and the fourth, as the Fenway crowd lost some of that World Series excitement and settled in for just another ballgame, just another struggle over the course of nine innings. The Twins threatened with one out in the fourth when Ken Harrelson misplayed a fly ball hit by Uhlaender into what the official scorer graciously ruled a triple. As Harrelson and center fielder Reggie Smith converged in right-center, the ball struck Harrelson's glove and caromed off Smith's left shoulder. But Jerry Zimmerman struck out and Perry hit a fly ball to Smith for the inning's final out.

In the fifth inning, Smith's double to left center pumped some life back into the crowd. With Russ Gibson scheduled up, Dick Williams sent up left-handed-hitting Dalton Jones as a pinch hitter. Jones hit a slow roller to Carew that took a bad hop off the infield dirt and bounced off Carew's left shoulder. Jones was safe at first base, and Smith advanced to third with no one out. Williams let Santiago bat, and he struck out for the first out. That brought up Andrews, who also struck out. With two out, Jerry Adair barely got his bat on the ball and looped a lazy fly toward short right field. Carew slipped momentarily on the grass, still wet from Friday's rain, and the ball dropped in for a single to score Smith with the tying run. Runners were on first and second, and Carl Yastrzemski was coming up. Ermer left Perry in the game, and Yaz pulled a grounder on a 3-and-2 pitch between Killebrew and Carew. Killebrew made the first attempt at fielding the ball, but it got past him. Carew was behind him, moving toward first base, and came up with the ball. But Perry, forgetting one of the first pitcher's rules of fielding, did not break for first base on the ball hit to the right side of the infield. Carew got himself into position to make a throw to first, but there was no one to throw to. Yaz was safe on the infield hit, and Jones scored to give Boston a 2–1 lead. Perry got out Harrelson to end the inning.

With one out in the Minnesota sixth, Bob Allison worked out a walk. Carew struck out swinging for the second out. Uhlaender singled to keep the inning alive, and Rich Reese, pinch hitting for Zimmerman, singled to bring home Allison to tie the score at 2–2. Frank Kostro, pinch hitting for Perry, walked to load the bases. But Santiago struck out Versalles on a sidearm curve to end the inning.

Ermer brought in Ron Kline, with a 7–0 record and a 3.60 ERA. Kline's last appearance against the Red Sox, exactly two months earlier, had been a disaster—two-thirds of an inning, giving up four runs on five hits. George Scott sent Kline's first pitch over the Green Monster for his 19th home run and a 3–2 Boston lead.

In the bottom of the seventh, Williams left Santiago in to hit against Kline, and watched him make the first out. Andrews then hit a dribbler back to the mound on a check swing, but Kline couldn't make the throw, and Andrews was safe at first. Adair followed with a bouncer back to Kline again. Kline had plenty of time to make the throw to shortstop Zoilo Versalles at second base for what might be an inning-ending double play. But Versalles, with his left foot on the bag and leaning off toward the shortstop side of the base, somehow dropped the throw to leave runners at first and second with one out. Ermer went to the bullpen again, this time summoning left-handed starter Jim Merritt for his second relief appearance of the week. In two starts against the Red Sox, Merritt had allowed only one run in 10 innings. Ermer wanted Merritt to pitch to Carl Yastrzemski.

As Merritt warmed up, Tony Conigliaro called Yastrzemski over and warned him that Merritt would come at him with a breaking pitch. Yaz agreed, noting that Merritt had gotten him to hit into three groundouts on sliders when Merritt shut out Boston in July. The first pitch was, indeed, a slider, outside for a ball. Yastrzemski was then thinking fastball, assuming Merritt couldn't afford to get too far behind in the count. But Merritt came right back with another slider, which missed for ball two. With the count in his favor, Yaz decided to wait on a fastball as long as he could. The next pitch was another slider, also low, putting the count at 3 and 0. Yastrzemski looked down to third-base coach Eddie Popowski, who gave the sign to hit away. But at 3 and 0, it would have to be the absolutely perfect pitch for Yaz to hazard swinging. Merritt's next pitch was a fastball down the middle, but Yastrzemski took it for a strike. Yaz was guessing fastball again on the 3-and-1 offering. Merritt came in over the plate with just that, and Yastrzemski sent the ball sailing into the Twins' bullpen in right center for his 44th home run of the year, just as he had promised Santiago before the game. Three Red Sox fans could not contain their joy over the home run and rushed out onto the field to congratulate Yaz as he rounded third base. More important than giving himself a one-homer edge over Harmon Killebrew for the league lead, Yastrzemski gave Boston a 6–2 lead with two innings to play. Even Hubert Humphrey rose and applauded Yaz's blast.

With Santiago having thrown 120 pitches, Williams dispatched Gary Bell to nail down the victory. He retired the side in order in the eighth inning and got out pinch-hitter Rich Rollins and Versalles for the first two outs of the ninth. But Cesar Tovar kept alive Minnesota's faint hopes with a double into the left-field corner. Killebrew came up next and could only manage to foul off Bell's curveballs. Yastrzemski, in left field, realized he was one ahead of Killebrew in the home-run race and considered the merits of Killebrew's walking with first base open, which would still leave the tying run in the on-deck circle. Killebrew worked the count to 2 and 2, and Bell tried to sneak a fastball past him on orders from Williams. Killebrew launched it over Yastrzemski's head, over the Green Monster, even over the screen, for a two-run homer that cut the Red Sox's lead to 6–4. Tony Oliva then lined out to Adair at third for the final out. After 161 games each, the Twins and Red Sox were figuratively joined at the waist, with records of 91–70, with one game to play.

Afterward, Cal Ermer moaned that just about everything had gone against his club—allowing Santiago to escape the first inning allowing only one run, Kaat's injury, Versalles's error, Perry's mental lapse. Calvin Griffith, present in the clubhouse, shared Ermer's feelings, shook his head, and said, "I guess it wasn't our day."

Yastrzemski had all but clinched the batting and RBIs titles. He was 3 for 4 to improve to .322. In Cleveland, Frank Robinson played his first game after five days off, went 0 for 4 and dropped to .311. In twenty-seven days, Yastrzemski had made up 33 points on Robinson. By knocking in four runs to Killebrew's two, the RBI title seemed secure, 119 to Killebrew's 113. The only category left unresolved was home runs, where Yastrzemski and Killebrew stood even at 44. If Yastrzemski retained status quo in all three departments, he would still be recognized as the Triple Crown winner even though he didn't sweep the categories outright.

In Detroit, Tigers veteran reliever Hank Aguirre provided some much-needed pregame levity before the pressure-packed doubleheader against the Angels. Aguirre noted that if he could pick up a win against California, he could make his own claim of a Triple Crown. After all, that would leave him 1–0 for the season, for a winning percentage of 1.000. His earned run average was a tidy 2.06; he had worked only 39 1/3 innings. And with one hit in two at-bats all year, his batting average of .500 was far superior to Carl Yastrzemski's.

Despite his limited contribution, Aguirre had found his niche with the Tigers. A professional ballplayer starting in 1951, he knew the ropes—and was more than glad to show them to newcomers. When Jim Price had first hit the majors that spring, Aguirre and fellow veterans Larry Sherry and Johnny Podres were happy to escort him through the don't-miss night spots on trips to New York and Los Angeles. Aguirre was appreciative of finally having a chance to get to a World Series. A tall right-hander from Southern California, he had signed with Cleveland and worked his way up to the Indians in 1955, the year after they went to the World Series. But he was shuttled between Cleveland and the minors for the next two years before being traded to Detroit before the 1958 season. By 1960 Aguirre was in the majors for good. He finished 16–8 in 1962, combining with Jim Bunning to give Detroit a solid one-two starting combination. He remained in the Tigers' starting rotation until the 1966 trade that brought Earl Wilson from Boston. By spring training '67, Aguirre had become a marginal member of the Tigers' pitching staff. He pitched fewer than seven innings during the first two months of the season. But even though he had worked so little, Aguirre knew that he and every other pitcher on the Detroit staff had to be ready to pitch during the final tumultuous weekend.

The Tigers opened Saturday's doubleheader with left-hander Mickey Lolich. His infamous ten-game losing streak was now as distant a memory as the midsummer riots. Lolich had won eight of his last nine starts with four shutouts. He took the mound to the cheers of 20,421, a crowd held down by the recent foul weather. The cheers grew even louder after Lolich retired California in the top of the first without a run.

In the bottom of the inning, Willie Horton cracked a two-run home run, his first homer since August 20, off Angels starter George Brunet to provide Lolich with an early cushion. Detroit added two more runs in the second. Don Wert doubled and scored on Eddie Mathews's single. Mathews moved to second base on a single by Mickey Stanley, advanced to third on a sacrifice bunt by Lolich, and scored on a sacrifice fly by Dick Tracewski. The Detroit lead increased to 5–0 in the fourth inning when Tracewski tripled and scored on a single by McAuliffe.

Lolich, meanwhile, continued to slice his way through the California batting order. He allowed only three hits, just one for extra bases, and struck out 11 as the Tigers won, 5–0. For Lolich, that meant nine wins in 10 starts and an ERA of 1.20 since the ten-game losing streak. With another game still to play that afternoon, Detroit actually was in first place. Its 90–69 record produced a winning percentage of .566 compared with .565 for the Twins and Red Sox, tied at 91–70. Between games, Willie Horton got a phone call in the clubhouse. It was from Boston's George Scott, who was playfully wishing Horton and the Tigers good luck for the second game of the doubleheader. Horton didn't appreciate the greeting and proceeded to tear the phone out of the wall. Earl Wilson, leading the AL with twenty-two wins, would start for Detroit against Jack Hamilton. Wilson, in three previous starts against California in 1967, had never failed to reach the seventh inning.

Wilson retired California without harm in the top of the first, and the Tigers quickly went to work on Hamilton. McAuliffe, starting at shortstop, led off with a single. Hamilton then walked Jerry Lumpe, Al Kaline, and Willie Horton to give Detroit a 1–0 lead and left the bases loaded with no one out. That was enough for Angels manager Bill Rigney. He immediately replaced Hamilton with Curt Simmons, the spot starter acquired early in the season from the Cubs. Simmons hit Jim Northrup to force in another run to give the Tigers a 2–0 lead. Rigney returned to the mound to lift Simmons and bring in Bill Kelso, a short reliever who rarely pitched more than two or three innings. Actually, Rigney was just hoping to buy some time. He had gotten starter Jim McGlothlin up in the bullpen, but Mc-Glothlin couldn't get ready as quickly as a standard reliever. Bill Freehan delivered a sacrifice fly to give the Tigers a 3–0 lead. Kelso got out of the inning without giving up any more runs, but it was hard to convince most of the fans at Tiger Stadium that this game wasn't over. Most of them surely thought the Tigers were assured of taking a half-game lead into the final day of the season, and that the Tigers would need only a split of Sunday's doubleheader to advance to a playoff game Monday against the winner of Sunday's Minnesota-Boston game.

Jim Fregosi got California on the scoreboard with a solo home run in the third inning, cutting the Tigers' lead to 3–1. In the fourth, Roger Repoz singled home another run to pull the Angels within 3–2. Kelso had kept Detroit in check through the second inning, and McGlothlin shut out the Tigers on only a walk through the fourth inning, when an intermittent rain began to fall. Bob Locke came in to pitch the fifth inning for California, and a throwing error by Fregosi on what looked like an inning-ending double play gave Detroit another run and a 4–2 lead.

Wilson walked Jimmie Hall to open the Angels' sixth. That was the second walk by Wilson to go along with six hits. Tigers manager Mayo Smith came out to the mound and, with Fred Lasher warming in the bullpen, asked Wilson how he was doing. Wilson told him he thought he was fine. "Tell you what," Smith told Wilson. "We're going to make a change because if this thing gets down to the wire and we have a playoff game Monday, you're the pitcher." Wilson reluctantly replied, "You're the manager," realizing that there was little reason to think about a playoff game if this game got away. But in all fairness, the Tigers did have a fresh bullpen, having not played since Wednesday. Lasher had not pitched since the previous Sunday, when he allowed three runs in 2⅓ innings in the demoralizing loss at Washington. Lasher retired California in the sixth and seventh. And when Northrup belted a two-run home run with Al Kaline aboard in the seventh off Minnie Rojas, Lasher took the mound in the top of the eighth with a 6–2 lead.

Fregosi opened the California eighth with a single and moved up to second on a walk to Hall. Don Mincher followed with a single that scored Fregosi and sent Hall to third base. Rick Reichardt singled to right, bringing home Hall and sending Mincher to third to cut Detroit's lead to 6–4. With the go-ahead run coming up with no one out, Smith brought in Hank Aguirre for his first appearance since working two-thirds of an inning twelve days earlier against the Red Sox. With runners at first and third, Bubba Morton hit a nubber back to the mound. The ball was hit too slowly for Aguirre to think about turning a double play. Aguirre's play should have been to look Mincher back to third base, then make the throw to first to retire Morton. Instead, Aguirre simply turned to first base to make the throw. Tigers catcher Bill Freehan yelled at Aguirre to throw home, but it was too late. As Aguirre made the throw to first, Mincher charged down the line to score. California had cut the lead to 6–5 and had the tying run, Reichardt, on second base with only one out.

Aguirre then walked Buck Rodgers, putting runners at first and second. Smith returned to the mound to yank Aguirre in favor of Fred Gladding, who, like Aguirre, had not pitched in twelve days. Bobby Knoop greeted Gladding with a bouncer back to the mound that Gladding was unable to get his glove on. The infield hit loaded the bases, putting the go-ahead run at second base with one out. With left-handed-hitting Tom Satriano scheduled to bat, Smith replaced Gladding with left-hander John Hiller, who was being considered to start one of Sunday's games. Rigney stuck with Satriano, and his faith paid off. Satriano sliced a single to left field to score Reichardt with the fourth run of the inning, tying the score at 6–6. "Hawk" Taylor pinch hit for Rojas and struck out, leaving the bases loaded and two out as Fregosi came up for the second time in the inning. Fregosi smacked a liner to center that barely cleared Dick McAuliffe's glove for a hit, scoring Rodgers and Knoop to give California an 8–6 lead. Hiller got Hall to pop out to first, but California had scored six runs on six singles and two walks given up by four Detroit pitchers.

Jim Weaver, who had pitched three scoreless innings for the Angels in the opener after the game was out of reach, returned in the nightcap and shut down the Tigers in the eighth and ninth innings without allowing a base runner, to earn his first major league save. The Tigers, who had been two innings away from a half-game lead, now were faced with the prospect of having to sweep California on Sunday just to earn a tie with the winner of Sunday's Minnesota-Boston game.

Hank Aguirre was not talking after the game about his personal Triple Crown. He sat at his locker, his hands trembling. In a season in which dozens of plays could be scrutinized as costing a team a pennant, Aguirre's failure to check Don Mincher at third base in the eighth inning suddenly stood out as the most glaring. "I've made that play a thousand times, a thousand times," Aguirre told reporters. "That's the thing about it. I should have looked at Mincher. It was a dumb play for Mincher to run, and it was a dumb play for me not to look at him. There were two dumb guys out there."

Mayo Smith sat at his desk in the Detroit manager's office, a cigarette dangling from his fingers. "If he'd thrown Mincher out," Smith said of

Aguirre, "the inning would have been different." Instead, the pennant race was different. "There's no tomorrow after tomorrow," Smith said, presaging the oft-used Yogi Berra cliché. By using Hiller in relief, Smith had committed himself to starting Denny McLain, who had not pitched in almost two weeks, on Sunday.

SUNDAY

For all of Jim Lonborg's scientific background and academic interests, he remained tethered to superstitions like most other ballplayers, who didn't know pi from cheesecake. Since he thought he was a better pitcher on the road, Lonborg decided to make this final Sunday at Fenway Park a road game of sorts. He arranged to spend the preceding night "on the road," or at least at Ken Harrelson's room at the Sheraton-Boston Hotel, within walking distance of the ballpark. He took along appropriate reading material—*The Fall of Joplin* by William Craig—and settled in for a quiet evening.

In Detroit, the Tigers' final doubleheader against the Angels began at 1:30 P.M., about half an hour before the Minnesota-Boston game began at Fenway. Because of Boston's vast improvement in one season, national attention had been drawn to the Red Sox's quest to win their first pennant since 1946. But the Tigers' pennant drought was a year longer. Detroit had not even had any close calls in the intervening years. The Tigers had displayed some awful timing, particularly in 1961. That year Detroit had equaled a club record by winning 101 games. It was the year that Norm Cash won the AL batting title hitting a spectacular .361. But the accomplishments of Cash and the Tigers were lost in history. For 1961 forever would belong to Roger Maris and his 61 home runs, and to the '61 Yankees, who easily beat out the second-place Tigers by eight games. Since winning its last pennant in 1945, Detroit had finished within ten games of the top only twice. Since Al Kaline had emerged as one of baseball's great hitters in the midfifties, he never had been able to enjoy the thrill of a true pennant race. Until 1967. And now, facing what appeared to be staggering odds against pulling out a pennant on the final day of the season, Kaline might have to confront his own forced absence from the team during midsummer—when he broke his hand in anger— as a contributing factor to finishing a game or two behind Minnesota or Boston.

Detroit would face left-handed rookie Clyde Wright in the opener. Coming up from Class AAA Seattle in midseason, Wright's first game with California had been a start against the Tigers at Anaheim on June 9, in which he was lifted after pitching shutout ball through seven innings and earning the victory. He had defeated the Tigers again ten days later at

Tiger Stadium, holding Detroit scoreless through 7²/₃ innings. Overall, he brought a 5–4 record and 3.16 ERA into Sunday's game.

As was the case in both of Saturday's games in Detroit, the Tigers got off to an encouraging start. Joe Sparma disposed of the Angels in the first inning without any damage. Dick Tracewski, starting at shortstop for the Tigers, opened with a leadoff single. After Dick McAuliffe and Kaline were retired, Willie Horton belted his 19th home run, into the lower deck of the left-field stands, to give the Tigers a 2–0 lead.

California struck right back in the second inning, when Don Mincher homered to right to cut the lead to 2–1. Sparma put himself in further trouble in the second inning with a pair of two-out walks, but he struck out Wright to end the inning.

With two out in the bottom of the third, Horton hit a fly ball to left center that dropped in when left-fielder Rick Reichardt and center-fielder Roger Repoz collided, with Repoz being charged with a two-base error. Bill Freehan was walked intentionally to bring up Don Wert. The strategy backfired when Wert slapped a single to left. Reichardt tried to throw out Horton at the plate, but his throw sailed over the head of catcher Buck Rodgers. That allowed Horton to score, increasing Detroit's lead to 3-0, and sent Freehan to third and Wert to second. Eddie Mathews followed with a line single to right field, bringing home Freehan and Wert for a 5–0 lead.

Rodgers homered to right in the fourth inning, only to have the run matched by the Tigers in the fifth on a double by Horton and an RBI single by Freehan. Another run would have scored in the inning, were it not for a rare base-running mistake by Kaline. He led off the inning with a single, considered trying to stretch the hit into a double, changed his mind and was thrown out trying to get back to first base. With four innings left in the opener, Tigers manager Mayo Smith enjoyed a 6–2 lead and had not yet had to dip into his bullpen. The improbable task of sweeping a doubleheader to earn a tie for first place looked more likely.

Sparma took the mound in the eighth, having more than done his job for the day. He had allowed two runs on five hits, striking out three and walking two. Three times in September, he had failed to last through the third inning, but now he was prepared to hand all or part of the last two innings over to Fred Gladding if need be. Two batters later, that's just what happened. Jimmie Hall led off the Angels' eighth with a single, and Mincher hit his second home run of the game, his 24th of the year, to pull California within 6–4 and rekindle memories of the Tigers' eighth-inning collapse of a day earlier.

Smith wasted little time yanking Sparma in favor of Gladding, who faced only one batter on Saturday. Gladding retired Reichardt and Repoz, gave up a single to Rodgers, then struck out Bobby Knoop to end the inning and leave the tying run at the plate. Gladding never faced the tying run in the ninth, mowing down pinch-hitter Tom Satriano, Aurelio Rodriguez, and Jim Fregosi—the latter on a grounder back to the mound—to end the game. For Gladding, who opened the year as one of baseball's hottest pitchers, it was the ninth save of the season but the first since May.

The Tigers returned to their clubhouse, as they did Saturday, seeking the sweep. Only this time there was no margin for error. A loss would end their season, a game short of the pennant. And Mayo Smith was placing the Tigers' hopes on the right arm—and injured left toes—of Denny McLain. Owner of a 17–16 record, McLain had not pitched since being knocked out two batters into the third inning by Boston on September 18. He had not won a game since August 29, working five unimpressive starts in September. But Smith felt he had no choice. The option of using swingman John Hiller realistically evaporated when Hiller was needed in relief Saturday. And Smith was prepared Sunday to lift McLain early, to use every available pitcher on the roster in relief. He even asked Mickey Lolich, who had pitched a complete game Saturday, if he could pitch in the nightcap. Lolich said he would be available.

Jim Lonborg may have been among the best pitchers in the league, but his mastery didn't extend to Minnesota. The Twins had beaten Lonborg in each of his three starts against them. Lifetime against Minnesota, Lonborg was 0–6. But with the season whittled down to a single game, Lonborg was the logical choice. Red Sox manager Dick Williams had won his gamble, surviving Saturday's game with Santiago and saving Lonborg for the finale. Lonborg's results would be viewed by a good part of the nation. Because of the passion that had grown nationwide for the AL race, NBC set up a special Sunday baseball telecast of the Boston-Minnesota game.

Minnesota, too, had saved its best for last. While Jim Kaat had been the Twins' hottest pitcher during September, Dean Chance was the team's most dependable pitcher throughout the season. He had been acquired from California in December 1966 in order to give the Twins enough pitching to win the pennant. That assignment may have been seen in vague terms throughout the season, but it was translated clearly into this final game: Chance was expected to pitch the Twins to the pennant on the last Sunday of the season. And there was no forgetting the individual drama involving Carl Yastrzemski and his pursuit of the Triple Crown. One Fenway fan simply described it all in a banner that read: Is YAZ GOD?

Among the guests in Tom Yawkey's private box was Sam Mele, who had begun the season as the Twins' manager. Throughout his baseball career, Mele had maintained his permanent home in the Boston area. It was there that he returned after being fired by Calvin Griffith in June. Mele had come to an unofficial agreement with Yawkey to join the Boston organization as a scout after the season. As he watched batting practice from the Red Sox owner's box Sunday morning, his loyalties were divided. He hoped his future employer, Boston, could advance to its first World Series in twenty-one years. But he also was rooting for his former Minnesota players to get back to the Series, where he had managed them only two years earlier. He ate dinner Saturday night with Chance and Twins rookie pitcher Jim Ollom.

With the Tigers leading, 2–1, in the second inning of their opener at Detroit, Lonborg took the mound at Fenway having written the figure "$10,000" in the pocket of his glove, a reference to the amount of money each of the Red Sox would figure to be guaranteed if they made it to the World Series. He began strong, retiring Zoilo Versalles and Cesar Tovar before walking Harmon Killebrew on four pitches. Then Tony Oliva made Lonborg pay for pitching carefully to Killebrew, lining a double over Yastrzemski's head in left field. Killebrew lumbered from first base toward third, and third-base coach Billy Martin sent him home. Martin was challenging the arm of Boston center-fielder Reggie Smith, who backed up Yastrzemski on the play. Smith made a good throw back to the infield. But the cutoff man, first baseman George Scott, threw his relay to catcher Russ Gibson high and off the plate, allowing Killebrew to score a two-out run and give Minnesota a 1–0 lead. The play was scored a double for Oliva and an error on Scott. Lonborg got Bob Allison to end the inning, and Chance headed to the mound for the first time already leading by a run.

Minnesota added to its lead in the third inning, again taking advantage of a two-out walk. This time Lonborg walked Tovar. Killebrew followed with a single to left that got by Yastrzemski and rolled all the way to the wall. Tovar rounded the bases for the second unearned run scored off Lonborg, giving the Twins a 2–0 lead.

Chance held Boston at bay through five innings, striking out two, walking none, and allowing three hits. Behind 2–0 and with a bullpen full of available arms, Red Sox manager Dick Williams sent Lonborg up to lead off the bottom of the sixth. Lonborg noticed that Tovar was playing him deep at third base. And since Chance had started him off with a fastball in his last at-bat—which he'd turned into a single—Lonborg figured he would see a fastball first again. So Lonborg crossed up the Twins in one of the gutsiest moves of the year and bunted a two-strike pitch down the third-base line, catching Tovar completely by surprise for a base hit. Chance, like most people at Fenway, was stunned by the maneuver and really couldn't blame Tovar for being caught off guard.

Who would have figured the opposing pitcher to pull a stunt like that, trailing by two runs in the sixth inning?

The Fenway crowd, which had been muted by Chance's effectiveness, suddenly came to life and started a chant of "Go! Go! Go!" as Jerry Adair stepped to the plate. Williams had no intention of having his lead-off man bunt with nobody out to get his pitcher in scoring position. Adair went up swinging away and responded with a sharp grounder just to the right of second baseman Rod Carew that scooted into center field for a hit, with Lonborg stopping at second base. Now the crowd was roaring, the tying runs were on base, and Chance couldn't believe his luck. A bunt and a bleeder, and suddenly he was in trouble. Veteran reliever Al Worthington got up in the Minnesota bullpen to start throwing. Boston's next batter, Dalton Jones, attempted a sacrifice bunt to get the tying run in scoring position but fouled off Chance's first pitch. The Minnesota infield shifted for the sacrifice possibility on the 0-and-1 pitch, but Jones swung away and slapped a single between Tovar and Versalles into left field to load the bases.

The Fenway frenzy grew as Yastrzemski stepped to the plate. Yaz had always had a hard time with Chance's sinker, so he couldn't afford to go up to the plate thinking home run. Chance's first pitch was a sinker inside. Yastrzemski was set for the sinker that tailed away from him and ripped Chance's next pitch into center field for a base hit. Lonborg scored from third base and Adair came in from second to tie the score at 2–2. The crowd grew even louder, supplementing its vocal support by tossing streamers from the stands. With Yaz at first and Jones at third, Cal Ermer stuck with Chance, though Worthington appeared ready in the bullpen. The next batter was Ken Harrelson. The Hawk worked the count to 3 and 2, then fought off a fastball in on the hands and bounced it to shortstop. With no one out, Versalles dismissed the option of turning a double play on Yastrzemski and Harrelson. Instead, he turned his body back toward home and threw to the plate to try to nail Jones, who had broken from third base on the hit. But Jones beat the throw, the Red Sox led, 3–2, and they had runners at first and second with no one out. The crowd just got wilder.

Chance was fuming as Ermer came out to the mound to replace him with Worthington, though he thought Versalles made the right decision. His rage was reserved for a Boston attack that had so far produced three runs—and maybe more—with what Chance considered only one legitimate base hit, Yastrzemski's hard single.

Worthington got set to face George Scott, a realistic double-play candidate. But on his first delivery, Worthington let loose with a wild pitch that allowed Yaz to move up to third and José Tartabull, running for

Harrelson, to second. The double-play possibility was off, and Worthington really needed a strikeout. But he threw another wild pitch, scoring Yastrzemski with the fourth run and sending Tartabull to third. Scott grounded out for the first out of the inning. Rico Petrocelli worked a walk, putting runners at first and third with one out. Reggie Smith stepped in and hit a sharp grounder to first base. Killebrew was unable to make the play, the ball bouncing off his left knee and coming back toward the plate. That allowed Tartabull to score, putting the Red Sox ahead, 5–2. Worthington got out of the inning without further damage, but Minnesota came to bat in the seventh inning needing at least three runs over the next three innings to keep its season alive.

Fenway Park organist John Kiley broke into a rendition of "The Night They Invented Champagne" as the Red Sox took the field for the start of the seventh. Lonborg retired the Twins without a run, and the Twins brought in Jim Roland to pitch the bottom of the seventh. Roland promptly loaded the bases without getting a batter out. Mudcat Grant, a star of Minnesota's '65 pennant winner but a forgotten man on the '67 team, came in and retired three straight batters to keep the Twins in the game.

In the top of the eighth, Rich Reese was sent up to hit for Versalles and reached on a single. Tovar followed with a ground ball to second base. Jerry Adair came up with the ball and tagged Reese in a jarring collision for the first out and threw to first base to complete the double play. But Adair was hurt in the collision, requiring seven stitches to close a cut in his leg, and was replaced by Mike Andrews. Adair's daring play turned out to be a key one. With two out, Killebrew, Oliva, and Allison hit consecutive singles to produce a run and cut Boston's lead to 5–3. But the inning ended when Allison tried to stretch his hit into a double, only to be thrown out by a perfect throw from Yastrzemski. Allison tried sliding away from the base, but he was tagged out by Andrews when he reached back for the bag. Had Allison held at first base, the Twins would have had runners at first and third, trailing by two runs, with Ted Uhlaender coming up.

Grant set down the Red Sox with only one hit in the bottom of the eighth. The Twins came to bat in the ninth inning with Uhlaender, Carew, and catcher Russ Nixon scheduled up. Uhlaender hit a grounder to shortstop that took a bad hop and struck Petrocelli just beneath the right eye for a base hit. The tying run was coming to the plate in the person of Carew, the rookie hitting sensation who was 0 for 3 in the game. Carew hit a grounder to second base. Andrews played it much like Adair had done on Tovar's grounder in the eighth. Andrews scooped up the ball and tagged out Uhlaender, who alertly knocked Andrews to the ground.

But before Andrews crashed, he flipped the ball to first base to get Carew and complete the double play.

Only one out stood between Boston and at least a share of first place. The security forces at Fenway Park realized it would be an impossible task to keep the fans off the field after Minnesota made the final out. Ermer called back Nixon and sent up Rich Rollins as a pinch hitter. On Lonborg's first pitch, Rollins hit a soft pop in on the hands to shortstop that Petrocelli thought took forever to get to him. It finally arrived, and Petrocelli squeezed his glove around it to end the game—and begin the celebration.

Petrocelli had concentrated so hard on catching the ball that it escaped him for a split second just what the Red Sox had done. It didn't take long—about the time it took third baseman Dalton Jones to come charging over to him—for Petrocelli to realize what was going on. Hundreds of giddy fans stormed the field; a couple of dozen even charged in the opposite direction, perilously climbing up the netting above the box seats behind home plate like a bunch of monkeys. Other fans vented their energies on the manual scoreboard in left field, assuming that no one in the ballpark any longer cared that Pittsburgh was leading Houston, 8–3, in the sixth inning. One fan fell into the Minnesota dugout, where he had to be removed by stretcher.

The mob was such that even Petrocelli and Jones could not make it to the mound before a swarm of wellwishers did. Lonborg was hoisted onto the shoulders of Mike Andrews and George Scott, then the boisterous crowd took over. While Rollins was miraculously able to jog back across the infield to the safety of the Minnesota dugout unscathed, Lonborg was unable to wade through the sea of humanity to reach the Boston dugout. Instead, he drifted toward first base, where he was lifted aboard a caravan of anonymous shoulders and carried out to right field. When he finally did make it to the clubhouse, he had lost his baseball undershirt—though his outer jersey somehow remained intact. Like the meeting of Stanley and Livingstone reenacted in the Boston dressing room, Petrocelli finally reached Lonborg and presented him with the winning ball that he had guarded preciously through the dangerous journey coming off the field.

The Red Sox fans in McCarthy's Tavern in Boston were possibly the most dedicated. Their attention remained focused on Sunday's game while the rear of the building was going up in flames.

Though the Red Sox still had to await the outcome of the Tigers' second game—which was a few minutes away from starting—to learn their own fate, they managed to get in a not-so-dry run of a celebration. The Great Western champagne remained on ice, but the players doused themselves with beer, decorated each other's faces with shaving cream, and consented to reporters' interviews in a madhouse of a clubhouse. A group of players, led by Joe Foy, set out to tape up the clubhouse boy in mummy fashion. Team owner Tom Yawkey, resplendent in a short-sleeved shirt and an ear-to-ear grin, made his way throughout the maze of players to offer his heartfelt congratulations on a great season. Manager Dick Williams indulged himself in the horseplay, exchanging hugs and thank-yous throughout the room, then retired upstairs to the executives' lounge to listen to the broadcast of the Detroit game, which had been picked up locally on WHDH radio. Before leaving the dressing room, he reminded pitcher Lee Stange to take it easy on the celebrating. If the Tigers won the nightcap, Stange would start Monday against Detroit.

Many of the pats on the back in the Boston dressing room were reserved for Carl Yastrzemski. With his closing 4 for 4, Yaz had completed one of the best personal stretch runs in baseball history. Over Boston's last nineteen games, he had hit .444 with 26 runs batted in. He had 10 hits in his final 13 at-bats. His final batting average of .326 was 15 points better than that of Frank Robinson, who sat out the Orioles' finale at Cleveland. Over the final four weeks of the season, Yastrzemski made up 37 points on Robinson. After September 3, Yaz hit .430 (37 for 86) to Robinson's .231 (21 for 91). Yaz and Killebrew were shut out of home runs on the final day, leaving each with 44. And with Yastrzemski adding two RBIs to none for Killebrew, Yaz finished with 121—tops in the majors and 29 more than his previous best—to earn the Triple Crown. Were that not enough, Yastrzemski also led the league with 360 total bases and in slugging percentage at .622.

Frank Robinson's statistics were dramatically divided by the June 27 collision with White Sox infielder Al Weis. Before the injury, Robinson was threatening to win another Triple Crown: .337 batting average, 21 home runs, and 59 RBIs in sixty-eight games. In the sixty-one games he played after suffering the concussion and subsequent double vision, Robinson hit .282 with 9 homers and 35 RBIs.

The wild scene in the Red Sox's dressing room was being shared mostly by people who hadn't had to endure the chronic losing that was associated with the Boston Red Sox through the years. Kids like Reggie Smith and Mike Andrews had come up from a winning program at Toronto. Even quasi-veterans like George Scott and Jim Lonborg had avoided the worst of times. But there were two individuals who had suffered through the worst of the losing, two individuals who shared a special appreciation for a first-place finish—or at least a tie for it. Owner Tom Yawkey groped through the chaotic clubhouse, through the hugs and beer baths, and finally reached his target, Yastrzemski. This was more than Carl

Yastrzemski, Triple Crown winner and certain American League Most Valuable Player. This was Carl Yastrzemski, lightning rod for everything that had gone wrong for the Red Sox through the early sixties, when fans across New England expected him to be the second coming of Ted Williams. No, he wasn't Ted Williams. And he no longer had to be. Tom Yawkey had tears in his eyes when, to be heard above all the commotion, he practically shouted into Yaz's ear, "I don't know how to thank you." Dick Williams joined in the "private" celebration a few moments later. This didn't reflect Williams's attitude toward Yawkey. He actually resented the fact that the club owner had begun to make himself more visible around the clubhouse during the final weeks of the season. Where were you when we were seven games out in June, Williams wondered.

Over in the visitors' clubhouse, Twins manager Cal Ermer had solemnly addressed his team before facing the postgame reporters, many having traveled across the country to follow this chapter of the three-team drama: "I told them they had nothing to be ashamed of. I told them they gave it a battle, and they lost. I'm proud of them. I thanked them for the job they did." Minnesota pitcher Jim Kaat, still emotionally crushed after having to leave Saturday's game with an elbow injury, came over to the Boston clubhouse and congratulated the victors. Kaat's mind wandered back to the July game in which he had the Yankees beaten until Mickey Mantle homered with two out in the bottom of the ninth, a game that was suspended moments later by a sudden thunderstorm, a game that ultimately was lost by Kaat in August, 1–0.

Zoilo Versalles was left to defend his throw home that contributed to Boston's five-run uprising. "I always play for the money," Versalles said. "So I throw home, It was the only play I had."

Dean Chance had watched the final innings from the stands, too disgusted by the turn of events to rejoin his teammates. He had left a note in the clubhouse that said he would be flying back home to Ohio instead of taking the team flight to Minnesota. If the Twins came back to win, to play in a playoff or the Series, the note continued, they would know where to find him. After Rollins popped up for the final out, Chance walked out of the park and caught a cab for the airport.

Within minutes of the Red Sox victory, the Tigers and Angels began the second game of their doubleheader. The Angels matched rookie Rickey Clark against McLain. Clark was 12–11, his only previous outing against Detroit being a 2–1 loss on August 29 at Anaheim. Clark was a Michigan native who had signed with the Tigers out of Western Michigan University in 1965. His brief stint in the Detroit organization wasn't distinguished. He led the New York–Penn League in wild pitches in his pro debut that year and appeared in only three games for Montgomery in 1966. He was drafted by California in November '66, made the Angels' roster in spring training, and was impressive enough in an early spot start to earn a regular position in the rotation for the rest of the season.

And within minutes of the Red Sox victory, NBC viewers nationwide were shocked to be watching an American Football League game between the Oakland Raiders and the Kansas City Chiefs. While NBC had never made any plans to show the second Detroit-California game after the Minnesota-Boston game on Sunday as it did Saturday, many viewers just assumed the network would take that course with a pennant on the line. NBC officials estimated they received four hundred calls complaining about the football telecast, which the network was contractually bound to show.

The Angels broke on top in the second inning as McLain was done in by his usual nemesis, the home-run pitch. This shot, courtesy of Rick Reichardt, landed in the left-field seats with one out. But Detroit countered against Clark in the bottom of the second. Eddie Mathews led off with a double to left center. Then Jim Northrup followed with a mammoth home run that sailed directly over the 415-foot sign in dead center field. The blast charged up the crowd and gave the Tigers a 2–1 lead. Clark struck out Bill Freehan for the first out of the inning but allowed Don Wert to reach on a walk. McLain bunted Wert over to second base, leaving it up to Dick McAuliffe to get the run home. That he did, smacking a triple to center. Angels manager Bill Rigney wasted no time pulling Clark. He brought in lefty Curt Simmons, who had hit the only batter he faced in relief on Saturday. Mayo Smith made his own lefty-righty switch and lifted left-handed-hitting Jerry Lumpe in favor of right-handed Dick Tracewski. Simmons got Tracewski to pop out to second base to end the inning, the Tigers having grabbed a 3–1 lead.

But McLain, who had pitched a combined three innings in his last two starts, opened the third inning in shaky fashion. Bobby Knoop singled. Jay Johnstone, hitting for Simmons, also singled. Smith started action in his bullpen with John Hiller, whom he had considered to start the game. Roger Repoz followed with a shot down the first-base line that Mathews snared with a leaping catch, then righted himself in time to touch the bag and double up Johnstone for a spectacular double play. But McLain gave up a double to Jim Fregosi, scoring Knoop to slice the Tigers' lead to 3–2. Smith strolled to the mound to bring in the lefty Hiller, who had pitched 1 2/3 innings in Saturday's nightcap. Up stepped Don Mincher, who had homered twice in Sunday's opener. Rigney wasn't about to play the percentages and call back Mincher because he was a left-handed hitter. Rigney had showed his faith in left-handed hitters batting against Hiller in Saturday's victory. Left-handed-hitting Tom Satriano had delivered a slicing single to left field that contributed to the infamous six-run eighth inning.

This time, power against power, lefty against lefty, Mincher crushed Hiller's first pitch. He lined it off the railing of the upper deck in right-center for his third home run of the day, putting California ahead, 4–3. The Red Sox's clubhouse went wild as the news came out of the large speakers that had been set up at each end of the room. In case anyone there wasn't aware of what had just happened at Tiger Stadium, an ecstatic George Scott provided his own unique recap: "Mincher hit one right in the kitchen!" Scott screamed. "Right in the kitchen!" The books were officially closed on McLain: 2²/₃ innings, three runs (all earned) on four hits. The composite pitching line on McLain's last three starts was far from flattering. He had pitched 5²/₃ innings, allowing nine earned runs on 10 hits. He was 0–2 in five September starts, with no chance to be credited with a victory Sunday even if Detroit rallied to win.

With a one-run lead going to the bottom of the third, Rigney brought in starter Jim McGlothlin, who had pitched two scoreless innings of relief in the Angels' win on Saturday. McGlothlin set down the Tigers with little trouble in the third. Reichardt opened the California fourth with a walk and stole second base. After Satriano struck out, Buck Rodgers drew Hiller's second walk of the inning. With right-handed-hitting Bobby Knoop up next, Smith replaced Hiller with righty Mike Marshall with the intention of using Marshall simply to get the Tigers out of the inning. Marshall was another example of Smith's feast-or-famine bullpen. He had not pitched since September 18, when he gave up Dalton Jones's winning home run in the tenth inning against the Red Sox. Knoop hit a grounder to Wert at third that looked like the start of an inning-ending double play. Wert threw to McAuliffe, who had been moved back to shortstop for the second game, to force Rodgers for the second out. But McAuliffe's relay to first wasn't in time to get Knoop, leaving runners at first and third with two out. With a chance to build a comfortable lead by keeping the inning alive, Rigney allowed McGlothlin to hit for himself. McGlothlin, with seven hits in 55 at-bats during the season, responded with a grounder into the hole on the left side of the infield hit too deep for McAuliffe to make a play on, and Satriano scored to give California a 5–3 lead. That brought up lefty Roger Repoz, and Smith left in Marshall. Repoz ripped a long fly ball into deep right center for a triple, scoring Knoop and McGlothlin for a 7–3 lead.

The huge Tiger Stadium crowd was getting more restive as Smith called on his fourth pitcher in as many innings, right-hander Dave

Wickersham, to end this barrage and finally get the Tigers out of the inning. Wickersham was another pitcher who couldn't be blamed if he knocked rust off his arm while making his way from the bullpen. He had last pitched on September 17 and had neither won nor saved a game since late June.

Wickersham walked Jim Fregosi, putting runners on first and third. That brought up Mincher, public enemy No. 1 in Detroit with his three home runs. With lefty Hank Aguirre warming up, Smith hoped he could get out of the inning without changing pitchers again. But Wickersham fell behind in the count, 2 and 0, and Smith trudged out to the mound to bring in Aguirre immediately. Mincher grounded out meekly to Mathews, prompting a sickly cheer from the crowd. The Tigers had already gone through five pitchers in four innings and faced a 7–3 deficit.

While Smith was searching desperately for a pitcher who could get an out, Rigney sat back and watched McGlothlin ease through the Detroit lineup again in the fourth inning. Aguirre worked one more inning for the Tigers, giving up a run in the fifth. Reichardt hit a one-out double, and Rodgers delivered a looping, two-out single over McAuliffe to increase California's lead to 8–3. Smith was compelled to send Lolich down to the bullpen in the fifth inning. Detroit's frustration was typified by the actions of Mathews. He threw a ball at *Detroit Free Press* photographer Jimmy Tafoya after Tafoya nearly prevented Mathews from catching a foul pop up.

Fred Lasher managed to hold California without a run for two innings while McGlothlin pitched shutout ball into the seventh inning. While Tiger Stadium still was frenzied, hundreds of fans apparently lost the faith and began leaving the ballpark. With one out, Freehan and Wert hit consecutive singles to give Detroit runners at first and second. With Lasher scheduled to bat, Smith sent up Norm Cash. Benched in favor of Mathews, Cash had come to the plate only twice in the past week. He advanced the runners by hitting into a fielder's choice and received a mixture of catcalls and polite applause as he returned to the dugout. The crowd came to life when McAuliffe followed with a single that scored Freehan and Wert, pulling Detroit within 8–5. Rigney brought in Minnie Rojas to retire pinch hitter Gates Brown, who had not been to bat since September 18, to end the inning.

Pat Dobson came on as the Tigers' seventh pitcher to begin the eighth inning. Knoop walked and reached second base on a sacrifice. A fan suddenly leaped out of the stands along the first-base side, raced onto the field, and slid into second base. Smith made a less dramatic move, bringing in Lolich. Smith's maneuver proved more successful, as Lolich got the Angels out without a run. In the Detroit eighth, Al Kaline reached with a leadoff bunt single off Rojas but was stranded. Lolich retired the Angels in order in the ninth, recording three strikeouts of the four batters he faced in the two innings. Lolich had to contend with the further distraction of fans wandering onto the field. That included one woman who hopped out of the center-field stands and danced around Jim Northrup before being escorted from the field by the authorities. There was one fan in the upper deck in right field who climbed out of the stands and hung by his fingertips before he was pulled back into the seats.

For the Tigers, the season had come down to one more time at bat. Rojas had pitched 1 1/3 innings, but he often worked three innings during a relief outing. And he had pitched well during the closing weeks of the season, recording either a win or a save in each of his last five appearances. He was scheduled to face the bottom of the Tigers' batting order— Freehan (1 for 3), Wert (1 for 2), and a pinch hitter for Lolich. In case Rojas ran into trouble, Rigney was prepared. For the first time in his managerial career, he had three pitchers throwing in the bullpen at once.

One of those was starter George Brunet, the league leader in losses with nineteen who had lost Saturday. Brunet had a tendency to let himself go the night after pitching poorly. Rigney approached Brunet in the dugout late in Sunday's second game and asked him what he did Saturday night. Brunet didn't answer. "Hey, c'mon. I've got to know," Rigney pleaded. "Were you good? Were you awful? Half bad? Just tell me." Brunet sheepishly assessed his behavior as "not too bad," which Rigney immediately interpreted as bad. "Can you pitch one inning for me?" Rigney asked. Brunet said he could and was sent to the bullpen.

George Cantor of the *Detroit Free Press* left the press box and sat with his father and brother in the stands behind the visitors' dugout on the third-base side. As the Angels took the field and prepared for the Tigers to bat in the ninth, a fan climbed atop the Angels' dugout and dropped to his knees. At first Cantor thought this was simply one of the many inebriated fans who had gotten out of control. Then Cantor put his glasses on and realized this wasn't just some drunk. The fan was actually praying, and he was crying. This desperate fan, and hundreds like him, was trying to will the Tigers to win the game and a pennant that had eluded Detroit for twenty-two years. Other reactions to the Tigers' plight weren't as noble, as various objects were thrown onto the field. These ranged from pennies to a half-broken whiskey bottle that stuck in the ground like a knife. Angels first baseman Don Mincher even wore a batting helmet in the field as a precaution.

Freehan opened the inning with a double, providing the remaining fans with at least a temporary respite from what was fast becoming an ugly scene. Then Wert walked, bringing the tying run to the plate with no one out. Smith decided to warm up Earl Wilson, whom he had projected as his playoff starter on Monday, to pitch in the top of the tenth. Smith sent up left-handed-hitting Lenny Green, and Rigney countered by bringing in Brunet, a lefty. Major league rules require a pitcher to face at least one batter upon entering a game, but a pinch hitter can be officially announced into the lineup and replaced without reaching the batter's box. Smith called back Green and sent up Jim Price, a right-handed hitter, to face Brunet. Price hit a lazy fly ball to left field that Woodie Held caught for the first out.

In the bowels of Fenway Park, a group of soaked, exhausted Boston players howled and cheered for the Angels to get two more outs. In the dark streets outside Fenway, hundreds of Red Sox fans still milled around, hoping to participate in another, greater celebration with their heroes.

Dick McAuliffe stepped into the batter's box, having been the Tigers' most consistent hitter that day by going 2 for 3 with three runs batted in. McAuliffe had never had a particular problem against Brunet in the past. He was determined to get on base to assure an at-bat for Kaline. Freehan took his lead off second. Wert did the same off first. Brunet's first pitch was a low fastball. McAuliffe swung and hit the ball sharply but right at second baseman Bobby Knoop.

McAuliffe immediately realized the speed and direction of the grounder was just right for a double play that would end the inning, the game, and the season. From the play-by-play provided by Tigers radio announcer Ernie Harwell, the Red Sox realized the same thing. Knoop scooped up the ball and tossed to shortstop Jim Fregosi covering second to force Wert. Fregosi relayed to Mincher at first in time to get McAuliffe. After grounding into only one double play in the first 161 games, McAuliffe had done it again, in an at-bat that ended the American League season at 7:43 P.M. eastern daylight time on October 1.

McAuliffe's double-play ball set off an encore celebration in the Red Sox clubhouse and throughout the Back Bay. This time, beer was replaced by Great Western champagne, in honor of Boston's first pennant since 1946. Tom Yawkey, who had suffered along with his players for so many years, through the '48 playoff loss to the Indians, through the last-weekend collapse at Yankee Stadium in '49, through the dreadful years in the fifties and early sixties, asked for a paper cup. Yawkey, who had not drunk alcohol in four years, raised a cup of Great Western in a toast to his rookie manager, who had promised a winning season and delivered a pennant, and began to cry. Williams thanked Yawkey for giving him the chance to manage.

With the celebration continuing around him, Tony Conigliaro could only sit in front of his locker, facing the floor with a towel draped over his shoulders. Having missed the last five weeks of the season, Conigliaro felt separated from the ballclub, only a spectator to what had just taken place. It wasn't long before he broke into tears. Mike Ryan sat down next to Conigliaro and put an arm around him. Conigliaro said gruffly, "Just what the hell did I do? What did I contribute?" Yawkey noticed the exchange and joined in. "Tony, you helped," Yawkey said. "You were a big part of it." Conigliaro managed a forced smile but didn't remain in the clubhouse much longer.

There were other Boston players who felt as awkward amid the celebration as Conigliaro, maybe more so. Ken Brett and Gerry Moses were a couple of youngsters who had been called up to the Red Sox from Class AA Pittsfield during September and were basically spectators to the team's victorious finish. They were in the clubhouse wearing Red Sox uniforms, but they didn't feel like they belonged, didn't feel like they deserved to take part in the fun. They couldn't avoid being sprayed with champagne, but they didn't do any spraying themselves. Brett, in fact, never did put on the World Series ring he was awarded for being a part of the 1967 Red Sox.

There was champagne in the Tigers' clubhouse, but the corks weren't removed. The players dragged in from the field, most just sitting motionless in front of their lockers, not yet bothering to undress. The last player to leave the dugout was Earl Wilson, who sat there alone with his thoughts for some five minutes. A TV cameraman tried to follow the players down the runway into the clubhouse, but he was discouraged from completing his mission when Lenny Green threw a ball at him. Mayo Smith had a final message for the team before the clubhouse was opened to the media. The reporters who then entered made their way awkwardly around the room, waiting for a player to make the first sound instead of initiating a conversation. Denny McLain could only think that if he had pitched better in September, if he had pitched at all instead of sitting out with the foot injury, that the Tigers would be AL champions. This opinion, with more of an angry edge, was shared by other Tigers players. Veterans, like Hank Aguirre, wondered if, in the twilight of their careers, they had just watched their last shot at a World Series slip through their fingers. Through all of this, virtually nothing was said, certainly not enough to break the tension.

Finally Al Kaline, fifteen seasons in the majors without a World Series trip, voluntarily ended the silence. "We have nothing to be ashamed of," Kaline said. "We gave it all we got. We did the best we could." With

Kaline's words, the clubhouse began to come to life. Bill Freehan rolled an empty beer can toward the middle of the room and lamented that "the games we lost in May and June hurt as much as the two we lost this weekend." While that was true, it sure didn't feel that way to the Tigers.

Before the season, Mayo Smith had said he would "take" 95 wins, identifying that figure as the total necessary to win the pennant. Indeed, 95 wins would have delivered a pennant. As he sat in his office, his team having completed a 91-win season that came up a game short of tying for the pennant, Smith's hands were shaking and his lips were stretched tight. A reporter asked Smith what he told his team, but Smith indicated he wasn't yet ready to field questions. The man who had spent much of his efforts in recent weeks trying to buy some time for his depleted bullpen was doing the same for himself. He aimlessly shuffled a stack of papers on his desk, then finally responded. "I told them they went down battling like champions, and they are champions in my book."

For the Angels, there was the satisfaction that during the final week of the season they had won four of seven games at Minnesota and Detroit and contributed mightily to the Twins' and the Tigers' each finishing a game out. "We said we'd decide the pennant," Jim Fregosi said, "and we did."

As the tension in the Tigers' clubhouse began to disappear, some players tried to look at the season in perspective. The season had not been a total disaster, though it felt that way. The Tigers may not have realized it during the latter portion of the season, but interest in their pursuit of the pennant had gone a long way toward redirecting the energies of a city that literally had gone up in flames in June. As long as the champagne was there, the players decided to go ahead and break it open. Not to spray each other in victory, but to toast each other for a battle well fought.

Back out on the field, many of the remaining fans swarmed in a different tenor from their counterparts in Boston, though the results were similar. A couple of hundred stadium seats were ripped out of their frames and tossed onto the field. A telephone and a water cooler were ripped out of the visitors' dugout. Light bulbs were pulled out of the field-level auxiliary scoreboards. Among the fans who were arrested for galloping around the field, one was charged with assault and battery after hitting a police officer. One unwitting usher was knocked over from behind and was carried away on a stretcher. Home plate was torn out of the ground. The pitching rubber might have suffered the same fate had stadium security not turned on the sprinkler system, as had been done at Fenway. The Angels were greeted by an unruly mob as they left the visitors' clubhouse for their bus. Some Tigers fans swatted them with scorecards. Others broke out windows in the bus. Officers were called in to help the players get safely to the bus.

In Boston, a telegram arrived for AL president Joe Cronin. It was sent from the public relations director of the Hotel New Yorker: "I NOW KNOW HOW TO SPELL Y-A-S-T-R-Z-E-M-S-K-I." It was signed by Arthur Susskind, the former TV producer for the Yankees who had told Cronin, when he was with the Red Sox, about the young slugger from the potato fields of Long Island with the long Polish name that he could not spell.

Dick Williams sent two identical telegrams to Bill Rigney—one to Detroit and another to Anaheim. The telegram thanked Rigney and the Angels for their efforts. Williams also asked Rigney to inform Jim Fregosi that the "dietician" had won the pennant.

Before Rigney left the clubhouse, he received a call from Tigers general manager Jim Campbell. "When you're through," Campbell told him, "Mr. Fetzer would like you to come up and have a drink." Rigney couldn't believe that the people who had just lost a trip to the World Series because of the Angels wanted to toast the California manager. "We just want to tell you all of baseball appreciates how hard you guys played." Rigney accepted and went upstairs to join Fetzer, Campbell, and Smith after the rest of the Angels team left the ballpark.

Among the hundreds of telegrams that Williams received was one from Chicago: "YOU DID A REMARKABLE JOB. CONTINUED SUCCESS IN THE WORLD SERIES. WIN, LOSE, OR DRAW, YOU'RE THE GREATEST." The telegram was signed by Eddie Stanky.

Out in the Detroit suburb of Romulus, the last act of the American League season took place. At Metro Airport, a charter plane that was prepared for a Sunday-night flight to Boston was rolled back into its hangar.

FINAL STANDINGS, AMERICAN LEAGUE 1967

	W	L	Pct	GB
Boston	92	70	.568	—
Detroit	91	71	.562	1
Minnesota	91	71	.562	1
Chicago	89	73	.549	3
California	84	77	.522	7.5
Baltimore	76	85	.472	15.5
Washington	76	85	.472	15.5
Cleveland	75	87	.463	17
New York	72	90	.444	20
Kansas City	62	99	.385	29.5

11
AFTERWARDS

When word spread of the Tigers' defeat, firecrackers were set off in Kenmore Square, just a few blocks from Fenway Park. At the Pennant Grille across the street from Fenway, Joe Multoni of Medford, Massachusetts, vowed to down one beer for each of the Red Sox's victories that season. It probably would have been difficult to convince Multoni that Boston's total of 92 was the fewest for an AL pennant winner since the 1945 Tigers earned the flag winning only 88 games.

The Minnesota Vikings were playing the Chicago Bears at Metropolitan Stadium that afternoon, but there was one fan at the Met who never entered the stadium. During the second half of the football game, with the Bears threatening inside the Vikings' ten-yard line, Ralph Belcore packed up his belongings near the main gates to the Met and headed home for Illinois. Belcore, who had been counting on attending a World Series featuring the Twins, no longer had any reason to maintain his vigil at the stadium.

Don Fillmore, who operated the flag department of Vaughn's, in the Twin Cities, sighed with disappointment over the Twins' defeat. But in a way, he felt relief. Fillmore had been prepared to silk-screen hundreds of small pennants featuring the World Series logo to be used at Metropolitan Stadium. But after the Twins lost on Saturday, Fillmore decided to wait until after Sunday's finale before producing the special shipment. No such shipment was necessary.

Some crimes being considered more heinous than others, Connecticut state police must have taken things in stride when they read Robert Craig, twenty-five, his Miranda rights after arresting him on Route 101 in the town of East Lyme. It seems Craig, from adjoining Lyme, felt compelled to quit his car and paint the words *Boston Red Sox* right there on the highway.

The Twins, it turned out, didn't vote a Series share to former manager Sam Mele after all. The New York *Daily News* reported that Mele initially was voted a token share, but a group of players led by Jim Kaat and Ted Uhlaender persuaded the rest of the players to exclude Mele. Milt Richmond of United Press International identified twelve Minnesota players and coaches—Billy Martin, Harmon Killebrew, Tony Oliva, Dean Chance, Rod Carew, Earl Battey, Cesar Tovar, Dave Boswell, Sandy Valdespino, Mudcat Grant, Al Worthington, and Zoilo Versalles—as deciding to make their own contribution to Mele to make up for the lost share. With each team member earning about $1,171.33 for finishing in a tie for second place with Detroit, each of the twelve would contribute about $97 to Mele.

For the White Sox, Friday night's elimination didn't end their final-week skid. They also lost the two remaining games of their series with Washington. They were shut out on five hits by Frank Bertaina, 4–0, and dropped the finale, 4–3. Starting the season's final week at 89–68, one-half game out of first place, Chicago lost its last five games to Kansas City and Washington to finish 89–73, three games out in fourth place. And the White Sox failed at the box office, too, falling short of the million mark. Their season's total was 985,634, the worst in nine years. Of the 63 home dates, the White Sox attracted twenty thousand or more fans to Comiskey Park on only sixteen occasions.

The Angels were the only other AL team to finish with a winning record, in fifth place at 84–77. In contrast to their effectiveness during the final week against Minnesota and Detroit, the Angels had been done in overall by their games against the four main contenders during the season. California was 30–42 against the "big four" for a winning percentage of .417. Against the AL's other five teams, which all finished with losing records, the Angels were 54–35, a percentage of .607.

On October 2, Tigers general manager Jim Campbell reported to work just as if it were any Monday morning. But soon after settling in, he asked his secretary to get Dick O'Connell, his Red Sox counterpart, on the telephone. "Dick!" Campbell shouted into the receiver. "Congratulations! You guys did a hell of a job. . . . Sure, we'll be in 'Bahstan.' . . .

Thanks, see you Tuesday." Campbell hung up the phone and shook his head.

"Amazing," he told a visitor. "Who would have thought that team would go from ninth to first?"

A few days later at a news conference, Mayo Smith defended his handling of the Detroit pitching staff, in particular the bullpen. "We never found two who could do the job at the same time," Smith explained. He attributed Fred Lasher's problems down the stretch to relying too much on his fastball. He offered the possibility that slugger Norm Cash, the former batting champ who was benched throughout the final weeks, might not be his regular first baseman in 1968, that Eddie Mathews might be the Tigers' long-term answer at first base.

Some Red Sox fans feared the World Series against the St. Louis Cardinals would be an anticlimax after such a long, taut struggle to win the pennant. While there *was* something of a letdown, Boston didn't lie down and die; they extended the Cardinals to seven games before losing. The highlight was Jim Lonborg's one-hit victory in Game Two at Fenway, which tied the Series at one win each. In St. Louis, the Cardinals won the next two games to grab a commanding 3–1 edge. Lonborg kept Boston alive with a three-hitter in Game Five to send the Series back to Fenway. The Red Sox forced a seventh-game showdown matching Lonborg and Bob Gibson, each with two Series victories. Lonborg was working with one day less of rest than Gibson, and the Cardinals finally got to him for a 7–2 win. Gibson—with his three wins, 26 strikeouts, and earned run average of 1.00—was voted the Series' most valuable player. With the defeat, Red Sox fans still had not celebrated a world championship since Carl Mays and Babe Ruth had each won two games against the Cubs in 1918.

Conspicuous by his absence during the Series was Ted Williams, who Yawkey dearly hoped would return to share in Boston's success. Instead, Williams merely wired his congratulations.

Carl Yastrzemski was the runaway choice for American League MVP. But his selection by the Baseball Writers Association of America wasn't unanimous. With two members from each major league market voting in their respective leagues, Yaz came up with nineteen first-place votes and one second-place vote. The writer who dropped him to second was Max Nichols of the *Minneapolis Star*. Nichols chose the Twins' Cesar Tovar, who played six positions and hit .267. Nichols' selection prevented Yastrzemski from becoming only the fifth AL player to earn unanimous election since the writers began selecting MVPs in 1931. It marked Yaz as the only AL Triple Crown winner not to unanimously be named MVP. A few weeks after the season, Yastrzemski was rewarded with a new contract featuring what was then baseball's magical annual salary of $100,000. The only Red Sox player ever to be paid more was Ted Williams, who had earned $125,000 during the last five years of his career.

Yaz remained with the Red Sox for twenty-three years, a rare privilege at a time when many aging players were coldly released and then tried to extend their careers by signing with other teams. His Hall of Fame career ended in 1983 with 3,419 hits and seventeen appearances for the AL All-Star team. In contrast to Ted Williams's cool departure from Boston—failing to tip his cap on a last-bat home run—Yastrzemski circled the field and touched hands with as many fans as he could on his final day in a Boston uniform.

But the coveted world championship eluded him. He and the Red Sox returned to the World Series in 1975 but lost to the Cincinnati Reds in a classic seven-game series. In 1978 the Red Sox looked like they had the kind of talent to win the Series. But the Yankees rallied from a fourteen-game deficit in July to tie the Red Sox for the AL East title and beat Boston in a one-game playoff at Fenway. The game ended with Yastrzemski hitting a foul pop-up caught by Graig Nettles, leaving the tying run at third base.

On October 18, 1967, Charlie Finley was given official approval by his fellow American League owners at a marathon meeting in Chicago to move the A's to the Oakland–Alameda County Coliseum. The length of the session was caused not by indecision about what to do with the A's but by how to deal with the certain outcry from officials in Kansas City and Missouri over leaving Kansas City abandoned. U.S. senator Stuart Symington of Missouri had all but promised congressional action against baseball, in the form of elimination of the sport's valuable antitrust exemption, if the A's were allowed to move.

The announcement of Finley's move was accompanied by the awarding of two AL expansion teams to Kansas City and Seattle to begin play by 1971. National League officials didn't immediately commit themselves to equivalent expansion and tabled the issue for baseball's annual winter meetings scheduled for Mexico City in December 1967.

But Symington wasn't satisfied with a promise to return baseball to Kansas City in the next three years and demanded quicker action. Kansas City mayor Ilus Davis told AL president Joe Cronin he was returning home the following day and planned to file an injunction to block Finley from moving the Athletics. Cronin hastily convened another owners meeting after midnight, and the group voted to move up the expansion to 1969.

Finley received a hero's welcome upon his arrival in Oakland. A group of about four hundred people met his plane at the airport, to which Finley applied the needle: "In Kansas City, we played practically all of our games before groups of this size."

At Mexico City the National League voted to join the American League at twelve teams starting between 1969 and 1971. The owners reviewed applications for expansion teams from Buffalo, Dallas–Fort Worth, Milwaukee, San Diego, and two Canadian cities—Montreal and Toronto—as well as an informal bid from Denver. Milwaukee, as part of its bid, agreed to give up its attempts to force the Braves to move back from Atlanta. The NL subsequently awarded its new teams to San Diego and Montreal, the latter making history as major league baseball's first team located outside the United States, with the new teams also beginning play in 1969.

Having twelve teams in each league presented problems both with scheduling—with ten teams, each club played every opponent nine times at home and nine times on the road for a total of 162—and with interest. Many baseball executives believed there was little chance that a team could be supported while laboring in eleventh or twelfth place. That raised the question of divisional play, which was used by each of the other professional sports. Each major league voted to divide into two six-team divisions, with the division winners meeting in a best-of-five playoff to precede the best-of-seven World Series. Beginning in 1969, it would be possible that the best teams in each league would sit home during the World Series.

With the number of baseball-hungry cities craving major league teams in the late sixties, there was no question that expansion and the subsequent divisional realignment were inevitable. But Charlie Finley, and his shift of the A's to Oakland, turned out to be the catalyst.

In Oakland, all of the pieces finally fell together on the field for Finley and the A's. He had quality pitchers, like starters Catfish Hunter, Vida Blue, and Ken Holtzman and relievers Rollie Fingers and Darold Knowles. Home-grown hitters like Reggie Jackson, Rick Monday, Joe Rudi, and Sal Bando were developed. The A's fought with each other and with Finley off the field but couldn't be stopped on the field. Sporting long hair, mustaches, and distinctive green-and-gold pullover tops to go with the now-accepted white shoes, Oakland won the AL West in '71, roared to world championships in 1972, '73, and '74, and added a fifth consecutive division title in '75 before losing the playoffs to the Red Sox. Finley's refusal to pay the going wage and the advent of free agency led to the breakup of the great A's teams soon afterward. Finley attempted to move the team again, this time to Denver in the late '70s, but failed. He eventually sold the team to Walter Haas in November 1980 and quietly left baseball.

Tony Conigliaro reported to spring training in 1968 at Winter Haven ready to play baseball. He was hurt to hear Dick Williams say the Red Sox had won the pennant in '67 without him and were prepared to do the same in '68. Even Williams was impressed with Conigliaro's first at-bats against a pitching machine. But in his first swings against live pitching, Tony C had a difficult time picking up the ball. The pitch would enter a fuzzy area, then disappear totally. In the Red Sox's first exhibition game against Oakland, Conigliaro singled and doubled. Four days later, after rapping an RBI single against the White Sox, Conigliaro was convinced he was going to make it all the way back.

But vision problems persisted throughout spring training. He was striking out often and looking bad doing it. He was waving harmlessly at pitches thrown right over the plate, even missing the ball in simple pepper games. A recheck of his left eye during a trip back to Boston revealed his vision was 20/300, making him legally blind in that eye. Conigliaro and his lawyer, Joe Tauro, put together and released a four-paragraph statement announcing Tony C's retirement from baseball.

But in June, Conigiliaro was encouraged by an examination that showed the vision had improved to 20/100. He arranged for a batting session at Fenway while the Red Sox were out of town, albeit facing the pitching of diminutive batboy Moe Rosenfeld, and did well enough to arrange to report to Boston's Instructional League camp that fall. But Tony C planned to return to the majors as a pitcher, convinced that his batting skills would never be the same. That plan was abandoned quickly, thanks to an 0–3 record, a sore arm, and his own improved hitting. The best news for Conigiliaro, though, was that his postcamp eye exam revealed the left vision was 20/20.

Conigilaro made his triumphant return to the Red Sox outfield in 1969. He hit .255 with 20 home runs and 82 RBIs, and earned the AL's Comeback Player of the Year award. In 1970 his numbers increased to 36 homers, 116 RBIs, and a .266 batting average. For these achievements, Conigilaro was rewarded with a trade, away from the team he had loved since childhood, to the Angels. His brother Billy, who had joined the Red Sox in 1969, believed the trade was precipitated when team officials learned that Tony C admitted to more vision problems, that he couldn't clearly see the ball while playing in the outfield at dusk. Conigliaro saw only part-time service with the Angels in 1971 for a number of reasons. He was hampered by a torn shoulder muscle and a pinched nerve in his neck, which combined to require twenty cortisone shots just to get him to the All-Star break. The left eye had deteriorated, back to 20/300. Nor was his cocky attitude accepted with the Angels as it had been back in Boston, where he was a boyhood hero. In June, Conigliaro arrived at Anaheim Stadium to discover his empty uniform laid out on a stretcher, covered with ketchup. On July 10, 1971, Tony C went 0 for 8 with five strikeouts in a 20-inning loss at Oakland. He was ejected in the nineteenth inning when, during his second argument with an umpire in the game, he flipped his bat in defiance. In seventy-four games, Conigiliaro was hitting .222 with four homers and 15 RBIs. He announced his next retirement from baseball the following day. "I have lost my sight and am on the edge of losing my mind," he admitted. Angels manager Lefty Phillips went so far as to say Conigliaro belonged in an institution.

Tony C returned home to Boston, where an eye doctor advised him that he should never play baseball again. He went into the restaurant business with Billy. He remained in shape and his vision improved again, leading him to consider yet another comeback in the winter of 1973–74 at age twenty-nine. It didn't hurt that the American League had adopted the designated hitter rule in 1973, allowing a player to bat for the pitcher in a regular spot in the batting order for an entire game without having to play in the field. The best offer he received was an opportunity to try out for the Angels' Class AAA Salt Lake City affiliate the following spring. Conigliaro declined.

Red Sox general manager Dick O'Connell offered Tony C a tryout as a designated hitter in spring training 1975. Conigliaro was back in the Boston lineup on Opening Day and thrilled the Fenway crowd by hitting a home run in his first at-bat. But the glory didn't last long. His hitting was awful. After twenty-one games, Conigliaro was hitting only .123 with two home runs and nine RBIs. He lost the regular DH job to rookie Jim Rice. On June 14, the Red Sox informed Tony C there no longer was any room for him on their roster, that he could choose between a demotion to Class AAA Pawtucket or an outright release. Conigilaro stubbornly chose the demotion, hit .220 for the Paw Sox, and on August 20, 1975, begrudgingly retired—for good. By the time Boston reached the final game of the '75 Series—buoyed by the heroics of Yaz and Carlton Fisk and Bernie Carbo and Luis Tiant and Fred Lynn and Jim Rice—it probably was forgotten by many Red Sox fans that Tony C had been in the starting lineup on Opening Day.

Having finally accepted the end of his playing days, Conigliaro wandered from job to job, working as a sportscaster in Providence and San Francisco, a sports agent, and the owner of a health-food store. In January 1982, at the age of forty-five, he auditioned for the analyst's position with the Red Sox telecast team on Channel 38 in Boston. The audition went well, and Tony Conigliaro expected to be rejoining the Red Sox, even if it meant in the TV booth. Two days later, he was riding to Logan Airport with Billy when he suffered a heart attack. He spent the next three weeks in a coma and required twenty-four-hour medical attention until he died of kidney failure on February 24, 1990.

The Impossible Dream did not live on for the Red Sox. It may have started to crumble on the ski slopes of Lake Tahoe on December 23, 1967, not long after Jim Lonborg became the Red Sox's first Cy Young Award winner. Lonborg took his planned ski trip, just as he had told author William Craig in July when Craig questioned taking such a risk. Lonborg tore ligaments in his left knee, and he was never the same pitcher afterward. He was lost for much of the 1968 season. Even with trades for starting pitchers Ray Culp and Dick Ellsworth, Boston lacked enough quality pitching to stay in the race. The Red Sox finished seventeen games behind the Tigers in 1968, though only six games off their pennant pace of '67. Lonborg returned to pitch in twenty-three games but only compiled a record of 6–10. Carl Yastrzemski repeated as the batting champ, as the only hitter in the American League to hit better than .300—.301, to be exact.

In 1969 the Red Sox were rolling on to their third consecutive winning season but had no chance to catch Earl Weaver's steamrolling Baltimore Orioles. A newspaper report quoted Tom Yawkey as giving Dick Williams a "good" grade on a scale of fair, good, excellent, or outstanding managing. The story turned frosty, the already cool relationship between Williams and Yawkey. Yawkey heard complaints from players about Williams's treatment. Discipline, which was seen as a welcome change in 1967, no longer was vogue in Boston. When the Red Sox returned home from a road trip in late September '69 with a record of 82–71, Williams was informed that management didn't intend for him or his coaching staff to return in 1970. The plan was for Williams to manage out the balance of the season. But when word leaked to the media, the Red Sox had no choice but to let go of Williams immediately.

Massachusetts Cooperative Bank realized its business relationship with Williams was over but had the keen marketing sense to film one last commercial. On a rainy Saturday morning, Williams walked out of the front door of his apartment, set two suitcases down by a U-Haul trailer, and said into a camera, "Hi, this is Dick Williams. When you're out of a job, it's certainly nice to have a savings account with the Massachusetts Cooperative Bank." The ad was shown the following season on Red Sox telecasts, but Williams made plenty of live TV appearances after leaving Boston. He managed six other major league teams and returned to the World Series three times, winning with Oakland in '72 and '73 and losing with San Diego in '84. The six stops did not include his abortive attempt to manage the Yankees beginning in 1974 for George Steinbrenner, a move blocked by Charlie Finley.

Lonborg remained with the Red Sox through the 1971 season, never winning more than ten games. He was traded to the Milwaukee Brewers (the former Seattle Pilots expansion team) and a year later to the Philadelphia Phillies, where he spent the final seven seasons of his big league career. Medicine did finally beckon; Lonborg returned to Boston and became a dentist.

Tom Yawkey never did live to see another world championship return to Boston. After losing the '75 Series, Yawkey was determined to make that final leap. In a deal that made the $1 million Herb Score offer of 1957 pale in comparison, Yawkey agreed on June 15, 1976, to the most expensive single transaction in baseball to date, to buy outfielder Joe Rudi and relief pitcher Rollie Fingers from Oakland for $2 million. This was part of Charlie Finley's baseball fire sale; he also planned to sell pitcher Vida Blue to the Yankees for $1.5 million. All three players would be eligible to become free agents after the season. Finley had no intention of either signing the players to huge salaries or watching them leave the A's without compensation. The sales were disallowed by commissioner Bowie Kuhn. The Finley shopping spree turned out to be Yawkey's last major move in his forty-four years as owner of the Red Sox. He died of leukemia on July 9, 1976, at age seventy-three.

Eddie Stanky's constant putdowns of his White Sox talent proved to be prophetic. Chicago, the mouse that scared the elephants in 1967, as Stanky put it, was never heard from in 1968. The starting pitching wasn't as strong, and the hitting showed no improvement. With the team stumbling along at 34–45, Stanky was fired, with Al Lopez being brought out of retirement to finish the season. Stanky returned to his hometown of Mobile, Alabama, and became the baseball coach at the University of South Alabama.

Nine years later, Stanky agreed to return to the majors as the manager of the Texas Rangers, the former Washington Senators expansion team that moved to Dallas–Fort Worth before the '72 season. He was introduced as the Rangers' new manager in Minnesota on the morning of June 22, 1977, replacing Frank Lucchesi. The fifty-nine-year-old Stanky won his Rangers debut that night against the Twins, 10–8. He headed back to the team hotel after the game and told Connie Ryan, one of the Rangers' coaches, to meet him for breakfast in the hotel restaurant at 8:30 the next morning.

At 8:30 Stanky was not in the hotel restaurant. He was on a plane headed to Atlanta, making his way back to Alabama. Earlier that morning, Stanky had called general manager Dan O'Brien back in Texas and explained that he was quitting after one game, that it was wrong for him to have left his wife and family behind. Thus, Eddie Stanky set a major league record for the shortest tenure for a so-called permanent manager—one game. Sixteen hours. Never did get to manage a home game. Stanky returned to coaching at South Alabama, sat out the 1980 season because of a heart attack, and retired in 1983.

Baseball didn't adopt Stanky's concept for looser substitution, as in his proposal to allow a pinch hitter to appear twice in a game. But the intention of increasing baseball's offense was appealing, especially after pitchers so dominated the 1968 season. The double pinch hitter died, but the designated hitter was born in the American League in 1973.

As for the White Sox, their attendance problems only worsened. In 1970 they attracted fewer than half a million fans. The Cubs established themselves as "Chicago's team" throughout the seventies and eighties, and there was a point when many baseball people believed the White Sox would be moved to St. Petersburg, Florida, in the late eighties. That was staved off by the construction of a new Comiskey Park, which opened in 1991.

The dislocated toes on Denny McLain's left foot were healed by the time he reached spring training in 1968. The Tigers reported to Lakeland determined not to let anything stand in the way of their winning the pennant. Many of the players had to go through the bittersweet experience of having opposing players tell them they were the best team in the American League in 1967; it was at the same time flattering and insulting to have peers tell them they should have won the pennant. The Tigers won easily in 1968, by twelve games over the second-place Orioles. But the real story was McLain, who became the majors' first thirty-game winner since Dizzy Dean had accomplished the feat with the 1934 St. Louis Cardinals. By the All-Star break, McLain already had won sixteen games while Detroit was running away with the league lead. He reached twenty wins on July 27 and won No. 29 on September 10. His first shot at thirty came on September 14 at home against Oakland, and Dean was on hand to be one of the first to congratulate McLain—though Dean was booted from the Tiger Stadium press box by veteran Detroit sportswriter Watson Spoelstra because he was not an officially accredited member of the media. But McLain gave up a pair of home runs to Reggie Jackson, and the A's proved to be rude foils by taking a 4–3 lead into the bottom of the ninth. The Tigers rallied for two runs, Willie Horton smacking the winning hit over a drawn-in Rick Monday in left field for the historic victory. McLain finished 31–6, and the Tigers went on to surprise St. Louis in a seven-game World Series after falling behind three games to one. Detroit staved off elimination in Game Five at Tiger Stadium, the final Series game scheduled for Detroit. The key play occurred in the fifth inning, when Cardinals speedster Lou Brock declined to slide coming home and was tagged out. The Tigers rallied to win the game, 5–3, then swept the last two games in St. Louis. In the seventh-game showdown, Mickey Lolich beat Bob Gibson for his third victory of the Series and was named the Series' most valuable player.

McLain had been usurped by Lolich during the Series. The runaway AL Cy Young Award winner in 1968, McLain shared the award with Baltimore's Mike Cuellar in 1969. McLain and Lolich never had a close relationship, in part because Lolich kept his associations with most team- mates at a minimum. But their relationship was strained in 1969, when McLain, a licensed pilot, arranged to fly Lolich and his wife round trip to the All-Star Game in Washington. McLain and Lolich miscommunicated on the travel plans, and the result was the Loliches' having to make other arrangements to get back to Detroit. Lolich was quoted as saying McLain "stranded" them in Washington.

The Lolich flap turned into one of the least of McLain's problems. Tigers general manager Jim Campbell had become concerned over McLain's difficulties in keeping up with his bills and asked the commis- sioner's office to look into McLain's financial dealings. The assignment was turned over to Henry Fitzgibbon, the head of security for baseball. He learned that a grand jury in Detroit was investigating McLain. In February 1970, *Sports Illustrated* published a story about McLain's gam- bling involvement during the '67 season. This included what proved to be a much more thrilling explanation of the injured-toes incident than McLain's version. According to the article, McLain was ordered to report to Detroit mobster Tony Giacalone to pay off for Williamston Kid's win at Detroit Race Course in August. To emphasize how much he wanted his money, according to the story, Giacalone brought his heel down hard on McLain's toes.

McLain admitted the bookmaking involvement to Kuhn but denied many aspects of the *Sports Illustrated* report, including the Giacalone incident. An investigation by Kuhn's office revealed no reason to believe McLain's bookmaking activities had any effect on his poor pitching per- formances in September 1967 that contributed to the Tigers finishing a game behind Boston. Kuhn suspended McLain indefinitely, which turned out to be the first half of the 1970 season.

Denny McLain returned to a hero's fanfare in June but was never a star pitcher again. After the '70 season, he was traded to Washington, where he became a twenty-game loser. He was sent to Oakland in the spring of '72, demoted to the minors in May, and traded to Atlanta in June. The Braves released him in March 1973 at age twenty-nine. He signed with Class AAA Iowa and went 1–4 in eight starts before agreeing to a demotion to Class AA Shreveport. He compiled a 6–4 record there, then retired as a player.

McLain stayed in baseball as the general manager of the Memphis minor league team before moving to Florida to get into real estate. The business brought him into contact with some shady characters, and in March 1984 he was indicted on five counts of racketeering, conspiracy, extortion, possession of cocaine with the intent to distribute, and conspiracy to import cocaine. He maintained his innocence but was found guilty of all five counts a year later and was sentenced to jail immediately following the trial. He spent 2½ years in prisons in Florida, Georgia, and Alabama before his conviction was reversed in August 1987.

Ken Harrelson, baseball mercenary in 1967, saw his best days in the majors after the '67 season. Playing every day in right field for Boston in 1968, Harrelson led the American League in RBIs with 109 while hitting 35 home runs. Combine that performance with his penchant for wearing Nehru jackets, gold chains, and long hair (even by 1968 standards), and Harrelson became something of a media sensation. But with the shakeup of the Red Sox after the '68 season, Harrelson was traded to Cleveland with pitchers Dick Ellsworth and Juan Pizarro for starter Sonny Siebert, reliever Vincente Romo, and catcher Joe Azcue. Before leaving Boston, Harrelson experienced first-hand Tom Yawkey's concern for his players. When Harrelson's son was ill with a rare kidney disease, Yawkey, unsolicited, was able to land a Boston specialist who previously had refused to take on the boy as a new patient.

With the Indians in 1969, Harrelson dropped off slightly to 27 homers and 84 RBIs. He played only sixty-nine games for Cleveland over the next two years and retired after the '71 season. Staying in baseball through broadcasting, he made an unusual transition in the late eighties by going from color analyst of the White Sox one year to general manager of the White Sox the next year—and back to analyst the following year.

Because of the odd circumstances surrounding Harrelson's 1967 release by the A's, major league baseball changed its waiver rules on December 1, 1967. Under the old rule, any team could have claimed Harrelson for a one-dollar waiver fee, but Harrelson would have had the option of rejecting the team that selected him. His signing with the Red Sox amounted to free agency because Charlie Finley was willing to get rid of him without getting anything in return. Under the new rule, that player becomes the property of the team that claims him first after being released. If Harrelson had been claimed first by, for instance, the Yankees, he would have been the property of the Yankees as soon as they paid a $20,000 waiver fee. And if he decided he wouldn't play for the Yankees, then other teams would have to deal with the Yankees if they believed Harrelson would play for them.

The California Angels continued to put together respectable teams but had a knack for coming up short. Dick Walsh came over from the Dodgers to take over the day-to-day operation of the ballclub before the 1969 season and proclaimed he was going to break up the Angels' country club. Bobby Knoop was traded to the White Sox. Buck Rodgers was farmed out to Hawaii. After the 1971 season, the front office decided to send Jim Fregosi to the New York Mets for a package of four players headlined by hard-throwing right-hander Nolan Ryan. The Mets planned to move Fregosi to third base, to solve a problem spot that had plagued them for years. But Fregosi broke a thumb during spring training and gained about twenty-five pounds through inactivity. Rodgers ran into him soon afterward and chided his old friend for the weight gain. "You're a pig!" Rodgers said. Fregosi explained that he had broken his thumb. Said Rodgers, "You didn't break your leg!" Fregosi was not the answer at third base for the Mets; he played two undistinguished seasons before being traded to Texas. Conversely, Ryan harnessed the power he had displayed in New York and went on to set major league records for strikeouts and no-hitters while pitching for the Angels, Astros, and Rangers.

The Angels always spent October watching some other AL team play in the World Series. In 1982 they led the Brewers two games to none in the best-of-five playoffs only to lose in five games. In the best-of-seven '86 playoffs, they were one out away from eliminating the Red Sox four games to one yet lost the series in seven games. Boston's Dave Henderson delivered the fateful hit, a game-tying home run in the ninth inning of Game Five off Angels reliever Donnie Moore. The disappointment of failing to nail down the pennant was something Moore was ultimately unable to live with; he later committed suicide.

Fred Gladding was right. On November 27, he was offically sent to Houston as the player to be named later for Eddie Mathews. He pitched six years for the Astros, leading the National League with 29 saves in 1969, and retired after the '73 season.

The best was yet to come for Harmon Killebrew, at least in terms of personal achievement. He rebounded from an injury-shortened 1968 season to become the AL's Most Valuable Player in 1969, leading the Twins to the Western Division championship. Killebrew led the league with 49 home runs, equaling his career high. He also set career marks and league highs with 140 RBIs and an astounding 145 walks. But Minnesota was beaten in the AL playoffs in three consecutive games by Baltimore, as was the case again in 1970.

Killebrew primarily played third base in each of those division-winning seasons, with Rich Reese manning first base. In 1970, Killebrew hit 41 homers, the eighth and final time he surpassed 40. His playing time decreased beginning in 1973 and his career was extended with the help of the designated hitter. After playing twenty-one seasons with the Senators-Twins franchise, he finished up as the Kansas City Royals' DH in 1974. His 573 career home runs rank fifth in major league history.

Dean Chance never pitched the Twins into the World Series, as the December 1966 trade was intended to do. He enjoyed another solid season in 1968, with a 2.53 ERA to go with a 16–16 record. But that was the last season in which Chance made a major contribution to the Twins.

Arm trouble limited him to 20 starts in '69, when he compiled a 5–4 record. Minnesota then traded him to Cleveland, where he was dispatched to the bullpen. He went 9–8 with the Indians before being sent to the New York Mets for the stretch drive. He pitched in three games for New York, which failed to catch Pittsburgh in the National League East, and was sent on to Detroit. Chance ended his career with the Tigers in 1971, splitting time between the starting rotation and the bullpen. His career batting average closed at .066.

Norm Cash remained the Tigers' regular first baseman well after the 1967 season, despite Mayo Smith's statements to the contrary following that final demoralizing defeat. He hit 32 home runs in 1971, one shy of the AL lead. Cash retired after being released by Detroit in August 1974, having hit 377 career home runs and playing more than two thousand games over seventeen seasons. The Detroit fans finally warmed to him, no longer holding it against him that he couldn't hit .361 every year. He never lost his light-hearted approach. During a game in which California's Nolan Ryan threw a no-hitter against the Tigers, Cash stepped to the plate armed with a table leg. He calmly explained to the home-plate umpire that there was no way he stood a chance of hitting Ryan with a conventional bat.

Cash suffered a stroke five years after retiring. Still, he tried to be a crowd pleaser. He returned to Tiger Stadium for Old Timers Day, though his mobility was so limited that a throw from outfielder Mickey Stanley struck him in the head. He was last seen shortly before midnight on the night of October 12, 1986, leaving the Shamrock Bar on Beaver Island, about thirty miles from his home at the northern end of Michigan's Lower Peninsula. It was a cold, rainy night in the area. Cash was returning to his cabin cruiser, the *Stormin' Norman,* and apparently slipped off the wet dock and into the icy waters of Lake Michigan. Divers recovered his body from the lake the following morning. There were no signs of another stroke or any other injury that might have caused the accident. Cash had a history for frolicking well into the night, but family friend Brendan LaBlance said Cash was not intoxicated at the time of the accident.

Managerial moves had little to do with the Tigers' romp through the American League in 1968. But once in the World Series, Detroit manager Mayo Smith did leave his stamp on the drive to the world championship. With four quality hitters playing in the outfield, Smith elected to move outfielder Mickey Stanley to shortstop against the Cardinals. Stanley performed adequately in the field and at bat, and Al Kaline hit .379 playing the full Series as the Tigers won in seven games.

Smith was rewarded after the Series with a new two-year contract, his annual salary increased from $40,000 to $55,000. But the Tigers were no match for the Orioles in the AL East the next two years. Smith was dismissed after the 1970 season, replaced by Billy Martin. He declined offers to remain in baseball and returned to his home in Lake Worth, Florida, to retire. There he died of a stroke in 1977 at the age of sixty-two.

Like Cash, Al Kaline never won a second batting title. But while the gregarious Cash somehow fell out of favor with Tigers fans, the stoic Kaline only grew in stature from year to year. He became a perennial All-Star and Gold Glove selection. He finally got to "see" his first World Series in '68, and didn't disappoint with his .379 performance. But the season overall was a difficult one despite the team's success. He played in only 102 games because of injury. He remained an integral part of the Tigers, helping win an Eastern Division title in 1972 and finishing his career in '74 as a full-time designated hitter. He retired with 3,007 hits, having played twenty-two seasons in a Tigers uniform.

Frank Robinson, the first player to win MVP awards in both leagues, rewrote baseball history in 1975 as the majors' first black manager. He had played on three consecutive pennant winners in Baltimore from 1969 through '71, then played for the Dodgers and Angels before being claimed on waivers by Cleveland during the final days of the '74 season. The deal was the setup for the more significant step of naming Robinson as the manager of the Indians for the '75 season. Twenty-seven years after Jackie Robinson broke the color line playing for Brooklyn, Frank Robinson became manager of the Indians—player/manager actually, though against his wishes. But while Jackie Robinson could count on his own ability to put up impressive statistics, Frank Robinson the manager could only be judged by the performance of his players. Cleveland didn't have the players to compete in the AL East, and in 1977 Frank Robinson became the first black manager to be fired. He later managed in San Francisco and back in Baltimore, being claimed by the familiar managerial axe each time, before moving into the front office with the Orioles.

Tommy John also went on to make major league history, though his feat can't be found in a baseball record book. He pitched with the White Sox through 1971, then three more seasons with the Dodgers. On July 17, 1974, he suffered an elbow injury while pitching to Hal Breedan of Montreal. Dodgers team physician Frank Jobe performed what has become one of sport's most famous operations to save John's pitching career. Jobe transplanted a six-inch tendon from John's right forearm to support John's left elbow. Jobe told John the chances of his pitching again were one in a hundred. Not only did John return, he pitched fourteen more years and made the All-Star team three more times.

Bill Robinson eventually found peace in the major leagues, though it wasn't at Yankee Stadium. He spent three seasons with New York, then was traded to Philadelphia. In three seasons there, he resurrected his career. He went on to play in Pittsburgh for seven years, and was an everyday outfielder for the '79 team that won the World Series. He stayed in baseball as a batting instructor, returning to the World Series with the Mets in 1986.

The 1967 pattern of voting for the MVP award was reversed in the Rookie of the Year balloting: a Twins player finished one vote from unanimous election, the lone dissenting voter choosing one of the Red Sox. Minnesota second baseman Rod Carew earned nineteen of the twenty votes, with the other going to Boston center fielder Reggie Smith.

Carew, the little boy from Panama who had learned to play baseball with a stick and bottle caps on the streets of New York, went on to become arguably the majors' best pure hitter of the seventies. He won seven AL batting titles from 1969 to 1978. He was neither a power hitter nor a speed burner. What Carew did was make the best use of his overall skills. He constantly adjusted his stance and swing to compensate for shortcomings. Out of the batter's box, he mastered one of the game's most difficult tasks—stealing home. Carew did it seven times in 1969 alone. He played on division winners in '69 and '70, each time being swept in the AL playoffs by Baltimore, and moved over to first base in the midseventies.

His landmark season was 1977, when he entered the final two months of the season with a realistic chance of becoming the first major leaguer to hit .400 since Ted Williams in 1941. National media flocked to watch an otherwise nondescript Twins team. Rod Carew, a quiet man who was typecast by many reporters as moody and withdrawn, was forced to cope with the media's magnifying glass as well as the daily pressure of pursuing .400. Carew finished the season hitting .388, and in the process tied his career high with 14 home runs and set a career mark with 100 runs batted in. Further examination of that year is necessary to appreciate Carew's performance. He led the league in hits with 239, runs with 128, and triples with 16. He also hit 38 doubles, giving him 68 extra-base hits. In the field, he led AL first basemen with 121 assists. There was no other choice for AL Most Valuable Player.

For all of his accomplishments on the field, what Rod Carew endured off the field proved more impressive. In 1970 Carew married the former Marilynn Levy. Rod is black; Marilynn is white. Rod converted to Judaism. The public disclosure of those facts prompted a torrent of criticism and hate mail. The adversity only helped strengthen Carew's resolve.

With Twins owner Calvin Griffith fearing Carew would leave Minnesota as a free agent following the '79 season, Carew was traded to California for four players in February 1979. With the Angels, Carew hit .300 for another five seasons and helped win two division titles, though still failing to reach the World Series. A free agent after the '83 season, Carew re-signed with the Angels for another two years, hitting .295 and .280, and passing the 3,000 mark in career hits. At age forty, Carew was again a free agent and wanted to continue his career in Anaheim, though he didn't enjoy the spotlight of LA. He thought he could play at least two more seasons. The club, though, had other ideas. What transpired was an awkward situation in which the Angels didn't pursue Carew and Carew didn't seek employment with any other team.

Through no desire of his own, Carew had retired. His career batting average was .328. The seven batting titles rank behind only Ty Cobb and Honus Wagner. His fifteen consecutive .300 seasons rank behind Cobb, Wagner, and Stan Musial. Then there were the seventeen steals of home. Carew was elected to the Hall of Fame in his first year of eligibility, in 1991.

Pedro Lopez Oliva—Tony to baseball fans—continued to be one of the most feared hitters in the majors. He again hit .289 in 1968, then pushed his average to .309, .325, and .337 from 1969 to 1971. But in 1971 his contribution was limited to 126 games. He hurt his right knee on July 29 when he dived for a line drive hit by Joe Rudi.

From that point on, knee operations became commonplace for Oliva. He went through seven of them and never played another full season. From 1973 to 1975 he managed to serve as the Twins' regular DH. He retired after the '76 season with a career batting average of .304, 1,917 career hits, and a right leg that he could not fully straighten. Without the knee problems, Oliva could very well have collected 3,000 hits. A statistic called "relative batting average"—comparing a player's output with league norms during his career—ranked Oliva as twelfth best in major league history.

BIBLIOGRAPHY

BOOKS
The Boston Red Sox: An Illustrated History by Donald Honig
Hawk by Ken Harrelson with Al Hirshberg
The Impossible Dream by Bill McSweeney
Yaz by Carl Yastrzemski with Al Hirshberg
Yaz: Baseball, The Wall And Me by Carl Yastrzemski and Gerald
    Eskenazi
No More Mr. Nice Guy by Dick Williams and Bill Plaschke
Strikeout by Denny McLain with Mike Nahrstedt
The Detroit Tigers: An Illustrated History by Joe Falls
T.J.: My 26 Years in Baseball by Tommy John with Dan Valenti
Extra Innings by Frank Robinson and Berry Stainback
Harmon Killebrew, Baseball's Superstar by Hal Anderson
The Dodgers Move West by Neil J. Sullivan
What's the Matter with the Red Sox by Al Hirshberg
Charlie O by Herb Michelson
Home Games by Bobbie Bouton and Nancy Marshall
Catfish: My Life in Baseball by Catfish Hunter and Armen Keteyian
Take Me Out To The Ballgame by The Sporting News
The Quality of Courage by Mickey Mantle

NEWSPAPERS/PUBLICATIONS

The Boston Globe
The Detroit Free Press
The Detroit News
The Minneapolis Star
The Minneapolis Tribune
The Los Angeles Times
The Kansas City Star
The Kansas City Times
The New York *Daily News*
The New York Times
The Dallas Morning News
The Sporting News
Sports Illustrated
Street and Smith's Official Yearbook 1967 Baseball

INDEX